BETTER BUSINESS RELATIONSHIPS

"Occasionally you come across books that are timely, utterly important and overdue. This book is one of them. Tasso holds the reader's interest by brilliantly presenting a persuasive argument that oscillates between the basics of psychology and selling. The importance of relationships in business is vital. *Better Business Relationships* is packed with useful advice which is well written and remarkably thoughtful."
Clive Lewis OBE, DL Business Psychologist; CEO, Globis Mediation Group

"Business leaders must be able to build real and meaningful connections with their clients, teams and communities – otherwise, are they really leaders? Today, there is definitely a lower tolerance for business leaders without a strong helping of EQ because of the demands of increasingly non-linear, global and network-based markets – you have to be able to work across boundaries and deal with diversity. In this context, *Better Business Relationships* is a timely, thought-provoking and engaging read."
Paul J English, Global Leader, Markets & Clients, Grant Thornton

"This book is an engaging read, written in a no-nonsense style and packed with helpful, practical tools and tips for building and maintaining effective business relationships."
Dr Kathryn Waddington, Course Leader MSc Business Psychology,
University of Westminster

"Kim explodes the myth that business relationships have to be cool and free of emotion. Her distilled wisdom and practical checklists show how best to enhance our natural human ability to communicate with others for mutual benefit."
Richard Chaplin, Founder & Chief Executive, Managing Partners' Forum

"For anyone whose business depends upon not only building, but maintaining and developing business relationships, this book is a must read. It's a key skill that almost everyone in business needs, but no one teaches you. Kim has a wealth of experience in this space and it shines through. It's a great reference book, but also one that you can dip in and out of and use just as a refresher – as I did! Building business relationships is fundamental to individual and collective success, and Kim's book is the ideal guide for anyone looking to develop or improve their skills in this fundamentally important area."
Chris Pullen, Business Development Director, EY Law

"Business relationships are not the same as social ones, requiring different skills and knowledge. Tasso provides a useful overview of theories, ranging from non-verbal communication, attitudes to change, creating rapport and why relationships sour."
Kiran Kapur, CEO, Cambridge Marketing College

"*Better Business Relationships* is a book for our time. Tasso captures a moment in our evolution where we could all do with refocusing back on what really matters: people. To discover your real self is the key to unlocking and developing engaging relationships with others. This book makes you realise – in an era driven by win-lose outcomes, mobile connectivity, advancing new tech, big data and constant automation – just how much we need to nurture and hold onto the value of building enduring, collaborative relationships. Ultimately, in business and in many ways life itself, people and their relationships lead to better achievements and results. Perhaps we stand accused today of forgetting this, so the timely reminder, advice and tips are of value to us all and especially those of us in leadership roles who would do well to take note. Who knows, the next decade may even see a return to human kindness, the essence of relationships."
Dr Sean Tompkins (D.Phil. & D.Eng.), Global CEO,
Royal Institution of Chartered Surveyors

BETTER BUSINESS RELATIONSHIPS

KIM TASSO

BLOOMSBURY BUSINESS

LONDON • NEW YORK • OXFORD • NEW DELHI • SYDNEY

BLOOMSBURY BUSINESS
Bloomsbury Publishing Plc
50 Bedford Square, London, WC1B 3DP, UK
1385 Broadway, New York, NY 10018, USA

BLOOMSBURY, BLOOMSBURY BUSINESS and the Diana logo are trademarks of
Bloomsbury Publishing Plc

First published in Great Britain 2019

Cover design by Eleanor Rose
Cover image © Getty Images

A catalogue record for this book is available from the British Library.

Library of Congress Cataloging-in-Publication Data
Names: Tasso, Kim, author.
Title: Better business relationships : insights from psychology and management for working
in a digital world / Kim Tasso.
Description: New York : Bloomsbury Publishing Plc, [2018] | Includes bibliographical
references and index.
Identifiers: LCCN 2018021276 (print) | LCCN 2018034226 (ebook) |
ISBN 9781472957009 (ePUB) | ISBN 9781472957023 (ePDF) |
ISBN 9781472957030 (eXML) | ISBN 9781472957016 (hardback)
Subjects: LCSH: Business networks. | Psychology, Industrial. | Success in business.
Classification: LCC HD69.S8 (ebook) | LCC HD69.S8 T377 2018 (print) |
DDC 650.1/3—dc23
LC record available at https://lccn.loc.gov/2018021276

ISBN: HB: 978-1-4729-5701-6
         ePDF: 978-1-4729-5702-3
         eBook: 978-1-4729-5700-9

Typeset by RefineCatch Limited, Bungay, Suffolk
Printed and bound in Great Britain

To find out more about our authors and books visit www.bloomsbury.com
and sign up for our newsletters.

For my children, James and Lizzie, who are my pride and joy.
And for Grant who is my rock.

CONTENTS

PREFACE

Who this book is for and how to use it

This book is for anyone – whether they are young or old, male or female, junior or senior, digitally-savvy or digitally-naive – who wants to know how to improve business relationships in our digital world. Those business relationships might be with your work colleagues – bosses and team members – or with those outside your organisation – customers, clients and referrers.

The book can be read from start to finish. And this is recommended if you are just starting to explore the world of business relationships. The DACRIE model begins with understanding difference and diversity, considers how we adapt and learn the fundamentals of communication and how relationships are formed, before moving on to improving internal and external relationships. Otherwise, you can go straight to your area of interest and the referencing system will direct you to what else you should read for basic explanations or more advanced ideas.

Introduction

The centrality of relationships in business

They don't teach you about relationships at school or college. It's assumed that you either already know – after all, you are a human being and an inherently social creature. Or you are expected to learn about relationships as you go – the trial and error method – which can cost you time, effort, some relationships and even your career.

In almost every job you need contact with other people. Even the most autonomous technology jobs will require collaboration with other tech folk, explanations with funders or discussions with clients or users.

Business relationships are important when you are trying to secure a job or interviewing a prospective recruit, when you are joining a team or trying to help a group perform better, whether you are trying to understand how to please your boss or develop the potential of those who work for you, whether you are seeking a promotion or trying to discipline someone, whether you are negotiating with suppliers or selling solutions to clients, whether you are providing great customer service or managing a client complaint.

You need to understand business relationships when you are influencing, persuading and motivating people or trying to change the way they think or behave. Nearly every aspect of business life involves effective business relationships.

Whether I am working with established business leaders or young people who are still in education, it seems to me that some basic knowledge and simple ideas about business relationships will at least save you some hassle and heartache and at best will accelerate your progress.

Combining psychology, communications and selling

My lifelong fascination with the interplay between psychology and business was truly ignited when I heard a futurologist back in 2012. Ian Pearson of Futurizon suggested that, in the future, the majority of jobs would be taken by automation and humans will be relegated to a parallel 'care economy' based on emotional skills, not physical or intellectual ones. His suggestion was that those who mastered human skills would be those most likely to still have jobs. As automation and artificial intelligence march ahead, we can see what he was talking about – those who will succeed in the future will be skilled in relationships.

So whilst I am not a leading expert in psychology or selling, I offer an unusual combination of psychology training, sales expertise and experience of helping many business people develop better business relationships. And I apologise in advance to psychology experts who may be horrified at the extent to which I have simplified some really complex concepts in order to make them accessible to readers with no psychology training.

Relevance for digital natives in online lives

My two grown children are from a different generation. I admit that it has been hard for me to understand what drives and motivates them and their different attitudes to life and work – it often feels alien to me.

Millennials can be a challenge for those who are in a business relationship with them. And they no doubt feel the same about us. So support to help make those relationships better has to be a good thing for everyone – after all, they will form the majority of the workforce in just a few years' time.

Digital natives (and I know that this is a term that some people really dislike) grew up in a different world. The digital world offers immediate access to almost infinite information, where there is no longer a divide between those who have information and those who do not, where people are inclined to share information and advice and where responses are expected in a moment rather than in days. They are used to typing (or videoing) their views and broadcasting to many people without effort. They are pretty good too at online dialogue with strangers. Yet they don't always get it when the response is not immediate or positive – or when they must navigate a real-time, face-to-face conversation or relationship where they don't have control or can't simply block someone or switch off the device.

In some respects, digital natives have an advantage over us older digital immigrants who struggle sometimes with the pace of communication and change. Yet they are also disadvantaged – they do not have the grounding in tackling real time, tricky interactions and relationships that are still the hallmark of modern business life.

As we make the transition from a commercial world dominated by digital immigrants to one full of digital natives, there is an urgent need to help these young people fast-track their learning and success in business relationships. And to help the older generation make the necessary adjustments for the new way of connecting with people in the digital world.

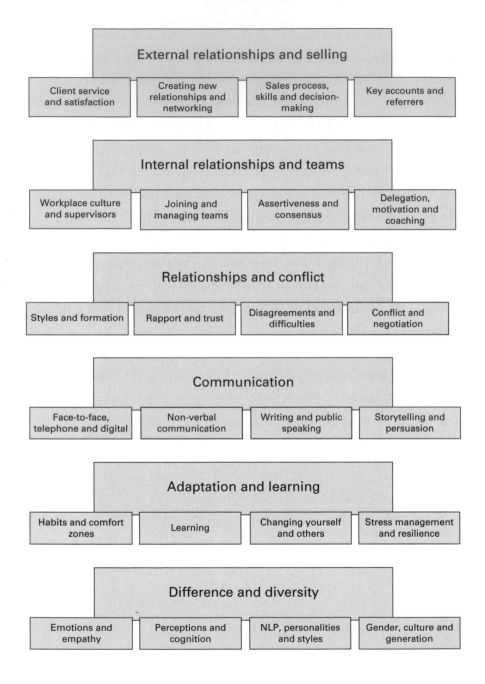

PART ONE

DIFFERENCE: UNDERSTANDING YOURSELF AND OTHERS

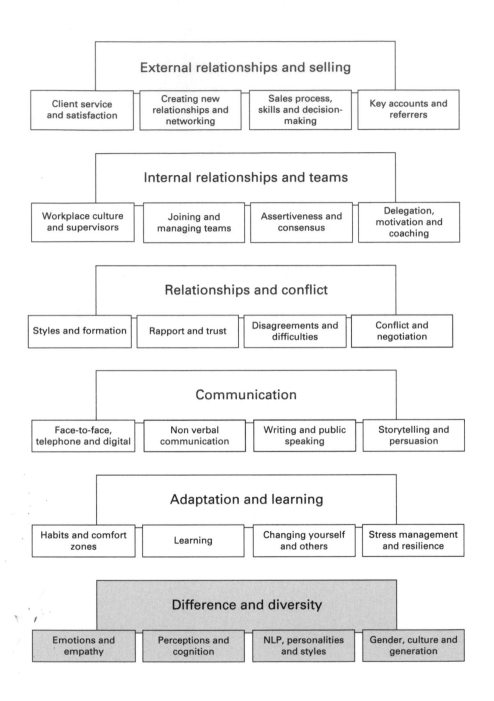

1

Introduction: Difference is good – perception and authenticity

Before we look at business relationships, we need to consider the components of those relationships – the people. So let's start by learning about ourselves and how we might be different from other people and how this might impact on how we create and sustain relationships.

It is easier to talk to and create relationships with people who are similar to us. Psychologists have suggested that we have a natural rapport (see p. 148) with 10–30 per cent of people we meet. It stands to reason that there is likely to be difficulty forming relationships with people who are different to us. And in business relationships – unlike in social relationships where we can choose with whom we associate – we have to deal with many different people.

People are different in terms of their demographics – their age or generation, gender, place of birth, culture, education, occupation, socio-economic status, race, religion and sexual orientation. But they are also different psychologically in terms of their personality, values, motivations, communication and thinking styles and the way they behave in relationships. Welcome to the world of neurodiversity.

People are also different in how they assimilate information, learn and make decisions. Some of these differences are based on what we inherit from our parents and some are shaped by the environment and experiences we had during critical stages during our early development. This is sometimes known as the '**nature versus nurture** debate'.

However, neuroscientists talk about '**neuroplasticity**' (as if our brains and the way we think are 'plastic' and can reform neural connections) – which means that we all have the ability to change. So we should not regard ourselves or others as being 'fixed' in any way.

There is a natural tendency in humans to avoid those with whom we are unfamiliar – the '**stranger danger**' our parents drilled into us. Humans have always had a preference for those who are in our tribe and naturally less inclined to those who are different and not part of our group.

The business world is unlike our social world where we can hang out with those who are like us. We have to work with people who are different to us. That can be off-putting – and even be frightening for some.

A starting point for better business relationships is therefore to increase our awareness and understanding of what we ourselves are like – our preferences and our way of seeing the world. And then understand better the differences in people around us with whom we need to form business relationships. Mutual understanding promotes better communication.

Once we recognize that people are different we can attempt to adapt our approach to ease the process of establishing a dialogue and a relationship. If we insist on believing that our way and style is the only way, then we will either fail to establish a relationship or experience conflict (see p. 156).

It would be a dull world if we were all alike. Diversity is good – it is better to have lots of different viewpoints, ideas and ways of thinking – it leads to better and more robust outcomes. Irving Janis coined the term '**Groupthink**' where those in a group all thought the same and preserved harmony sometimes at the expense of making good decisions. So we must recognize, celebrate and adapt to differences in people rather than ignoring, fearing or trying to eradicate them.

Perception and authenticity

Perception is how we interpret what our eyes, ears, noses, tongues and hands tell us – the sensory input. We perceive things differently. For example, one person may perceive tears as sadness and another person may see them as happiness.

Sometimes we only attend to some of the information in front of us – we may **filter** it to select information that supports our views or past experiences. This sometimes generates inaccurate or biased perceptions. We all know how frustrating it is when we try to do something good and others perceive that we have a hidden agenda and question our motives.

There are some things we think about that are in our conscious minds – we are aware of them. And there are some things in our **subconscious or unconscious** minds – we are not aware of these thoughts and feelings but they still affect the way we behave. Sometimes there are things in our subconscious minds – for example, a negative experience with a person that our minds have forgotten or repressed (stopped us being aware of) – that might still affect our behaviour. For example, this might happen when someone resembles someone from our past and – at a subconscious level – we attribute similar characteristics to this new person as we associated with the previous person. Psychologists call this **projection.** Stereotypes and prejudice might be other forms of subconscious thinking that can affect our behaviour. We will consider cognitive bias later. All we can do is make an effort to be mindful of what we are feeling and thinking so we minimize the impact of subconscious beliefs.

When we form business relationships we must guard against jumping to early conclusions or allowing stereotypes to rule our perceptions. But our brains will try to operate efficiently and use very few cues to make judgements and decisions about how to behave. This is especially the case when we are in new situations and have little experience of the type of people or behaviours we encounter.

Be aware too that what we think we are projecting may not be what is perceived by others. There is a famous saying that when two people communicate there are really six people involved – who we think we are, what we want to project and how this is information is received (how we are perceived).

We must be **authentic** – to be true to ourselves. We might want to modify our behaviour in order to ease the development of a new relationship, but we do not want to wear a mask or try to be someone different. Sometimes people suffer from **imposter syndrome** – this is where they are unable to accept their strengths and successes and feel that they are frauds.

We must be sincere. But also we must not allow our raw feelings to dominate. We need a careful balance.

2

Emotional intelligence and empathy: managing emotions in yourself and others

You would think that if we know rationally that we need to get on with other people – for example, if you get a new job and have to start working as part of an established team – then everyone would just do the rational thing and get on.

The part of the brain that manages this logical and rational thinking is the outer layer of the cerebrum and is called the cerebral cortex – and it is the newest part of our brains to have developed. The cerebrum in humans is far more developed than in other creatures. This is where we do what some have called 'slow thinking' – we analyse data and make rational decisions. But things are not that simple.

There are much older parts of our brains too – there's the limbic system ('mammalian' brain) which plays a role in long-term memory and emotions and regulates body temperature. There's also the brain stem – some call this the 'reptilian brain' because it automatically controls things such as sleep, breathing and heart rate.

These older parts of our brain do a lot of things automatically – like releasing the chemicals in our stomachs so that we digest our food, ensuring that our hearts beat and that our lungs continue to take in fresh air, extract oxygen and dispel carbon dioxide. Some consider it the 'fast thinking' part of our brain: we don't have to make conscious decisions about what is happening – it just happens. In a crisis, the older part of our brain takes over and our behaviour may be rather different to the rational approach.

Psychiatrist Steve Peters, in his book *The Chimp Paradox*, provides another way of thinking about these different brain systems. He says that there is a rational side of the brain (the ego or human part), the more emotional side (id or chimp) and the super-ego or computer which governs automatic behaviour and memory. These terms are similar to those used by psychologist Sigmund Freud (see p. 50) but are not the same.

Human beings are intrinsically emotional creatures. Most of what we feel and do is driven by chemicals in our bodies causing sensations, and we experience and interpret these things as emotions. For example, when we experience anxiety or fear, our bodies generate chemicals such as adrenaline and cortisol. Sometimes these chemicals are called 'stress hormones'. These chemicals enable our bodies to get more blood to our arms and legs so that we can run away or fight (see **fight, flight or freeze** response on p. 61), and in doing so they change the way we breathe and the way we think.

We learn to interpret the various sensations in our bodies as emotions. Neuroscientist Lisa Feldman Barratt has said, 'Emotions are guesses your brain constructs in the moment where billions of brain cells are working together.' Our experience and environment have an impact: for example, we might interpret a churning stomach as hunger or as anxiety. The way we interpret our emotions and those displayed by others is therefore individual. However, it suggests we have the ability to reinterpret and control our emotions.

For many years, I wrongly thought that being 'professional' and to succeed in business relationships meant that I had to suppress my emotions and act in a cool, emotion-free way. However, if we look at the work of many experts in leadership, management and motivation we see that conveying emotions the right way is important. If we convey our emotions in an authentic way then we are more likely to be trusted (see p. 148).

So returning to our example at the beginning of this section, when we join a new team we need to be aware that there could be a number of different emotions in play that don't always result in rational behaviour. For example, some people may experience negative emotions as they are uncomfortable with a change to the team, some may feel threatened by the arrival of a new team member and some may be shy and anxious about getting to know someone new. There may also be more positive emotions – some may be excited at a new team member, others may welcome the prospect of a new social connection and others may feel that the new joiner can help them succeed.

Emotions are important. You, as the new team member, will be experiencing a variety of emotions that will impact on the way you behave. And each of the existing team members will be experiencing emotions that will impact on the way that they behave. Somehow you have to understand and navigate these emotions – in yourself and others – and the behaviour they generate in order to become an accepted and productive member of the team. Timothy Gallwey, who wrote the book *The Inner Game*, suggested that a first step in managing your emotions could be achieved by using **STOP**:

- Step back
- Think
- Organize your thoughts
- Proceed when you know your best action

Human beings are social creatures and **emotional contagion** can occur. The behaviour of a team leader can lift or deflate the team and a shared mood unites a team. Research shows that teams with a positive joint experience perform better. Positive behaviours such as empathy and mirroring create a connection between a leader's brain and the brains of others. Goleman and Boyatziz found that after one executive worked with a coach and role model to improve behaviour, employee retention and emotional commitment increased in the team and annual sales increased 6 per cent. In a nutshell, this means that if one person is sad, it is likely that others will become sad too. So adopting a cheerful demeanour increases the chances that others will 'catch' your happiness.

The ability to recognize and manage emotions in yourself and others is called emotional intelligence or EQ.

The importance of empathy and emotional intelligence (EQ)

Empathy is the ability to put yourself in the other person's shoes and see things from their perspective. It is one of the core skills in emotional intelligence – which is sometimes known as EQ. This is not to be confused with IQ – or Intelligence Quotient – which is a way to measure a person's cognitive, thinking or intellectual skills. The two measures are not connected – a person with a high EQ could have a low IQ and vice versa.

Seeing another person's perspective is important in understanding their view of the world. If we are empathic it is easier to imagine what might be driving or motivating them. And if we can understand what other people want or need then it is easier to help them see what they can achieve by adopting a particular course of action. Empathy is a vital part of influencing, persuading and motivating people. Empathy makes it easier to negotiate and to promote change.

Emotional intelligence experts divide the subject into four parts:

1 Recognizing our own emotions

2 Managing our own emotions

3 Recognizing emotions in others

4 Managing emotions in others (i.e. relationship management)

There are tests that you can do that provide a score for your abilities in each of these areas. And as we learned before, humans have the ability to change the way they think and behave, so emotional intelligence can be improved with training and practice.

How good are you at recognizing your own emotions? Some people may not be very self-aware. They may allow whatever they are feeling to be expressed in a raw form and that might be alarming or even threatening to those around them.

Imagine a small child who is told that they cannot have a sweet. The small child may be overwhelmed with anger and frustration and proceed to have a horrendous tantrum that embarrasses and upsets everyone. Any parent will tell you that there is little you can do when a small person is throwing themselves around in a rage and hitting out at everything. As we grow up, we need carers to help us recognize, understand and manage our emotions in a way that is appropriate for our society. Some cultures require all emotions to be suppressed while in other cultures it is usual to shout out immediate feelings with much passion. But some people do not receive this guidance.

EQ assessments can reveal that people are not good at recognizing or managing their emotions. **Emotional regulation** is where you can learn to reduce vulnerability to negative emotions. The basics require you to attend to your physical body – to avoid illness, to eat properly, to avoid mood-altering substances and to get enough sleep and exercise. Then you need to increase positive emotions by enjoying pleasant things in the short term and attending to goals and major changes in the longer term. The material on stress management and building resilience (see p. 70) as well as mindfulness techniques (see p. 69) will also help. Experiments on **mood freezing** show that we can simply tell ourselves that we don't need to express anger or other negative emotions.

We need to be more self-aware. If we are feeling sad then – unless we know how to manage our emotions – this is likely to change the way we interact with others. When sad, we may be lost in our own thoughts and not feel like speaking and we may not show any interest in those around us. If someone does not know that we are sad, they may perceive us as being cold, distant or even rude. So communication is important. We might say 'Excuse the way I am today – I am feeling rather sad about something. Apologies if I seem distracted.' That's good communication. Or we may acknowledge and manage our sadness and attempt to communicate in a way that the sadness doesn't affect the way we behave. But remember what was said about being authentic.

Humans experience many different emotions and to different degrees. For example, we might feel a bit restless, mildly irritated, annoyed, angry or enraged. A similar emotion is there but the strength of that emotion varies. Some people know themselves well and are adept at naming their different emotions (they have a good emotional vocabulary) – and the causes of those emotions – and managing those emotions effectively.

There is much in the media at present about **mindfulness**. Mindfulness is about being in the moment and concentrating on what our bodies are telling us – how we are feeling, how we are breathing and so on. A few moments to concentrate on our physical and mental state can help us to recognize our emotions and the way they are making us behave and to calm or soothe ourselves better.

It will be much more comfortable to talk or work with someone who is aware of and managing their emotions than someone who is not. Someone who does not recognize or manage their emotions is likely to be erratic and unpredictable, which means that it may be difficult for others to trust them and to form good working relationships with them.

The other skills relate to how well we recognize emotions in others. Obviously we need to pay attention to what others are saying and doing. It is important to think about *how* they say things and not just *what* they are saying. It is helpful if we look at their non-verbal behaviour (some call this body language, although it extends to things like voice as well) to see if it is **congruent** or the same as what they are saying.

However, non-verbal behaviour is culturally dependent. Some cultures encourage people to be very still and not display any facial expressions or use their hands for gestures. It is easy if you are only familiar with one culture to then misinterpret the expressions or gestures of someone from a different culture.

Emotional intelligence also measures how well we manage emotions in others. For example, you may realize that someone is angry but you may not know what to do about it and simply avoid them. Or you may get angry in response. Someone with strong skills in this area may simply reflect back what they are observing: 'It looks to me as if you are angry.' This is showing that you are paying attention and **validating** – or recognizing their right to have these emotions. Or you may take a less direct approach and simply encourage the other person to talk, such as by saying, 'Some people would feel angry in this situation – what are you feeling right now?'

As I am sure you have figured out already, empathy and emotional intelligence are immensely important subjects for business relationships and you will read further about them in this book.

3

Know yourself and adapt to others: NLP, cognitive styles, personality, gender, generation and culture

Neuro-Linguistic Programming (NLP) – a sort of applied psychology – was developed in the 1970s by a group of psychologists (Richard Bandler, psychologist; John Grinder, linguist; and Gregory Bateson, anthropologist) who studied successful people.

'Neuro' relates to the brain and what happens in your mind; 'linguistic' relates to language and how you use it; and 'programming' focuses on the patterns of behaviour that you learn and repeat. In essence, NLP is about using the language of the mind to consistently achieve specific desired outcomes. Some of its ideas and concepts could be considered the power of **positive thinking**.

A key idea is that we each form a unique internal **mental map** of the world as a result of the way we filter and perceive information absorbed through our five senses. Some of NLP's ideas are mainstream. For example, it suggests that people differ in the way that they prefer to receive and organize information – their representational system. Many schoolchildren in the UK are tested to determine their preferred representational system so that they can be helped to learn in the way that suits them best, and lessons are structured in a way to appeal to as many preferences as possible.

The **representational systems** – and you can find out yours by completing an online assessment – are as follows:

Representational system	The types of words used by people with this system	Aspects of their behaviour to help you detect their preferred system
Visual	Draw, Look, Perspective, Pattern, Picture, Recognize, See, Vision, Watch	• Appearances are important • Breathes from top of lungs • Difficulty remembering verbal instructions • Draws diagrams • Eyes up • Head and body held erect • Memorizes by seeing pictures • Organized and tidy • Possibly disturbed by noise • Sits forward in chair
Auditory	Hear, Listen, Loud, Noisy, Quiet, Say, Sounds, Words	• Breathes from middle of lungs • Distracted by noise • Eyes move sideways • Interested in what you have to say • Learns by listening • Likes to be told how they are doing • Memorizes steps and procedures • Repeats things back easily • Talk to themselves
Kinaesthetic	Cold, Feel, Grasp, Hard, Hold, Sense, Texture, Touch, Warm	• Breathes from bottom of lungs • Moves and talks slowly • Needs to 'feel right' • Responds to touch • Stands close to people
Auditory Digital	Motivate, Recall, Remember, Think	• Exhibits characteristics of other systems • Needs to know 'it makes sense' • Talk to themselves

Why is this useful in business relationships? It goes back to the point that we are all different and that recognizing and adapting to other people can smooth the creation and maintenance of relationships. For example, if you are a visual person then you can adapt the way you speak or write in order to be more accessible to an auditory person.

NLP suggests that you observe people's non-verbal communication and their representational style so that you can **mirror and match** their behaviour. In this way you can increase your chances of establishing rapport (see p. 148) with someone.

NLP also suggests that if you observe people's eye movements, you can work out whether they are recalling or remembering visual, auditory or kinaesthetic information or constructing it or whether they are talking to themselves (i.e. self-talk). This might be useful in determining whether someone is reporting facts or creating a story.

There are many other ideas in NLP, but those that are most useful for business relationships are as follows:

- The core beliefs (pre-suppositions) of NLP include: 'You have within yourself all the resources you need to achieve what you want'; 'The meaning of communication is the response it elicits'; 'Mind and body are connected'; and 'There is no failure, only feedback.' These positive ideas are empowering.

- **Circle of excellence**: This is a technique for mentally rehearsing a future situation. Our minds cannot tell the difference between what is really happening around us and things that we imagine – and it releases the appropriate emotional chemicals accordingly. It is used to help people overcome nerves and to feel more confident (see p. 264).

- Enabling and **limiting beliefs**: Our beliefs are self-fulfilling, so whether we think positive thoughts or negative ones, they will affect the outcome. This is partly to do with our brain's ability to filter out and only receive information that supports our internal ideas (hypotheses).

- **Filters**: People unconsciously use filters to transform experiences into thoughts. Common filters are deletion, distortion and generalization. NLP offers questioning techniques to help you achieve better communication with people using each of these filters.

- **Positive intent** suggests that all behaviour is the result of a good reason – people may do or say strange things, but the trick is to understand their positive intentions so that you can communicate and work together better.

- **Positive**: The brain deletes negatives and works more efficiently with positive commands. So, rather than saying 'Don't shout' use 'Stay calm.' We've all experienced what happens when someone says 'Don't think about an elephant!'

- **Reframing**: This is one of my favourite techniques and I find it helpful for dealing with people with whom I am experiencing difficulty. It suggests that we try looking at a person or situation in a completely different way. For example, instead of seeing someone as being difficult and argumentative, reconsider them as being highly creative with novel ideas. The technique relates back to the idea of filters. If we consider someone negatively, our brains are likely to only perceive and remember information from them that supports this negative view. If we change the way we perceive them then we receive different information about them. What's also interesting is that you can create a change in the relationship dynamics simply by thinking about someone differently. Your different view causes you to behave differently and they are then likely to respond to you differently.

Cognitive and communication styles and personalities

There are other ways in which we are different. We can only review a few of the most important ideas here.

There are suggestions that people differ in the way that they process information. **Attentive** people (sometimes referred to as the involved group) take a central route through information and focus closely on what you are saying. They develop counterarguments and respond, deciding what they think. On the other hand, **distracted people** take a peripheral route and focus on irrelevant parts that randomly interest them – they prefer simple language.

In NLP we considered the way that our brains prefer to receive information. Harrison and Bramson suggested that people think in different ways and therefore the way we present information and ideas to them should alter.

Cognitive style	What they are like	What you should do to work effectively with them
Synthesist	• Curious • Creative • Speculate with 'What if?' questions	• Listen until they have finished • Show interest in their ideas • Build on their ideas – use 'and'
Idealist	• Ambitious goals • High standards • Seek agreement and consensus	• Link your ideas to broad, quality goals for the greater good
Pragmatist	• Flexible • Resourceful • Practical • Seek immediate reward/pay-off	• Provide short-term objectives • Focus on quick wins
Analyst	• Accuracy and attention to detail • Gather data before making decisions • Methodical	• Provide a logical plan with supporting data • Check that there are absolutely no errors
Realist	• Fast moving • Like to do things • Rely on sight, sound, taste, smell and touch	• Provide a three-paragraph executive summary

Later on we will consider a similar idea about how people have different learning styles (see p. 44).

Another model – developed by Dr Michael Kirton – considers cognitive style in a different way. He has a scale – called the **Kirton Adaptor-Innovator Inventory (KAI)** – which suggests that one-third of people are adaptors and one-third are innovators (with the rest somewhere in the middle). This model might be useful in business relationships when you are trying to work on problem-solving together or on sharing ideas.

Adaptor – Uses rules	Innovator – Breaks rules
Ideas based on the original problem and the original likely solutions	Has many ideas – some may not address the original problem
Likes ideas that are more readily accepted by other people	Redefines, reconstructs or reframes the problem
Does more comprehensive searches of one or two ideas	Presents many but less carefully worked out ideas

Seeks solutions within the structure of a problem and in the ways that are tried, understood, safe, sure and predictable	Provides less expected and potentially less acceptable solutions which challenge accepted practice
Likes ideas which are low-risk and maintain as much continuity and stability as possible	Presents ideas that may be very different to prevailing models and which are likely to be strongly resisted

There are many different models about **personality**. Some of these models are quite complex but are supported by the psychology community. For example, the **NEO model** uses a detailed questionnaire to understand the mix of different personality characteristics:

Neuroticism: identifies individuals who are prone to psychological distress:

- Anxiety – Level of free-floating anxiety
- Angry hostility – Tendency to experience anger and related states (frustration, bitterness)
- Depression – Tendency to experience feelings of guilt, sadness, despondency and loneliness
- Self-consciousness – Shyness or social anxiety
- Impulsiveness – Tendency to act on cravings and urges rather than reining them in
- Vulnerability – General susceptibility to stress

Extraversion: quantity and intensity of energy directed outwards into the social world

- Warmth – Interest in and friendliness towards others
- Gregariousness – Preference for the company of others
- Assertiveness – Social ascendancy and forcefulness of expression
- Activity – Pace of living
- Excitement seeking – Need for environmental stimulation
- Positive emotion – Tendency to experience positive emotions

Openness to experience: the active seeking and appreciation of experiences for their own sake

- Fantasy – Receptivity to the inner world of imagination
- Aesthetics – Appreciation of art and beauty
- Feelings – Openness to inner feelings and emotions
- Actions – Openness to new experiences on a practical level
- Ideas – Intellectual curiosity
- Values – Readiness to re-examine own values and those of authority figures

Agreeableness: the kinds of interactions an individual prefers from compassion to tough mindedness

- Trust – Belief in the sincerity and good intentions of others
- Straightforwardness – Frankness in expression
- Altruism – Active concern for the welfare of others
- Compliance – Response to interpersonal conflict
- Modesty – Tendency to play down own achievements and be humble
- Tender-mindedness – Attitude of sympathy for others
- Conscientiousness – Degree of organization, persistence, control and motivation in goal-directed behaviour

Competence: Belief in own self-efficacy

- Order – Personal organization
- Dutifulness – Emphasis placed on importance of fulfilling moral obligations
- Achievement striving – Need for personal achievement and sense of direction
- Self-discipline – Capacity to begin tasks and follow through to completion despite boredom or distractions

- Deliberation – Tendency to think things through before acting or speaking

Unfortunately, these complex models don't help us much in day-to-day life with business relationships (although they might be very helpful when used, for example, as part of an assessment before a job interview).

In the business world, a common model is **Myers-Briggs Type Indicator (MBTI).** This is based on the ideas of psychologist Carl Jung and you can do an online assessment to find out your type, which is defined as four characters – showing which of each of the pairs is dominant resulting in sixteen different personality types.

MBTI is based on four spectra:

- **Extraversion (E) – Introversion (I):** The extravert is directed outward towards people and objects, and the introvert is directed inward towards concepts and ideas. So an extravert might be action oriented, seek breadth of knowledge, prefer frequent interaction and gain energy from spending time with people. An introvert likes to think, seeks depth of knowledge, prefers substantial interaction and gains energy from spending time alone.

- **Sensing (S) – Intuition (N):** This relates to how new information is understood functionally. Sensing people trust information that is in the present, tangible and concrete that can be understood by the five senses, and they like details, facts and data. Intuitive people trust information that is more abstract or theoretical that can be associated with other information, and may be more interested in future possibilities and how things relate to patterns or theories.

- **Thinking (T) – Feeling (F):** This concerns decision-making and judging functions. Thinkers decide things from a detached viewpoint, measuring what seems reasonable, logical, causal, consistent and matching a given set of rules. Feelers decide by associating or identifying with the situation and looking at it from the inside to achieve the greatest harmony and consensus considering the people involved.

- **Judgement (J) – Perception (P):** A preference for using either the judging function (thinking or feeling) or the perceiving function (sensing or intuition). Those who judge show their preference for thinking or feeling and like to have things settled, whereas those who perceive prefer to keep decisions open.

Let's think how this might be useful in business relationships. If you were an ENFP ('Giving life an extra squeeze') and were trying to work with someone who is an ISTJ ('Doing what should be done') you would probably clash unless you recognized the difference and either modified your own behaviour or made allowances for the different style of the other person.

DISC is another commonly used personality assessment tool. The DISC model of behaviour was first proposed by Dr William Moulton Marston, a physiological psychologist, in his book *Emotions of Normal People*. The assessment tool was designed by industrial psychologist Walter V. Clarke and others. The model covers:

- Dominance (sees the big picture, can be blunt, accepts challenges, gets straight to the point)

- Influence (shows enthusiasm, is optimistic, likes to collaborate, dislikes being ignored)

- Steadiness (doesn't like to be rushed, calm manner, supportive actions)

- Conscientiousness (enjoys independence, objective reasoning, wants the details, fears being wrong)

Other personality models tackle the same differences but use different terminology. For example, Insight Colour Analysis categorizes people as being red, blue, green or yellow – and all have positive and negative traits. Another approach uses animal analogies – lion, owl, monkey and horse. But all these models serve a similar purpose – to show that people are different and that we all have strengths and weaknesses.

Another difference is in the way people prefer to communicate. This model looks at the extent to which people ask or tell and share emotions or controls. This results in four styles:

- Analytical (likes to write, aloof and sceptical)

- Driving (spoken/visual, blunt and impatient)

- Amiable (values human interaction, persuasive)

- Expressive (visual/spoken, dramatic and curious)

Having explored several common and formal methods of personality assessment, I still prefer the simplicity of a very basic model I learned at the start of my sales career in the technology sector. It focused almost entirely on non-verbal communication from facial expressions so you need to be aware that it may not work well in some cultures. Interestingly, somewhat later I learned that the three types mapped pretty well onto **McClelland's need theory of motivation**. I call it the **3D model**:

- Dependent – People who smile a lot and like social interaction. Their focus is on relationships. McClelland called this desire for interpersonal relationships 'affiliation'. Some refer to these rapport-oriented people as 'dogs'.

- Detached – People who have a neutral facial expression and like focusing on the task at hand. McClelland called this motivation 'achievement'. Some refer to these folk as independent 'cats'.

- Dominant – People who frown a lot and like to control and confront. McClelland said the motivation is 'power' and driven by the desire to influence the behaviour of others. I call these the bears!

Again, knowing your own style and recognizing and adapting to the styles of others can help you develop business relationships more easily.

Gender and generational differences

Whether men and women behave differently – gender differences – is a controversial topic that can be considered sexist if we are not careful. There are some indisputable biological differences – for example, male eyes are wired more for central acuity and female eyes have better periphery vision. Steve Peters suggested that men and women have different brains which give rise to different behavioural tendencies. But many other differences are the result of upbringing and culture. This takes us back to the 'nature versus nurture' debate.

There are obviously different chemicals in male and female bodies which can give rise to different behaviours and moods. How men and women experience and express emotions may alter too – although this is often due to cultural influences. For example, men may mask their fear with anger. Men tend to have more testosterone than women – which can give rise to aggressive behaviours. And women have to cope with monthly variations in oestrogen and progesterone which can alter mood and behaviour.

In business relationships, we use empathy to try to imagine how the other person might feel or see things. Obviously this is much more difficult if you are a woman trying to imagine how a man might feel if you have no experience of being a man! There's also a rather different dynamic because of the sexual angle. It can be tricky treading the careful line between friendly banter and appropriate behaviour in a work environment and there is much in the media at present about inappropriate male–female interactions in the workplace.

Generational differences also exist. This means that whole groups of people – as a result of their upbringing during a particular time – can share particular views and act in a certain way and this might be different for subsequent generations. Here are some general differences between the generations as reported by Ron Zemke:

- Veterans (born before/during the Second World War 1939–45)

  ○ Attracted to workplaces with stability

  ○ Want employers who value experience

  ○ Loyal

- Baby Boomers (born 1940s–1950s)

  ○ Place a high value on effective employee participation

  ○ Do not object to working long hours

- Generation X (Born 1960s–1970s)

  ○ Enjoy ambiguity

  ○ At ease with uncertainty and insecurity

  ○ Require proper 'work–life' balance

  ○ Resistant to tight control systems and set procedures

- Nexters (Born 1980s)

  ○ Intolerant of all unfair discrimination

  ○ Serious-minded and principled

  ○ Prefer to work for ethical employers

Since this work, there has been a lot of talk about the **Millennials**. These are people who were born between 1980s and early 2000s. Sometimes these people are referred to as Generation Y, Echo Boomers or Generation Me.

In 1987, Strauss and Hawe indicated that this generation was categorized as: seeing themselves as special, being sheltered, confident (some might say overconfident), team players, conventional, pressured and driven to achieve. Some argue that whilst Millennials are more civic-minded, with a greater sense of local and global community, others have argued they have a sense of entitlement and are more narcissistic.

There's an interesting video by Simon Sinek about Millennials in the workplace where he talks about four aspects of this generation.

1   Parenting – He argues that their parents told them that they were special and that they could do anything they wanted. With 'rewards' for just participating, they developed a lower sense of self-esteem (see p. 266).

2   Technology – The use of social media meant that they see others' social media personas as being 'perfect' lives which they felt they did not live up to. And unlike previous generations, where there was movement through adolescence, learning to form relationships with peers, in the digital age these 'relationships' were often more superficial digital interactions, so the relevant people skills were not learned. Hence this generation finds it harder to form deep, meaningful relationships. Sinek also argued that the dopamine (a feel-good hormone) released from each 'like' or 'share' becomes addictive, so that Millennials spend even more time online.

3   Impatience – They grew up in a world where everything – information, films, music, TV series and even dates – could be obtained instantly. This instant gratification means that the generation do not know how to work hard at something over time which is needed both to achieve an impact (something else important to Millennials) and job satisfaction.

4   Environment – When Millennials move into the corporate world they find that it is driven by short-term financial goals and that they cannot achieve everything quickly and without effort. Sinek suggests that businesses therefore have a responsibility to counteract the poor parenting Millennials have received and provide more feedback and involvement to help them adjust to the work environment.

Gary Hamel suggested that in order for organizations to attract, retain and engage Generation F (the Facebook Generation), they need to understand the following:

1   All ideas compete on an equal footing

2   Contribution counts for more than credentials

3 Hierarchies are natural, not prescribed

4 Leaders serve rather than preside

5 Tasks are chosen, not prescribed

6 Groups are self-defining and self-organizing

7 Resources are attracted, not allocated

8 Power comes from sharing information, not hoarding it

9 Opinions compound and decisions are peer-reviewed

10 Users can veto most policy decisions

11 Intrinsic rewards matter most

12 Hackers are heroes

Partly as a result of our digital world, young people are reported to suffer from **churning** – a series of on-and-off relationships – which can leave them vulnerable. It is likely therefore that it will be more difficult for Millennials to form meaningful business relationships. And those from different generations need to appreciate that they may have different values and beliefs to those from other generations. Bridging the gap – through empathy, discussion and listening – will support the development of good business relationships.

Cultural and international differences

Another important difference between people is their culture. This spans issues such as nationality, race and religion. In an ideal world, we would study the culture of each person we meet in order to gain a better understanding of their view of the world and how this affects their behaviour – but that would take too much time.

So there have been studies to see if there are general trends in cultures. There was a famous study by Geert Hofstede who identified a number of themes where cultures differed.

Individualist	Collective	The extent to which people act in their own interests or towards others in a group or society
·Masculine	Feminine	Traditional male and female stereotypes with feminine seen as more inclusive and nurturing
Low-power distance	High-power distance	Low-power distance means people regard each other as equals whereas high-power distance people will have much more respect for seniority
Weak uncertainty-avoidance	Strong uncertainty-avoidance	Those with strong uncertainty-avoidance like to be given specific instructions and are less comfortable taking the initiative
Short-term orientation	Long-term orientation	

Hofstede showed how these components combined for different nationalities:

- Strong uncertainty-avoidance (Japan, Portugal) vs Weak uncertainty-avoidance (Denmark, Singapore)

- Collective (Asia, China) vs Individualistic (UK, USA)

- Feminine (Scandinavia) vs Masculine (USA, Austria, Japan)

- High-power distance (India, Venezuela) vs Low-power distance (UK, Israel)

What this demonstrates is that even when people might look similar – or there may be a perceived similarity – nationality can have a huge impact on how you communicate and build relationships.

A more complex model – with seven dimensions – was created by Trompenaars and Hamden-Turner:

1	Universalism (consistency)	Particularism (flexibility)	What is more important – rules or relationship?
2	Individualism (individual creativity)	Communitarianism (team work)	Do we function as individuals or as a group?
3	Specific (analytical, low-context)	Diffuse (synthesis, high-context)	Involvement, commitment and context – how separate do we keep our private and working lives?

4	Neutral (control)	Affective (passion)	Do we display our emotions?
5	Achievement (egalitarian, doing)	Ascription (hierarchy, being)	Do we have to prove ourselves to receive status or is it given to us?
6	Past (sequential)	Future (synchronic)	Do we do things one at a time or several things at once?
7	Internal (push)	External (pull)	Do we control our environment or are we controlled by it?

This might explain why it is particularly difficult to form effective business relationships with those from different parts of the world and different cultures. Many organizations which have culturally diverse employees offer training in cultural sensitivity to support the creation and maintenance of cross-cultural relationships.

4

Relationship styles and team roles

As well as internal, personal differences such as the way we absorb information, think and behave, we also differ in the way that we relate to other people and form relationships.

Of course there are lots of different types of relationship. Fiona Elsa Dent suggested that there were different types of business relationships depending on your work team, functional duties and social relationships. She observed that the level of intimacy might differ between acquaintances, colleagues and your 'inner circle' of close friends.

Dent suggested that the way we connect with people at work depends on both work-based need (the extent you have to communicate with others in order to do your job) and personal connection (the extent you want to communicate more personally).

Dwayne D. Gremler suggested that there were the following types of business relationship:

- Formal – based on the role occupied by individuals (e.g. the managing director)

- Personal – based on the knowledge each person has of each other (e.g. Joe in accounts)

- Communal – based on the concern for the welfare of others (e.g. we want all staff to be happy)

- Exchange – based on the giving and expectation of benefits (e.g. I'll spend time with this supplier as I anticipate a good discount and extra support)

Elias Porter – in what is known as **Relationship Awareness Theory** – suggests that all behaviour is driven by motivation (see p. 245) and that this changes in conflict (see p. 156). He suggested that personal weaknesses are overdone and that strengths and personal filters are of influence. He identified seven ways of relating to others when things are going well:

1 Altruistic – Nurturing

2 Assertive – Directing

3 Analytical – Autonomizing

4 Flexible – Cohering

5 Assertive – Nurturing

6 Judicious – Competing

7 Cautious – Supporting

Returning to Dent, she suggested a simpler approach. She saw an interplay between the extent to which people are reserved or outgoing and whether they focus on the task to be completed or the importance of relationships. She produced a chart that classified people as having the following relationship styles:

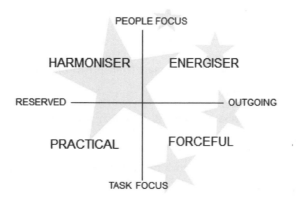

What this means is that if you are a harmonizer you may find it challenging to work with someone who is forceful, and vice versa. It suggests that you may have to adapt your style or be more tolerant of other people's style if you want to create and maintain a productive working relationship.

This preference for task- or people-focus is important in leadership styles too. It is a good idea to identify your preference and to learn to develop the others so that you can get on with the maximum number of people in as many different situations as possible. How business relationships are formed in tackled in detail in Part 4 (p. 127).

Types of team and team roles

What do we mean by 'team'?

Morgan suggested that 'A team is a distinguishable set of two or more individuals who interact interdependently and adaptively to achieve specified, shared and valued objectives.'

Cohen and Bailey elaborated on this: 'A team is a collection of individuals who are interdependent in their tasks, who share responsibility for outcomes, who see themselves and who are seen by others as an intact social entity embedded in one or more larger social systems and who manage their relationship across organisational boundaries.'

But just putting people together doesn't make a team. Bruce Tuckman argued that a team takes time to form and goes through stages:

1 Forming – Members feel tentative and insecure about their roles

2 Storming – Members try to assert their positions and jockey for seniority and control

3 Norming – Members agree and establish working practices and processes

4 Performing – Members work positively and productively together to achieve the goals

There is another difference between people – their different roles within a team. This is a popular model proposed by Meredith **Belbin**. Again, there are no rights or wrongs here and a team ideally needs a mix of people if it is to be productive. There are online assessments where you can learn your preferred team roles:

- (SH) Shaper – Focus on task to be completed
- (CO) Co-ordinator – Leads the team
- (PL) Plant – Has ideas
- (RI) Resource Instigator – Gets things
- (ME) Monitor Evaluator – Checks and ask questions
- (TW) Team Worker – Promotes harmony
- (IMP) Implementer – Systematic approach
- (CF) Completer Finisher – Does the job
- (SP) Specialist – Brings expert knowledge

Your business relationships will have to adjust for the different roles that you and others play in a particular team. And to add complexity, you may have different team role preferences in different situations and teams! There's more about teams in Part 4.

SECTION SUMMARY

IN THIS FIRST SECTION we have explored how people differ – in the way that they perceive, think and process information, in their personalities and within teams to name a few. We also considered the impact of differences created by gender, age and culture.

We considered how it is important to develop your awareness of your own preferences, approaches and styles – and their strengths and weaknesses – as well as learning to recognize how others might be different. We touched on the role of NLP in understanding and adapting to difference.

In order to understand others better, we looked at the importance of emotional intelligence – the role of emotions and how we manage them in ourselves and others. We also considered how our view of the world shapes what and how we perceive people, things and situations. Empathy – the ability to see other people's point of view – was shown to be crucial in building better business relationships.

Finally, we touched on different types of relationships and how people differ in the way that they work in teams. As adaptation – while remaining authentic – is such an important part of the process of building successful business relationships, in the next section we will explore adaptation and change – in ourselves and others – before looking at the fundamentals of good communication and relationships.

PART TWO

ADAPTATION: LEARNING HOW TO CHANGE

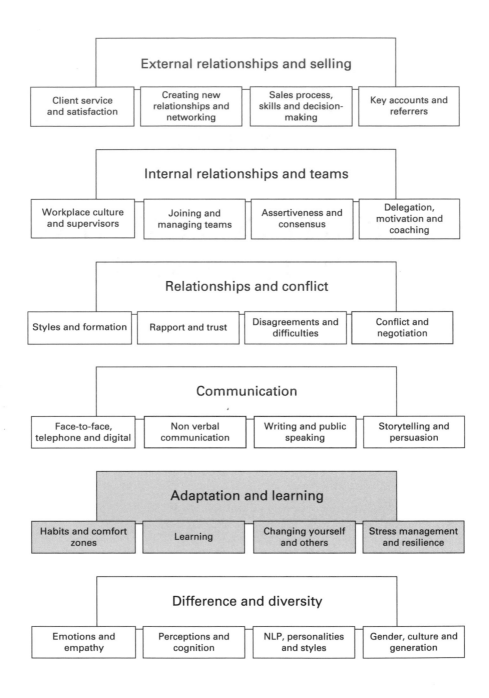

External relationships and selling

| Client service and satisfaction | Creating new relationships and networking | Sales process, skills and decision-making | Key accounts and referrers |

Internal relationships and teams

| Workplace culture and supervisors | Joining and managing teams | Assertiveness and consensus | Delegation, motivation and coaching |

Relationships and conflict

| Styles and formation | Rapport and trust | Disagreements and difficulties | Conflict and negotiation |

Communication

| Face-to-face, telephone and digital | Non verbal communication | Writing and public speaking | Storytelling and persuasion |

Adaptation and learning

| Habits and comfort zones | Learning | Changing yourself and others | Stress management and resilience |

Difference and diversity

| Emotions and empathy | Perceptions and cognition | NLP, personalities and styles | Gender, culture and generation |

5

Why change is important but difficult: attitudes, habits, comfort zones

In Part 1 we considered some of the many ways in which we are different from other people. We also recognized that if we wanted to form better business relationships then – while remaining true to ourselves and being authentic – we might need to adapt our views, attitudes or behaviour in order to get on with those who are different.

Adaptation is a temporary change. Learning how to change is therefore important – whether it is temporary or a permanent change. Although we are always keen to find ways to change other people's attitudes and behaviours – what we call change management in the business world – it is easier to start with the changes that we can make to ourselves.

When we change, others are likely to respond differently to us and so some degree of change in them is achieved. There is a saying that if you continue to do what you have always done then you will always achieve the same result. Some say that doing the same thing again and again and expecting a different outcome is a form of madness. Change is necessary if we want a different outcome – for example, getting on with someone with whom we have found building a relationship difficult in the past.

The link between attitudes and behaviour

Let's start by looking a little more closely at the link between what we think and how we behave.

An **attitude** is 'certain regularities of an individual's feelings, thoughts and predispositions to act toward some aspect of his or her environment' (Secord and Backman). Attitudes refer to a particular target (e.g. a person, a group, an object or an idea). Attitudes are evaluative – they filter and self-define. Remember the material in Part 1 about filters and perception?

Attitudes are cognitive representations that help us to structure our social world and our place within it. There is a link between what we feel (our emotions), what we think (our cognitive thoughts) and what we do (our predispositions to act in a particular way). Personality reflects predispositions or attitudes that remain consistent across a range of situations.

Creatures of habit

We humans are creatures of habit. It would take too much time to absorb all the information about a situation every time we experience it – so we take cues from what we see and tap into our memories and pull out something similar. As we saw in Part 1, some of our thoughts and behaviours are automatic or unconscious – we don't think about things too deeply if we feel it is familiar. So habits make us efficient – but they can also keep us locked into old ways of thinking and behaving.

Neuroscience shows that we have two ways of reacting to the world and change. Our **reflexive system** is automatic and based on habit. The **reflective system** is thoughtful or mindful – it's where we examine what we are thinking and why before acting.

Kevin Ochsner estimates that humans act on habit 70–90 per cent of the time. Some suggest that it takes twenty-one days to break or make a habit – there's value in repetition. So for people to change they need to create a new habit. This means you must set goals, create a strategy and maintain the personal motivation to change. In simple terms, we need to think about the positive consequences of a change in the future to reduce cravings to act in the old way.

Growth or fixed mindset?

Carol Dweck argued that people have either a fixed or growth mindset. People with a **fixed mindset** assume that intelligence and talents are innate – that you are born with them. These people hire other people for their capabilities. **Growth mindset** people assume that they can improve through working hard, practice and learning, and so they explore and persist. They hire people for their potential. If you have a growth mindset then you are likely to want to try to learn and change. The fact that you are reading this book suggests that you have a growth mindset!

A third adapt more easily

Psychologist Salvatore Maddi and telecommunications executive Carl Horn challenged some advice indicating that to avoid stress you should avoid change. Maddi's research on creative people revealed that **creativity**, insight and originality were more likely to come from people who enjoyed stimulating experiences and fluctuating environments (the 'openness to experience' characteristic on personality assessments – see p. 20).

Through a period of intense change management in a commercial organization, they found that one-third of people ('**the adaptive third**') thrived whilst the majority suffered. The simple difference in behaviour of the adaptive third was that whilst everyone else looked back at what had happened and why, they focused on the future. Maddi described this as 'existential courage'.

This linked to work by Roxane Silver who studied victims of bereavement, abuse and terrorism. She found in studies over many decades that a consistent one out of three trauma victims will not search for a reason to explain why they are experiencing misfortune.

The simple difference of the adaptive third was that whilst they asked themselves what the change meant, rather than trying to make sense of what they had done to deserve the experience, they tried to make sense of what they could do now that it had occurred. The adaptive third asked 'What can good people do when bad things happen?' instead of 'Why do bad things happen to good people?'

Moving out of your comfort zone

Alasdair White described a **comfort zone** as 'a state where you are not experiencing any anxiety because you are using a limited set of behaviours to deliver steady performance without any sense of risk'. He suggested it was a form of mental conditioning where a person creates and maintains mental boundaries that provide a sense of security.

When you step out of your comfort zone – as you do when embracing any change – your anxiety levels will increase and a stress response occurs (see below, p. x). A little anxiety and stress is good as it creates a higher level of concentration and focus. Some people thrive on stress and find it hard to function without some pressure such as an impending deadline.

However, with too much stress you are in the danger zone and performance is impaired. Each person has a different comfort zone so whilst you may be content with a small change, others may have a more severe response. So in business relationships you need to be aware that you may be responding to a situation differently to other people.

6

How to learn effectively: learning process and learning styles

If adaptation and change are so important, then it figures that it would be helpful to understand how people learn new information, attitudes and behaviours.

Are you ready to learn and change?

We will look at motivation in detail later (see p. 245). However, we need to be ready to learn. Often, when people are not achieving what they want they will simply do more of the same – only harder.

Some people will react to change, perceived threats and the unknown by 'going rigid' – by not doing anything. Psychologist Kurt Lewin suggested that in order to change, people must go through the following process:

- Unfreeze – reduce risk, threat and fear by feeling psychologically safe
- Movement or change – accept new knowledge and develop new skills and behaviours
- Re-freeze – adopt those new behaviours for the future

Lewin also suggested that those people least likely to understand and accept changes are those who are unsuccessful. Charles Darwin made a famous comment about this: 'It is not the most intellectual of the species that survives; it is not the strongest that survives; but the species that survives is the one that is able to adapt to and to adjust best to the changing environment in which it finds itself.'

In a business environment, individual behaviour is powerfully shaped by the organizational roles that people play. This means that whereas it seems just fine for a junior person to admit that they have a development need and request some training, it may be more difficult for a senior person or someone who has been in the role for a long time to reveal a weakness or ask for help.

Edgar H. Schein had a related theory which suggests that people experience two types of anxiety: **learning anxiety**, when they recognize the need to learn something new; and **survival anxiety**, when they experience pressure to change. Obviously, the survival anxiety has to be higher than learning anxiety to encourage the change. But Schein also said that when people are facing changes they might have a fear of temporary incompetence, a fear of being punished for getting things wrong, a fear of loss of their personal identity or a fear of loss of group membership.

The learning process

There is a model of competency:

- Unconscious incompetence – where you are unaware that you are unable to do something

- Conscious incompetence – where you are aware that you are unable to do something

- Conscious competence – improved performance as you work hard at the new thing you have learned

- Unconscious competence – high performance where you act in a natural, automatic way (a bit like the habits mentioned above)

Let's relate this to business relationships. At first you were not aware that there were particular knowledge and skills that you could learn to improve your business relationships. Then you realized that there were knowledge and skills that might help you. Once you have read this book you will make an effort to apply the new knowledge and skills. After practice you won't have to make a conscious effort as the knowledge and skills will become part of your natural behaviour.

David Kolb suggested that to learn we must progress through a four-stage cycle:

1   Concrete experience (CE) – we actually experience something (feeling)

2   Reflective observation (RO) – we think about something that happened (watching)

3   Abstract conceptualization (AO) – we think about a future situation or possibility (planning)

4   Active experimentation (AE) – we have a go at trying to do something (doing)

During this learning process, we use different types of thinking:

1   Diverging – considering new ideas to what we know during CE and RO

2   Assimilating – incorporating new knowledge into internal mental models during RO and AO

3   Converging – bringing things together and drawing conclusions during AO and AE

4   Accommodating – expanding existing mental models to make room for new ideas during AE and CE

Playing is another learning method and children will use a number of learning strategies, including repetition, rehearsal and play-acting.

In learning, general concepts are easier to remember than details – so when introducing a new idea our brains grasp the big picture of what we're learning rather than the details.

Traditionally, we learn through 'block practice' – where we focus on a single topic for a while. Researcher Bob Bjork found that **interleaving learning** was better for information retention and recollection. This suggests that you might switch between topics – in creativity we are urged to 'go on an excursion' and think or do something different before returning to a problem or idea.

Different learning styles

A variant of this model is provided by Peter Honey, who suggested that there are differences between people in how they prefer to learn:

- Activists like to get on and experience something
- Reflectors like to review what has happened
- Theorists tend to form conclusions about what has happened
- Pragmatists prefer to plan what they might do

So, in an ideal learning situation, there will be a mix of activities that appeal to these different preferences. It is also good to strengthen your own ability in those methods that are not your preference.

Reflection

What is important about all learning is having time to reflect – to allow the new information to become embedded. The process for reflective thinking is as follows:

1 Description – What happened?

2 Feelings – What were you thinking and feeling?

3 Evaluation – What was good and bad about the experience?

4 Analysis – What sense can you make of the situation?

5   Conclusion – What else could have been done?

6   Action plan – If it arose again, what would you do?

This follows the dynamics of the reflective space which moves between internal and external energy for: disaggregation, framing, implication analysis, insight, reframing, options and action. Use these steps to think about a recent situation where you successfully formed a new business relationship.

7

Changing yourself and others: the change process, goal-setting, models of human behaviour, change management, reframing

Before attempting to change other people, it is a good idea to examine whether and how you might adapt or change yourself.

Recognize that change takes time

The learning models above suggest that change takes time. And that change is not always straightforward: you are likely to experience a range of emotions as you embark on your change journey and sometimes you will return to earlier stages – or relapse – before progressing.

Psychologist William Bridges proposed that you had to **transition** – to tackle the end of what you were and the old way of behaving before you can move on to a new way of being:

- Endings
  - Disengagement
  - Disidentification

- ○ Disenfranchisement
- ○ Disorientation
- The neutral zone
  - ○ Taking time out
  - ○ Disconnected from the old ways and the new ways
  - ○ Frightened
- The new beginning

You need to prepare yourself for negative feelings before you start to feel more positive about the new things you learn and the new ways of behaving. This model was elaborated on by psychiatrist Elisabeth Kübler-Ross – in her work with bereavement – to show the following stages in the **change cycle**:

- Shock
- Denial – a feeling that the change is not relevant or not necessary
- Anger – feelings of anger, blame, resentment and conflict
- Depression – self-blame, lack of confidence, low energy and poor performance
- Acceptance – letting go of old habits
- Experimentation – trying to do things differently, learning and obtaining feedback
- Success – adopting new ideas and skills with confidence

When grieving or bereaved you might experience other feelings, such as numbness, yearning, outbursts, depression and sadness, before letting go. It is helpful to remember that whenever we adopt new behaviours we have to allow ourselves time to 'grieve' for the old, comfortable ways of doing things.

Decide why, what and how you want to change – goal-setting

Before changing, you need to think about what you want to achieve – your goal. It needs to be something that you want or desire if it is to be motivating. There may be a rational element to this goal such as 'I need to be better at establishing better business relationships' as well as an emotional element such as 'I will feel more confident and will progress my career faster if I get better at establishing business relationships.'

You might find it helpful if you set some specific objectives (SMART – Specific Measureable Achievable Realistic Time-specific) so that you can monitor your progress and know that you are succeeding. For example, you might set an objective to meet five new people in another department or to meet ten people at an external client organization. Or you may decide that you want to have at least one meeting each week with someone new or to add a further five connections on LinkedIn each week.

You need to assess whether the goal is achievable – to test it against reality. Perhaps you do not have enough time, perhaps other people don't have time to spend with you, perhaps you haven't identified what sort of people you want to establish business relationships with or where you might meet them, perhaps you are still feeling shy or perhaps your job does not provide the right opportunities. You might also ask people for some **feedback** – to check whether your perceptions and self-awareness are correct. At this stage, you may have to return to your goals and modify them.

Feedback can be important to help you see your 'blind spots'. There's a popular model called **Johari windows** – created by psychologists Joseph Luft and Harrington Ingham – that helps people understand themselves and their relationship to other people better.

	Known to self	Unknown to self
Known to others	Arena	Blind spot
Unknown to others	Façade	Unknown

You need to consider what options there are to achieve your goal. Some may be good and/or easy and others may be more difficult. You will need to decide which option is best or most palatable for you. Then you must decide on the small, specific and manageable steps that you must take in order to move towards your goal. Don't try to eat the elephant – break tasks down into smaller, more manageable pieces.

The final step is to be motivated to try out the new behaviour. And you need to maintain momentum in doing so. The best ways to maintain interest and motivation is to measure your progress against your original goals or get feedback from others.

These steps are what are sometimes used in coaching situations – John Whitmore created the GROW model (Goal, Reality, Options, Will to act) and this is explored further in Part 5.

As you attempt to change yourself, you will experience a wide range of emotions. This is good as it will give you real insight and empathy into how those you are trying to change will feel so that you will be in a better position to support them.

Changing others

Changing yourself may be all that you need to do in order to change the dynamic between you and others sufficiently so that you can forge better business relationships.

In Part 1, we considered the various ways in which people differ and how this can have an impact on how you build better business relationships. But the picture is more complicated because psychologists have different explanations of how people develop to become the people they are and do things the way that they do. So it follows that those psychologists will have different approaches to changing people. I will try to explain these approaches simply.

Psychological models of human behaviour

There are four main schools of thought in psychology and each perspective would suggest a different approach to create change in people – especially in **change management** programmes.

Behavioural

You may have heard stories about how rats and pigeons can be trained to press buttons when lights are flashed in order to get food. This is done by providing a reward each time they start to do something towards the desired behaviour – for example, looking towards the light or moving towards a button. This is referred to as shaping behaviour.

The **Behaviourist** approach suggests that people should be rewarded for good behaviour and punished for bad behaviour. It is closely aligned to thoughts about motivation (see p. 245) – people will do things to get food if they are hungry and other things to avoid negative situations.

If you subscribe to this view of people, you would try to achieve change by offering rewards for the behaviours you want and deterrents for the behaviours you want to avoid. Sometimes this is called the '**stick and carrot**' approach. In business relationships, you want to ensure that people perceive a benefit from the relationship rather than any negative impacts – that's obvious. But how do you know what they will find attractive or unattractive? The answer there lies in empathy (see p. 7) and in asking sales-related questions (see p. 295).

Psychodynamic

Most people will have heard of Sigmund Freud and his work analysing people's dreams. His model proposed that we have conscious and unconscious thoughts:

- The id holds our underlying urges

- The superego is our conscience from values absorbed from our parents, family and society

- The ego is the rational and conscious part of us acting as a go-between in relation to the id and superego managing our behaviour

This model suggests that we are the product of our experiences as a young child and how we navigated various developmental milestones such as toilet training and puberty. Changing people from this perspective involves understanding what early experiences shaped them and drives their present behaviour. Obviously this is really difficult to do – even if you are a fully qualified psychotherapist.

But the interesting insight for us when we consider business relationships is that we may witness behaviour that surprises us but is natural for that person because it's the same as when they were young – or they are unaware that they are even doing it. Sometimes we see quite childish behaviour in adults – particularly if they are not good at managing their emotions. There is a helpful model about this in Transactional Analysis (see p. 146).

Humanist

The *Person-Centred approach* to psychology was pioneered by Carl Rogers. He argued that everyone has a drive to become the best that they can possibly be – to **self-actualize**; and that each person has the necessary resources within themselves to self-actualize although sometimes people get 'stuck'. And whilst he didn't really offer an explanation of how people develop, he suggested that good relationships were built on three important principles – empathy (seeing the other person's point of view), authenticity and congruence, and something he called Unconditional Positive Regard (UPR). I like this idea a lot. It means that you accept people for whatever they are – making no judgements.

You will notice that these three ideas occur repeatedly in this book because they are the foundations of really good relationships – working really hard at understanding the other person, accepting them for what they are and being true to yourself.

Cognitive

This approach almost ignores the material that is so important to some of the other models – the stuff that is unconscious or from the past or based on instinctual drives such as the need for food, shelter and sex. Instead it sees human beings as rational creatures who set goals and act to achieve those goals.

There are a lot of change situations in business that fail miserably because they assume that if you tell people there is a rational reason for them to behave a certain way or set them a target then they will do it – because this misses out those emotions! In business situations we know that rationally we need to get on with other people and form productive relationships. But it isn't that simple is it?

Different approaches to changing others

So, depending on your beliefs and preference for the different models, your approach to changing others will vary. These are the management approaches inferred from the model you adopt:

Behavioural

- Performance management
- Reward policies
- Values translated into behaviours
- Management competencies
- Skills training
- Management style
- Performance coaching
- 360-degree feedback

Cognitive

- Management by objectives
- Business planning and performance frameworks
- Results-based coaching
- Beliefs, attitudes and cultural interventions
- Visioning

Psychodynamic

- Understanding change dynamics
- Counselling people through change
- Surfacing hidden issues
- Addressing emotions
- Treating employees and managers as adults

Humanistic

- Living the values
- Developing the learning organization
- Addressing the hierarchy of needs
- Addressing emotions
- Fostering communication and consultation

In this book I adopt an integrated approach – drawing on models and ideas from all of the different perspectives.

Are they ready for change?

We need to consider whether or not other people are ready to change. Partly, this is about motivation (see p. 245) and partly this is about communication (see p. 73) and engagement.

Proachaska and Scoular proposed the following model of readiness for change – suggesting that there are stages and that your actions need to be different in each:

Stage	Characteristics	How you can help?
Pre-contemplation	• Unaware of the need for change • Oblivious to any issues	• Raise awareness of the need to change with communication • Provide evidence and examples • Explore reasons and options • Ask for opinions and views
Contemplation	• Thinking about changing but taking no action	• Help them take responsibility for acting • Listen to and reflect back their feelings and hesitation • Avoid forcing the issue
Preparation	• Making the first steps towards the change	• Develop their commitment by giving positive feedback on what they have done • Ask them what they will do next • Get them to agree to what they will do next
Action	• Taking regular action to change	• Explore how to integrate the new action into their day-to-day activities • Ask them how things are going
Maintenance	• Getting results and feeling positive about the changes	• Recognize and celebrate the successes • Help them to consider new and more stretching goals
Relapse	• Returning to old behaviours	• Reassure them that occasional relapses are a normal part of the change process • Consider what triggered the relapse so that it can be avoided in the future • Remind them about past successes; ask how these were achieved and try to repeat them

There is a view that most people take about six attempts before they achieve a long-term change in behaviour.

Creating a safe environment for change

In the above section on comfort zones, I mentioned how it was important to reduce risks and increase psychological safety when individuals are trying to change.

Psychologist Michael Kahn offered ways in which to create a safe, holding environment in a therapeutic setting which is useful in other change situations. He said that people needed opportunity, desire and competence to change.

A holding environment is where there is an optimum level of anxiety, trust, a balance between empathy and objectivity, resilient boundaries, competent receipt of emotions and positive experiences and outcomes. The twelve holding behaviours Kahn mentioned included:

Containment

1 Accessibility (being there for them)

2 Attention (listening to them)

3 Inquiry (asking questions)

4 Compassion (being sympathetic)

5 Acceptance (don't judge)

Empathic acknowledgement

6 Curiosity (asking questions)

7 Empathy (seeing their point of view)

8 Validation (recognizing and accepting their feelings)

Enabling perspective

9 Sense-making (helping them to understand)

10 Self-reflection (helping them to think about what they are feeling)

11 Task-focusing (focusing on specific things that must be done)

12 Negotiated interpretation (forming a joint view of what happened and why)

Amy Arnsten argued that when people feel that they have no control or options the prefrontal cortex of their brains functions less and in some cases shuts down entirely (a 'blank mind'). But if people have a choice or even perceive that they have a choice, cognitive functions are preserved. Even a small number of options or options which are not particularly attractive can change people's perception of an event from stressful to tolerable.

Appreciating people's differences and validating their emotions are important elements of business relationships – and key in promoting change in other people. Creating an appreciative environment and providing feedback in a constructive and sensitive way is also critical for those trying to adopt different behaviours, and these topics are addressed later in Part 5 (p. 225).

Change management processes

Many management experts have suggested models that show the change management process as a series of phases or steps. One of the most popular was created by John P. Kotter of Harvard Business School:

1 Establish a sense of urgency
    – Why must this change happen now? Some people refer to the need for a 'burning platform'.

2 Create the guiding coalition
    – Who are the people leading the change programme?

3 Develop a vision and strategy
    – Create a compelling vision of what it will be like when the change is completed and a strategy – or the steps necessary – to get there.

4 Communicate the change vision
    – Talk about the future persuasively and passionately.
    – Encourage people to give their views and ask questions.

5 Empower people for broad-based action
    – This means giving people permission, confidence and skills to make whatever changes they need to help achieve the vision.

6 Generate short-term wins

- Ensure that some results can be seen quickly – even if the main vision or longer-term results will take some time to achieve.

7   Consolidate gains and produce more change
  - Recognize and reward effective changes and build on them to achieve even more.

8   Anchor new approaches in culture
  - Embed the change into the day-to-day life of the people – a bit like making habits stick, as we discussed above.

One of my favourite books on change management was written by Chip and Dan Heath. In the book there's a simple, elegant model that requires just three steps for achieving change. They use the analogy of an elephant who is being directed by a rider.

1   The rational reason – This is what the rider wants to achieve.

2   The emotional reason – The elephant is a large and powerful beast – he or she is emotion. It doesn't matter how rational the reason, there needs to be a powerful emotional reason for the elephant to move or do something: for example, to receive food or to avoid a punishment.

3   The path – The specific small step that people need to take to start the journey of change. So rather than asking the elephant to walk to another region, we simply point out whether he or she turns right or left next. Think about the Chinese saying 'The journey of 1,000 miles starts with a single step.' You need to think about the small, specific and immediate step that they need to take to start the change journey.

A change team

If you are trying to make a major change amongst many other people then it is likely you will be working as part of a team. We will look at teams in detail later in Part 5 (p. 218), but it is worth considering who you might need to help you when you are trying to change others. There will be different business relationships with these people. Alan O'Neill suggested that there were four key roles needed for successful change:

1 The Sponsor – The person who has the authority to make change happen. This might be your boss or the head of a division. This person has legitimate power by nature of their position in the organization. You need to convince the sponsor to support you and your change plans.

2 The Implementer – The person who implements the change – who actually makes it happen by changing the process or the systems or by running the change programme.

3 The Change Agent – Someone who facilitates the change. It might be a senior person acting as a good role model. It might be an external consultant who runs workshops and training sessions.

4 The Advocate (or Champion) – Someone who likes and has ideas about the change and who has an infectious enthusiasm for the project.

Of course, there may be other people in your change team but these are just some of the different roles that people might adopt. It is interesting that sometimes the more power that someone has, the less influence they have. So achieving effective change isn't just about someone telling people to do something.

Managing change in organizations is tough. There is much talk nowadays of learning and agile organizations. Peter Senge described the **learning organization** as those where 'people continually expand their capacity to create the results they truly desire, where new and expansive patterns of thinking are nurtured, where collective aspiration is set free and where people are continually learning to learn together'. He said that there were five characteristics of a learning organization: systems thinking, personal mastery, mental models, a shared vision and team learning.

Millennials and change

There is a generational aspect to change. We considered Millennials earlier (see p. 25). Millennials are more adaptive by nature, so they may react more positively to change than older generations. In fact, they actually have a desire for challenge and change.

They like mobile, video and social media, so communication about change needs to adopt these methods. Millennials are less comfortable with a 'command and control' model of management and respond better to co-operative **leadership** (see p. 252) – where they feel more involved and are consulted and empowered.

Millennials are also more likely to be confident about asking questions and challenging their bosses and supervisors. And as Millennials like to see how their work will have an impact, you need to demonstrate how their participation and contribution will have a meaningful result for others as well as themselves.

Positive thinking – reframing

At this stage I think it's worth mentioning one idea that I have found to be helpful whether you are trying to change yourself or change others. It relates back to the material about our internal view of the world (see p. 14). When trying to solve problems, many people adopt the method of looking at things from a different perspective.

Let me share a story with you. I was working with a team of very clever lawyers in the City of London. We had a shared responsibility for an important function in the business. I got on with everyone in the team apart from one individual who caused me problems. This was because he often went off on tangents, encouraged team members to talk about things that weren't on the agenda and would sometimes railroad and crash conversations. I started to see this person as being difficult and felt that he was deliberately trying to upset me.

At each meeting I would watch him and pick up on all of his negative – to my mind – behaviours, and seethe. As a result, when I spoke to him I was curt, defensive and, I imagine, rather dismissive and aggressive. I adopted a combative stance. Not surprisingly, the situation got worse and his interruptions and sidelining had an increasingly detrimental impact on the work of the team. Others could see that there was friction between us.

So I decided to reframe him. Instead of seeing him as a negative interferer (an enemy), I reframed him as an innovative thinker (an ally). With my new view of him, I invited him to give his view on things before asking others for their views or presenting my ideas. I thanked him for his different perspective and additional ideas. As a result, he became a more productive member of the team and our relationship improved. So what really changed here? I changed my views and as a result my behaviour changed and then so did his reaction to my behaviour. The Chinese symbol for problem is the same as the symbol for opportunity, and that's what we try to do with a reframe – see the same situation in a positive rather than a negative light. We change our filters and perceive different things.

8

Managing stress, mindfulness and building resilience

Learning and change can be stressful. We know that some stress can help us be more productive, but too much of the wrong kind of stress not only impairs performance but can cause long-term and serious psychological and physiological damage. Difficult business relationships can be a source of stress – and you will not be in the best position to create new business relationships if you are stressed.

What happens when we experience stress

Each time we feel stressed, our bodies react as if there is a real physical threat to our safety and we go into '**fight, flight or freeze**' mode, which floods our system with chemicals including adrenaline and cortisol. Too much of these chemicals reduces the white blood count and impairs our immune system as well as causing problems with blood pressure and heart function. Stress can have a real impact on our overall physical and emotional wellbeing.

And stress is not just about what or how much you have to do – it is how you react to different situations. Each individual will have a variety of different stressors (things that cause stress). Some people are stressed when they have too much to do, others when they don't have enough and others may feel stressed when faced with a new or challenging situation. The meaningfulness of what you are doing will also have an impact.

Meeting new people and developing new business relationships can be stressful to some people. **Social anxiety** is quite common – some estimates suggest that one in eight people suffer from it. In some respects it isn't surprising as in many cultures young children are warned about 'stranger danger' and to avoid contact with people they don't know.

In extreme cases there is a condition called **anthropophobia** (which literally means 'fear of humans'), which is also called interpersonal relation phobia. Anthropophobia is an extreme, pathological form of shyness and timidity which may manifest as fears of blushing or meeting others' gaze and awkwardness and uneasiness when appearing in society. Some cases are mild and can be handled, while more serious cases can lead to complete social withdrawal and the exclusive use of written and electronic communication.

There's evidence to suggest that our personality affects how we manage stress. On the NEO personality assessment (see p. 19), the Neuroticism aspect might indicate how vulnerable and prone to stress individuals might be. For example, are you an:

- Emotional inhibitor (Do you bottle things up?)

- Emotional ruminator (Do you dwell on past upsets?)

- Toxic achiever (Are you overly competitive, showing anger and hostility?)

There are management actions that increase stress during change programmes when you often need people to be creative: announcing changes piecemeal; allowing people to learn about changes from rumours or the media; refusing to explain reasons for changes; being untruthful; not providing a vision of where the organization is going; and increasing uncertainty by long delays between announcing changes and telling those affected. Effective communication addresses most of these issues.

Not all stress is bad – the links to creativity and happiness

Not all stress is bad. There is evidence of an optimum stress level. Harvard Business School has conducted a long-term study of the relationship between stress and creativity which indicates that the absence of stress can lead to complacency and disengagement. There are four stress conditions suggested:

- On a mission – an optimum situation for creativity in the workplace is when there is the pressure of a deadline with meaningful work

- On an expedition – although there is little pressure here, creativity flows as the work is meaningful

- On a treadmill – a common scenario where there is high pressure but meaningless work as a host of repetitive, uninspiring and/or administrative tasks pile up

- On autopilot – people have low engagement in this situation and often switch off

There is a well-established correlation between happiness and creativity and this is particularly relevant in the area of **empowerment**. A happy state of mind engenders productivity, creativity and motivation.

Henley Management College reported that 'There appears to be a positive correlation between an atmosphere of "human playfulness" (i.e. humour) in the workplace and the improvement of innovative activity and creativity . . .'. A feeling of positivity in the workplace is linked to the '**progress principle**' (Professor Teresa Amabile of Harvard Business School) – the high correlation between making progress and feeling good at work.

The **happiness model** suggests that we are stressed when there is too much challenge, and bored when there is too little, and that the route to happiness is finding the right balance between challenge and confidence. The model sees four levels of happiness:

1. Pleasure (immediate happiness)

2. Achievement (short-term happiness)

3. Contribution (long-term happiness)

4. Ultimate good (enduring happiness)

Too much stress can become anxiety

If you experience too much stress for too long, the result can be **anxiety**. Whereas depression is a negative focus on the past, anxiety is a negative focus on the future. Everyone feels anxious occasionally and often it is helpful – it helps us prepare for and to assess and avoid real risks. But too much anxiety and worry can cause problems and stop you doing what you want to do.

Anxiety can affect the way we feel, the way we think, the way our bodies work and the way we behave. Needless to say, it will be difficult to form effective business relationships if we are feeling anxious. Stress and anxiety can have profound effects on our bodies – and these can be frightening, which causes a vicious circle where the feelings get worse and worse.

How to beat stress and anxiety

So how do you beat stress? This is a huge question which merits a serious response. There are issues to do with your general wellbeing and how happy you feel with your life overall, to the relationships with people around you and whether you feel that you are in control.

There are a number of steps involved in managing stress and anxiety:

1   Understand your stress and anxiety better

2   Reduce the physical symptoms

3   Alter the thoughts related to stress and anxiety

4   Change the behaviours related to stress and anxiety

Obviously, if the stress and anxiety you are experiencing are overwhelming then you must seek professional help – from your doctor, from a support charity or a trained counsellor or therapist. They may suggest you try something called **CBT** (**Cognitive Behaviour Therapy**). This might involve keeping a diary of when you feel stressed or anxious and how strong the feeling is and trying to identify what triggers the stress.

You might be offered problem-solving techniques – to identify the core issue, develop a range of possible solutions and select the best option. Relaxation techniques – such as yoga or controlled breathing – may also help. Sometimes stress and anxiety are caused by distorted thinking – by exaggerating the threat, jumping to conclusions or disaster (catastrophic) thinking. Trained therapists can help you achieve more balanced thinking.

However, for less extreme situations I would like to recommend a book that I found both amusing to read and helpful – *Crazy Busy – Overstretched, Overbooked and About to Snap*, by Dr Edward Hallowell, which I first read in December 2007. It is full of strategies for handling a fast-paced life, but many of the ideas have remained so vibrant to me as I have witnessed, amongst my clients and colleagues, a growing and worrying tendency to manifest some of the problems outlined as the digital age matures.

Just over half the book describes the problems with modern life that many of us are only too familiar with. There's the increasingly fast-paced life that we all lead and the challenge of trying to take back control, identify the important things and concentrate on them. Hallowell looks at the medical disorder **ADD** (**Attention Deficit Disorder**) – where people rush, feel impatient, lose focus mid-task, bubble with energy but keep forgetting what they're doing, feel powerless with all the stuff around them and have great ideas but fail to complete any of the many tasks they undertake.

The author mentions the **control paradox** – by trying to control life as much as possible, you run yourself ragged, thus losing control in the process. He suggests that we stay busy to avoid looking into the abyss but this can keep a person from keeping up with the issues that matter. Acceptance, not busyness, brings us to a peaceful place.

Hallowell tackles the myth of **multi-tasking** (which he calls 'frazzing') and reminds us that in sports, the better the player you are, the more focused you become. And so he advises us to put our smartphones away and focus on the task, or person, at hand: 'Lingering is a lost art . . . if we're not careful we'll get so busy that we'll miss taking the time to think and feel.' He says it is the renegade spirit of people which loves to play – with ideas, numbers, algorithms and programmes – and if we are too busy we lose this ability.

The author refers to two great thinkers: Mihály Csíkszentmihályi, who showed that our state of highest functioning as well as greatest joy – a state he called '**flow**' – is where we rely on the special talent that Malcolm Gladwell described in his book *Blink: The Ability to Think Without Thinking*.

Hallowell addresses the oxymorons of modern life – connected anonymity (the ability to connect online intimately yet remain completely anonymous) and social disconnection. This is a real problem if you are trying to develop more business relationships. He says that virtually every person who consults him as a psychiatrist suffers from some form of disconnection. This, with social isolation, can lead to or exacerbate depression, drug and alcohol abuse, poor tolerance of frustration and a tendency toward violent behaviour. He suggests that we count the number of minutes we spend each day with live human beings. As humans, we are hard-wired to be social creatures – to hang out with humans.

Hallowell advises that emotion is the first key to the best of modern life. He says that the small actions such as shaking hands and maintaining eye contact set a positive emotional tone which in turn brings out the best in people. At the heart of making the most of life today is the ability to treasure and protect your connections to what you care most about, and thus the main problems in modern life today are caused by neglecting what matters to you most. He mentions numerous studies of successful people in business which emphasize the importance of focusing on what you do best and sticking with it.

The second key is rhythm – his word for the complex set of neurological and physiological events that create the apparent effortlessness of a person doing complicated work well. As a person practises any activity, the planning and executing of it moves gradually from one part of the brain to another (the cerebellum acts as the automatic pilot of the brain). We touched on these ideas earlier.

Hallowell talks a little about the need to find hope when you're down (positive thinking). He describes the phenomenon of *gemmelsmerch* – a force that tugs at our attention all the time and distracts us from whatever we're doing. He then talks about the F-state – frantic, frenzied, forgetful, flummoxed, frustrated and fragmented – and warns you to make sure that you do not merely make your life faster and more full of data – more difficult to follow and keep track of – in an effort to make it more fulfilling and suggests you look at the paradox of labour-saving devices that take up so much time.

The author talks about 'screensucking' – wasting time engaging with any screen; 'leeches' – people or projects that waste your time and attention; and 'lilies' that make you feel fulfilled and satisfied. 'Doomdarts' are obligations you have forgotten about which suddenly pop up into your consciousness like a poisoned dart. EMV – Email Voice – refers to the unearthly tone a person's voice takes on when it is reading an email while talking to you on the telephone. 'Gigaguilt' refers to the guilt a person feels over missing something even while knowing that keeping track of everything is impossible and having enough time to please everyone is equally impossible. 'Taildogging' is about going faster or pushing harder – yourself, your children, your business, your spouse – simply because other people are doing so.

'Pizzled' – a combination of fed up and puzzled – is how you feel when a person, without asking or explaining, brings out his or her phone to make a call while you are together (others now call this phubbing). Hallowell also coined the term 'blind baseball' – where the players have blurry vision and the field is in constant motion.

He goes on to some strategies and remedies to achieve the C state (calm, cool, collected, concentrating, creative, co-ordinated, courteous) such as OHIO – Only handle it once – using your morning burst (or whatever time of day that you feel mentally at your freshest); minimizing junk time, conversation interrupts and pile-on (Just say 'No'). There is material on assertiveness on p. x.

Hallowell cautions against being an 'Info Addict' – so alert to what is going on in the world that you fail to do anything yourself – and the 'Spray Effect' – when you try to put your attention on too many things at once. He suggests that you keep alert to the warning signs that you are about to become overloaded (know your juggling limits) – and take a break at that point. He also emphasizes the need to deal with toxic worry (sometimes depression starts with a lack of mental focus).

One of the author's most memorable statements is that 'Attention is like money. If we don't watch how we spend it, we waste it.' He talks about how our brains are becoming stuffed with stunning information that we will soon forget and that instead of the thoughtful life they savour, people are in danger of living superficial, sound-bite lives they barely notice. He unpicks the common association that fast is smart – and describes the differences between people who are fast processors and those who are slow processors.

Hallowell challenges us to consider where we do our best thinking. He says that many people find answers in the shower or in the car and suggests that this is because what a person does at work is too goal-directed and contaminated by *gemmelsmerch* to allow the free play of ideas that great and **creative thinking** requires. A shower promotes good thinking because it induces a state of comfort, calm and relaxation and stimulates all five senses and your mind is free to go where it wants. Today's world provides us with too much information and not enough thought – what separates a great innovator from the mere data gatherer is the ability to stop gathering data and think about what has been gathered.

The central solution is to have a system to make sure that you do what matters to you and find the right balance between control and lack of control. He says that most sages urge us to make the most of the moment and to never forget that any day might be our last. Hallowell urges us to constantly ask ourselves, 'Am I doing what I really want to do?' and 'Am I doing what most matters to me?' He warns that once fear starts to govern your use of time, you cease to be true to the best of who you are and, paradoxically, you give up your chance to live a genuine life.

Towards the end of his book, Dr Hallowell suggests that you do a systematic assessment of your use of time and assess the value received for the time invested. He goes beyond the usual work-based categories and considers electronic time, intimate time, wasted time and creative time. He then argues that you consider the effort in order to assess the 'worth it' factor.

Hallowell identifies ten key principles to managing modern life:

1 Do what matters most to you

2 Create a positive emotional environment wherever you are

3 Find your rhythm

4 Invest your time wisely to get maximum return

5 Don't waste your time screen sucking

6 Identify and control the sources of *gemmelsmerch*

7 Delegate (see p. 239)

8 Slow down

9 Don't multitask ineffectively

10 Play

There is much advice on how to improve your ability to pay attention – for example, get enough sleep, watch what you eat, exercise, reduce distractions, balance structure and novelty, do what you want to do, build variety into your career, vary individual tasks, have human moments (that's where relationships come in), don't expect your attention to last indefinitely, stretch your brain every day, combine work and play, encourage deep thinking by engaging in active debate and find joy every day.

Become mindful

Hallowell hints at something called **mindfulness** when he mentions 'slowing down'. Mindfulness is the basic human ability to be fully present, aware of where we are and what we're doing, and not overly reactive or overwhelmed by what's going on around us. It's where we allow our reasonable mind to understand our emotional mind a little better so that we have a wise mind that integrates both.

There are lots of ways to practise being mindful. You can focus on your breathing: this really slows you down, brings you back into your body and helps you focus on the moment – the here and now. Some psychologists call this grounding.

The first step is to observe what you are experiencing – to really concentrate on one feeling at a time and let go of distractions and other thoughts. The second step is to describe the experience by putting words to the experience without evaluating or judging. The final step is to participate: becoming one with your experience and completely forgetting yourself – letting go of negative or destructive thoughts and feelings and concentrating on more positive emotions.

This links back to our earlier consideration of emotions. With good emotional intelligence skills you can learn to stop for a moment and really concentrate on what you are feeling within your body – tension, anger, fear and so on – which helps increase your awareness. You can then name that emotion and consider its cause – and whether your response is appropriate and proportionate, before trying to take a little more control over your feelings.

Alternatively, you can learn relaxation techniques or how to meditate. They all have similar aims – to help you reconnect with yourself and ground yourself within your body so that you feel less out of control.

Build your resilience

What is resilience and how can you be more resilient? A Harvard Business School report found that there are three fundamental characteristics that set resilient people and organizations apart:

- A capacity to face reality
- An ability to find meaning in testing times
- An ability to improvise

Psychological resilience is an individual's tendency to cope with stress and adversity – whether through bouncing back, not being affected negatively or developing better strategies for the future.

Resilience is a process rather than a personality trait (although scores on psychometric scales for things like anxiety, depression, vulnerability to stress, assertiveness, positive emotion and self-discipline may be indicators of resiliency). It is a two-dimensional concept spanning both the adversity and the positive attitude/behaviour adaptations. So two judgements are involved – the significance of the risk and the adaptation required.

Most research shows that resilience is the result of individuals being able to interact with their environments and the ways in which they promote wellbeing or protect themselves against risk factors – whether by themselves or supported by their relationships or policies.

There are many ways to develop resilience. The American Psychological Association suggests ten ways:

1 Maintain good relationships with family, friends and others

2 Avoid seeing crises or stressful situations as unbearable events

3 Accept circumstances that cannot be changed

4 Develop realistic goals and move towards them

5 Take decisions or actions in adverse situations

6 Look for opportunities for self-discovery after a struggle with loss

7 Develop self-confidence (see p. 264)

8 Keep a long-term perspective and consider the stressful event in a broader context

9 Maintain a hopeful outlook – expect good things

10 Take care of your mind and body – eat properly, exercise regularly and pay attention to your own needs and feelings

---

SECTION SUMMARY

WE STARTED BY CONSIDERING WHY the ability to adapt and change was important for business relationships. The link between attitudes, thoughts and behaviour was established and we explored ideas around habits and comfort zones. And we examined ways to learn more effectively – whether we are ready to change, the learning process and our different learning styles.

Then we examined how we can change ourselves – and that it may take time – as well as others and ideas around the change cycle. The four models of human behaviour were overviewed – along with ideas on how to promote change as we dipped into material on change management processes.

There was an analysis of how modern, digital life can cause stress and unhappiness. Whilst recognizing that some stress is valuable (for example, in creativity), we looked at ways to deal with negative stress and anxiety with ideas on positive thinking, reframing, grounding, mindfulness and building resilience.

PART THREE

COMMUNICATION FUNDAMENTALS

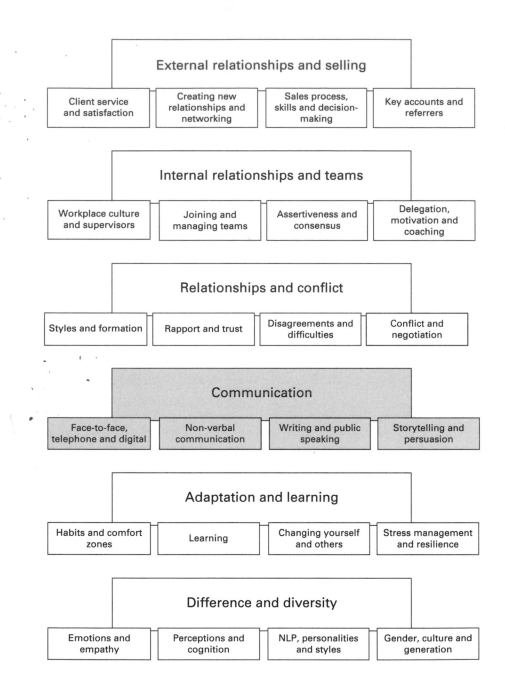

External relationships and selling

| Client service and satisfaction | Creating new relationships and networking | Sales process, skills and decision-making | Key accounts and referrers |

Internal relationships and teams

| Workplace culture and supervisors | Joining and managing teams | Assertiveness and consensus | Delegation, motivation and coaching |

Relationships and conflict

| Styles and formation | Rapport and trust | Disagreements and difficulties | Conflict and negotiation |

Communication

| Face-to-face, telephone and digital | Non-verbal communication | Writing and public speaking | Storytelling and persuasion |

Adaptation and learning

| Habits and comfort zones | Learning | Changing yourself and others | Stress management and resilience |

Difference and diversity

| Emotions and empathy | Perceptions and cognition | NLP, personalities and styles | Gender, culture and generation |

Having considered how people are different and how they learn, adapt and change in the previous sections, the next piece of the puzzle in building better business relationships requires us to understand communication.

Communication is the lifeblood of relationships – without communication there is no relationship. As humans we all communicate, so it should be easy – but many problems in business relationships are caused by poor communication.

Communication comprises a number of elements – first, the material, content or message; and second, how it is delivered by one person and received by another. Communication can be face-to-face, by telephone or in writing. In the digital age we also have to manage communication through teleconference, email, social media and instant messaging, where some of the traditional rules of communication have been eroded. The importance of non-verbal communication (NVC) also merits serious attention.

A frequent challenge for communication in business relationships is the style and level of formality. So we'll look at differences between informal communication – such as in casual, social conversations or on social media – and more formal communications such as those in business meetings, reports and presentations.

We'll also touch on some issues around written communications: how to get your message and meaning across accurately, particularly with regard to the ubiquitous email. And we'll start to explore how to influence and persuade people – which are important skills for business relationships both within our organization (Part 5) and those outside our organization (Part 6).

9

Face-to-face communication

Face-to-face communication

We start by exploring face-to-face communication even though in our digital world a lot of relationships are created and maintained online where there may be no face-to-face communication. Increasingly, face-to-face communication is through the medium of a screen using videoconferencing or social media. However, many of the same ideas apply whether there is face-to-face communication or not. And some would argue that a business relationship isn't properly formed until there has been some face time. Digital relationships – such as those formed and sustained on social media – are covered in more detail in Part 6 (see pp. 137 and 271).

Elements of communication

There is often a difference between the message that the speaker sends and what the listener or reader receives. There are stages in communication – many of which are hidden as they take place in people's minds. In Part 1, I mentioned that each person has a unique view of the world (mental map) created by their own experiences, education and cultural background. This unique mental model has an impact on every communication and interaction – because people perceive, filter and assimilate information differently.

There's a model by Shannon and Weaver that shows some of the potential areas of difficulty in a five-step process of communication:

1 The speaker gets an idea to communicate

2 The speaker encodes the idea into words

3 The communication travels through some medium to the receiver – there may be distortion on the way

4 The receiver receives and decodes the message using their mental model and perception filters

5 The receiver holds the idea

This shows why communication can be complicated and why misunderstandings arise – what you mean to express as the sender can be interpreted differently by the receiver. How you send the information – the elements of communication and the extent to which it is specific, authoritative, impactful, believable, relevant and timely – will influence how well it is received. There may be barriers to communication within the receiver – particularly how they are feeling, what they remember and understand and their attention – which may also affect how the message is received.

Effective communication is where:

• We get what we want – a positive connection

• We have been understood – from our point of view

• The other person seems OK with the exchange

Heath argued that there are six characteristics of effective communication. It must:

• Be simple, brief and profound

• Be unexpected and surprising

• Be based on concrete, real experiences

• Be credible and trustworthy

- Be emotional – so the other person feels as well as thinks

- Tell a story

I. A. Richards labelled four kinds of messages we receive in communication – sense, feeling, tone and intention. The sense of the message is what's on the surface – the words that are spoken or written. Feeling underlies the sense of the message. Tone relates to the relationship between the speaker and the listener. Intention relates to why the speaker is relaying the surface message.

Communication isn't simply about expressing our views. A key tool in any communication – and particularly when we are trying to influence or persuade – is that of empathy. We must anticipate how the other person is feeling and thinking and how they might react to the information. This understanding of other people's perspectives was discussed in Part 1 (see emotional intelligence on p. 7). Active listening – where you attend carefully to what is being said – is important in promoting good dialogue and in persuasion. This is addressed in more detail in Part 6 on selling.

In a business relationship, be aware of the difference between push communications – where we are telling or directing people what to do – and pull communications, where we take a more consultative or coaching approach to draw them in. We all know how different it feels between when someone tells us to do something (push) or asks us (pull). We can see this on a spectrum:

DIRECTIVE (Push)

- Tell someone what to do

- Solve someone's problems

- Give advice

- Offer guidance

- Ask questions

- Help them solve their problem

CONSULTATIVE/COACHING (Pull)

Some problems in communication

There are numerous things that can go wrong in communication and there are two particular examples worth mentioning here.

A **Freudian slip** is an unintentional communication error that is regarded as revealing subconscious feelings. The speaker accidentally uses a slightly different word to the one intended but conveys their real views. Sometimes there is a sexual undertone – for example 'He brings a lot of emasculate energy' (meaning weak) instead of 'He brings a lot of masculine energy' (meaning strong).

Interrupting someone or stopping them from speaking is annoying. It can even undermine their confidence and self-esteem (see p. 264), make them withdraw and may even break a business relationship if it happens frequently. There's a **gender difference** too – studies have shown that it's primarily men interrupting women. A study by Deborah Tannen at George Washington University found that when men were talking to women they interrupted 33 per cent more often than when they were talking with other men. Men seem to back off less often when they are interrupted too. Another study showed that both men and women interrupted women more when they were talking.

Tannen says that we learn conversational styles when we are children. 'High involvement' describes people who talk along to show enthusiasm whereas 'high considerate' describes people who believe only one voice can speak at a time. So there can be clashes of conversational style that compound any cultural differences. There are suggestions that you can use non-verbal communication to avoid being interrupted – for example, lean in, look focused and maintain eye contact.

It has been suggested that you should analyse the different types of interruptions before adopting a strategy to deal with it:

- Power play – The interrupter wants to throw the person off their game by making them flustered and defensive. Saying 'Did you have something to add?' is a better response than 'May I finish?', which confirms the power shift.

- Co-operative interjection – Although it's not intended to shut people down – and often comes from an ally – it can have a negative effect over time. This might require a private word with someone to say that you'd like to be heard more. Tannen suggests that in a high-functioning team in the workplace you should hear three nano-seconds of silence between each person speaking as evidence that there is enough listening.

- Uncontrolled outburst – This suggests that the interrupter is lacking self-control, so you should remain calm and turn your attention to the interrupter. Say that it seems to have evoked a strong response and encourage them to continue.

- Efficiency intervention – The interrupter keeps finishing your sentences and you feel hurried. Sometimes this happens when people are speaking too much or too slowly. Also avoid using disclaimers before you speak.

Communication in conflict is addressed in Part 4.

10

Non-verbal communication and telephone communication

What is communicated (the content or message) is not as important as how it is communicated (the delivery). It's not just what you say but how you say it. This relates to **Non-Verbal Communication** (NVC) – sometimes known as body language.

NVC holds the key to how you present a better impression of yourself and generate a more positive and confident perception amongst your work colleagues, customers or clients, family and friends.

NVC is an important element of any interaction between two people – whether they are meeting, networking, attending a first presentation, pitching for a new contract, negotiating, undertaking research or trying to build a business relationship. Developing your abilities in NVC can significantly enhance your performance as a salesperson, as a great communicator and as a leader and motivator of teams. NVC skills are valuable to all occupations but particularly those with a high level of people interaction – such as in marketing, human resources and senior management.

NVC can help significantly in your personal life too. It can make you look more confident in social settings – thus increasing the likelihood of you meeting and getting on with new people. It plays a critical role in the development of new romantic relationships as well. You can often detect a happy couple by the way in which their body language '**mirrors and matches**' each other and by the way their orientation and eye contact is focused. Preening and courting behaviours (e.g. fiddling with hair, adjusting clothing) are often non-verbal and unconscious signals of attraction. It can also help you understand better how your partner, children, friends and family are feeling – enabling you to overcome difficulties and focus communication in the right direction.

Early psychological research suggested that just a fraction of the meaning in any interaction is conveyed by the actual words spoken, while almost 70 per cent of the meaning is conveyed by non-verbal means – whether this is your appearance, the way you speak or your body language. Meharbian's results indicated that meaning is communicated as follows: 7 per cent by the spoken word, 38 per cent by the tone of voice and 55 per cent by other non-verbal cues. Perhaps this is not so surprising when you learn that the eye has eighteen times more neurons than the ear – we have much greater bandwidth for visual information than for auditory information.

More recently, Alexander Pentland of MIT has written about what he calls '**honest signals**'. His research confirms that people are dramatically influenced by how others communicate rather than by what they say. He also found that consistency in tone of voice and motion is taken as an indicator of people who really know what they are doing and is therefore important for trust (see p. 148) and respect.

Pentland's research demonstrated that when someone is pitching (see p. 309), it is possible to estimate the ratings they received purely by their **tone of voice**. He also found that the effectiveness of leaders could be measured and he could predict their success at certain tasks without knowing what they actually said – just by the way they said it. His research also indicated that more successful people are more energetic, talk more, listen more and spend more face-to-face time with people.

Some people may be concerned that the deliberate use of NVC is somehow manipulative and unethical. These fears are unfounded, mostly because people often use NVC in order to improve communication (by gaining a deeper insight into how other people are feeling), but also because research has shown that even those most skilled in NVC are unable to project an inauthentic or untruthful image for very long.

Types of non-verbal communication

Nine different types of non-verbal communication have been identified:

1   Facial expressions

2   Gestures

3   Paralinguistics (aspects of spoken communication that do not involve words, such as 'aah' and 'mmn')

4   Posture

5   Proxemics (the amount of space someone uses)

6   Eye gaze

7   Haptics (relating to touch)

8   Appearance

9   Artefacts (things that are held or used)

Edward G Wertheim, in his work *The Importance of Effective Communication*, identified five roles for non-verbal communication:

1   Repetition – repeating the spoken message

2   Contradiction – indicating a conflicting feeling to what is expressed verbally

3   Substitution – a gesture instead of a spoken word

4   Complementing – adding extra meaning to the spoken words

5   Accenting – highlighting or emphasizing elements of the spoken words

Cultural differences in NVC

Non-verbal communication is dependent on culture. Some cultures – for example, those in Southern Europe – may use a lot of movement and hand gestures whereas other cultures – for example in Japan – may be still, with few facial expressions and no hand gestures at all.

Different nationalities have different gestures and interpretations of gestures too. For example, a nod up and down means 'Yes' in European cultures but in some Indian cultures the same meaning is conveyed by the head moving from side to side.

Cultural differences in NVC are often the unrecognized reason why negotiations between, for example, Europeans and people from the Middle East are perceived as being more difficult than those with fellow Europeans. Examples of differences include the amount of eye contact, hand gestures and handshaking.

The body language of those from urban areas also differs from those from rural areas – those from rural areas tend to use much more space and speak more loudly than those from urban areas.

Gender differences in NVC

There are gender differences too in NVC. Research suggests that women might have a biological advantage in that they are generally much better at reading non-verbal communication than men. This may partly be due to their greater peripheral vision from the structure of their eyes or their reported greater ability to multitask than men. Men's eyes are wired for greater central acuity.

Yet women suffer from some biological disadvantages too: typically women are shorter than men – and height can convey power and authority. Women often have softer and higher-pitched voices than men and can be perceived as having less authority as a result. So women and men may need to develop different abilities in order to overcome these disadvantages. Most people know that Margaret Thatcher underwent voice training in order to bring the pitch of her voice down to a level usually associated with men.

Environmental context of NVC

Many non-verbal behaviours and gestures may be the result of environmental factors rather than a true reflection of someone's feelings. Whilst folded arms (effectively signalling a barrier between the person and others, and also some auto-contact – as if you are giving yourself a hug) and a scrunched-up body position may indicate discomfort, vulnerability or defensiveness, it may simply be due to the room being cold. Be aware of environmental factors in your interpretations. Consider clusters of gestures rather than focus on an isolated movement.

Voice

Research shows that those with a lower-pitched and louder voice and who speak quickly are perceived more positively than those with a high-pitched, softer voice or who speak very slowly. Your voice has a major impact on how you are perceived and the impression you create. People often assume louder voices convey greater confidence and authority and that speed of speech reflects intelligence (and nervousness if it's too fast!).

A study into surgeons' voices by Harvard University in 2002 found that there was a correlation between tone of voice and the likelihood of a surgeon being sued for malpractice. Out of interest, another study found that increasing time by as little as five minutes on diagnosis reduced the likelihood of malpractice. This underlines the importance of face-to-face contact and the need to be heard accurately.

Research also shows that some accents are perceived more favourably than others. Although it is difficult to change your accent, it certainly helps to understand how other people might react.

Space and NVC

You can also learn about people from the way in which they organize their work space. Does the desk provide a barrier? How much 'private area' (e.g. behind a desk) is there? Are guest seats the same height? Are there photos of themselves with important people or framed certificates on their walls? Is the area tidy or cluttered?

In business relationships, particularly in networking situations, the difference in how much space people from different cultures feel comfortable having between them becomes apparent. Personal body space for many Europeans is around 18 inches whereas it might be less for those from other cultures. Having someone 'in our space' (imagine being crushed in a packed underground train) makes us feel uncomfortable. We may then inadvertently project that discomfort onto the people we are meeting.

Open and closed stance

In European cultures we perceive those who use a lot of personal space as being more confident. Someone who is scrunched up into a small space, with arms and legs folded, gives the impression of a lack in confidence and disinterest in communication. Whereas an open body stance – head up, shoulders down, arms relaxed and unfolded and legs uncrossed – sends the message that you are keen to communicate.

A real smile – which reaches the eyes – is considered friendly and welcoming in many cultures. And although there is no visual contact during a telephone voice call, people can hear a smile in your voice.

Congruence and deceit in NVC

Non-verbal communication provides powerful insight into just how authentic people are. Does their non-verbal behaviour support and enhance their spoken words or do they seem at odds?

Watching for incongruent behaviour may make it easier to identify where someone is uncomfortable or trying to conceal the truth. Paul Ekman suggested that you can increase your ability to detect deceit by looking for contradictions in what people say, hesitations, vagueness of details or conversely too much detail. But he also said that you should look for clusters of indicators, patterns and changes in behaviour.

Indicators of deception include increased touching of the mouth and chin area (a remnant of when children cover their mouths when they lie) or a reduced amount of hand and arm gestures (it is difficult to falsify non-verbal communication) and different eye contact to usual. One psychology experiment required nurses to avoid telling patients and their relatives the truth, resulting in a dramatic reduction in their gestures and body language. It is as if your body is unable to lie even if that is what your mouth is doing.

Buying and distress signals in NVC

You can gain an insight into extent to which people are agreeing with what you are saying by considering their non-verbal communication. For example, a salesperson might watch for buying signals during meetings – when people suddenly sit forward or tilt their heads as if to listen more intently.

Head nods, eye movements, smiles and other non-verbal signs – paralanguage – while someone is speaking can indicate that they are paying attention, are interested and wish for the other person to continue speaking.

People will also sit forward when they wish to speak and will try to pick up the eye contact 'baton' to take over the conversation – this is where non-verbal communication is used as a cue. Similarly, if people sit back or fold their arms, you may have lost their attention and interest.

If someone freezes or becomes momentarily still, it may be that they perceive a threat in something you have said. The same has been observed when people receive bad news or a shock. In these types of situations people may clasp their hands and grip their chair as if they are holding on or anchoring themselves against further shocks.

Whereas glazed eyes, yawning or a head resting on a hand may indicate disinterest, loose energy or displacement activity (e.g. jiggling coins in a pocket, strumming fingers, pen- or foot-tapping, etc.) indicates a suppressed desire to remove oneself from the situation and can be a sign of impatience or anxiety.

Steepling (like the chap on the cover of this book) creates a barrier, revealing a sense of vulnerability, and can also be a sign of superiority – the apex of the fingers draws others' vision to eye level, which gives the person 'permission' to speak. Similarly, when people interlace stiffened fingers it may be a sign of stress or distress.

Rocking back and forth might be a sign of extreme distress. Researcher David Givens suggests that this is a primitive form of **self-soothing**. A closed mouth and tight lips are another gesture that indicates a level of discomfort. Joe Navarro wrote a number of books on non-verbal communication which addressed these 'reserved' behaviours.

Telephone communication

Whilst face-to-face communication is best for establishing business relationships, inevitably time and distance constraints mean that we have to use the telephone. In some jobs, for example in customer services, the vast majority of communication is by telephone.

While many of the same rules of good communication generally apply, we have a major disadvantage on the telephone – we cannot see the other person's non-verbal communication. We must concentrate on what is said and how it is said. Voice becomes even more important – and the pace at which we speak. And while people can't see us smile, they can hear it in our voices.

Although it is often easier, quicker and less intrusive to write an email (see below), the interactivity, immediacy, feedback and emotional connection achieved through a telephone call mean that calls are particularly important for developing business relationships.

To feel more confident about making calls, you need to prepare. Read and have any relevant information to hand. Know what you want to achieve and anticipate questions. But also be prepared to adapt in response to the reaction or questions of the person you are calling.

Avoid distractions. Allocate sufficient time and move to an environment where you won't be distracted or disturbed and where you can take notes. Some people feel that there is value in rehearsing what they plan to say – particularly if they anticipate a difficult call. The timing of calls can be important – some people are larks and prefer early morning interaction whereas others are owls and operate best towards the end of the day.

Starting calls. Think about the 'bookends' of the call: the personal small talk at the start and the end of the call. It can set or pick up on the tone or mood of the call. Your introduction should explain the reason for the call – and be mindful of its value to the person you are calling. Use empathy to build rapport and trust and an emotional connection. Be alert to non-verbal cues – such as hesitation – that might indicate the call should be rescheduled.

Structure of the call. Consider all the components of a good telephone call. Allocate the appropriate amount of time to each element: introductions, questions, interaction, summaries and endings.

Get on the other person's agenda. The essence of good selling is to use empathy and research to get on the other person's agenda. Focus on what is of interest to them rather than your own agenda. Professional selling is about identifying or creating needs and then proposing a solution and benefits (see Part 6).

Promote interaction through questions and active listening. The bulk of any relationship management telephone conversation should be interactive.

Curiosity is a valuable aid to selling – and so is the ability to tolerate silence to give the other person time to consider their response. The use of structured questions (the basis of many sales models) and active listening techniques is important in sales calls as much as persuasion (see below).

Ending calls. Part of the preparation for a telephone call is knowing your desired outcome. Where you are trying to gain agreement to something – sending further information or arranging a meeting – you may encounter objections (see p. 299). There are also different methods of closing conversations such as confirming everything has been covered or offering alternative courses of action.

Many organizations use voicemail. Your out-of-office message should be short, friendly and convey the right tone. It must be up to date and provide alternative contact details for emergencies.

If you need to leave a voicemail message, prepare what you will say in advance, but keep it short. Include your name, organization's name, reason for calling and telephone number. While many mobile telephones will show the number that dialled in, some organizations suppress their numbers so you might repeat your telephone number in order that that the recipient doesn't have to replay your message to get the number correctly.

Informal and formal communication (and etiquette)

The level of formality of a communication will depend on a number of factors.

In a work environment, you might expect informal communication with people during breaks and when chatting about personal interests. Communication will be more formal when you are in a meeting or talking to your boss or superiors or to customers and clients. Likewise, in a social situation – such as a reception or party at work – you might adopt a more informal style and tone. You might expect a text message, a phone call or an email to use less formal language than a letter or a report. The spoken word is less formal than the written word.

Another factor is the nature of the business relationship. If you have people reporting to you, the nature of your communication might be formal in a work environment and informal in a social environment. You would probably be more formal when you first get to know someone than after you have known them for a while. Similarly, you would expect to talk more formally to a client and perhaps to someone who is significantly older than you. Younger generations tend to favour less formal communication.

In some cultures, you would expect the tone to be more formal if you are addressing someone from a higher class or caste than yourself. Some cultures would find it inappropriate for you to share personal information about yourself at the start of a relationship or to ask it of a stranger, whereas in other cultures you might be expected to divulge information about yourself and exchange social pleasantries at length before you get round to discussing business. You may even need to show respect by refraining from speaking until you are addressed.

And herein lies a problem – how do you know when and how to switch from formal to informal communications? And vice versa? It can be as embarrassing to be too formal (where you might come across as aloof and disinterested) as it is to be too informal. Some people feel that once they reach 'the friend zone', where communication is typically informal, it is hard to start a conversation about more formal business matters.

Knowing the right level of formality comes with experience. There is much guidance on business etiquette. A British guide to etiquette in social situations with those from upper-class backgrounds in the UK is Debretts. But there are many online sources to help you navigate cultural differences and these are often referred to as 'Doing business with' guides. If you spend a lot of time in business relationships with people from other countries then it is probably advisable to look up the relevant guide or consider cultural sensitivity training.

Sometimes it is easier to watch and listen to the level of formality shown by those around and adapt your style to what they are doing.

11

Formal and informal communications, etiquette and storytelling

Whether you are meeting someone for the first time or whether you see them on a regular basis, you need to keep your communication natural and interesting. No one wants to risk being perceived as a bore. And a story can bridge the gap between informal and formal communication.

It is uncomfortable pushing information out to people (that's where the term 'being pushy' comes from) and much better to pull in their interest with questions, anecdotes and stories. Although again, there are significant cultural variations in business interactions – some cultures are much more direct than others, so take care not to misinterpret someone's style and intentions if they come from a different culture.

When social media burst onto our screens, there was a resurrection of interest in the power of storytelling, with much talk of campfires and communities. Storytelling is one of the oldest ways in which we humans communicate – pre-dating written words. The oral tradition still dominates in some cultures.

There's a wealth of information from the realms of neuroscience showing that stories are more memorable than facts alone:

- Stanford University found that stories were twenty-two times more memorable than facts
- OneSpot found that 92 per cent of consumers want to internalize words in the form of a story

- The human brain does not distinguish between reading or hearing a story and experiencing it in real life – the same neurological regions are activated
- An experiment found that five per cent of people remembered a statistic yet 64 per cent remembered a story
- The brain releases dopamine when it experiences an emotionally charged event, making it easier to remember and with greater accuracy
- A story activates parts of the brain that allow the listener to turn the story into their ideas and experience as a result of a process known as neural coupling
- During storytelling – when people connect – the brain goes through a variety of processes such as neural coupling, other cortical activity and dopamine release
- When processing facts, two areas of the brain are activated. A well-told story can engage other areas

Where people identify with stories, you benefit from the self-reference effect. People have a tendency to effectively recall information about themselves. Memories linked to what we think about most – i.e. ourselves – are held longer and recalled more easily. We saw earlier that strong emotions are an important part of how memories are stored in our brains.

Whatever your story, you need to understand the level of knowledge and interest in the person to whom you are speaking or writing. This requires the use of empathy (see p. 7). Then you can adjust the story so that it connects with the listener or reader.

There may be many different people listening to or reading your story – they may all have different personalities and styles and they may have different roles in the buying process (see material on the Decision Making Unit – DMU – on p. x). The story must be adapted to appeal to as many as possible. When writing a story you need to adjust to the channel or medium of communication that you are using – whether it is a blog, a client case study, a pitch or a formal presentation.

When we think about the most memorable and inspiring speakers we have ever heard, we often recollect their emotion and passion. Making an emotional connection is what storytelling is all about. Inject your personality or feelings into the story so that they can connect on an emotional level. But be authentic.

Our short-term memory works in chunks of two to seven pieces of information. And most people find it easiest to retain around three key pieces of information, so use the 'rule of three' by including three key messages that you want the other person to retain.

When you have to convey complexity, tell your story as if to a child. That way you automatically adjust for their level of knowledge and tailor the content to be more meaningful to them. Even the most complex TED (Technology, Entertainment and Design) lectures start from a simple idea and build up layers of complexity. Writing experts suggest that you should regard your reader as 'an ignorant genius' – they are clever but they need to learn new information.

There are seven basic story plots which you can use to structure and develop your stories:

1   Overcoming the monster

2   The quest

3   Journey and return

4   Comedy

5   Tragedy

6   Rebirth

7   Rags to riches

And there are seven basic story elements you should include:

1   A hero

2   The hero's character flaw

3   Enabling circumstances

4   The hero's ally

5   An opponent

6　The life-changing event

7　Jeopardy

Good stories follow the dramatic curve. They build tension to a conclusion and climax. Storybooks are often organized so that each chapter or section follows its own dramatic curve – so you are drawn onto the next part of the story.

The heroic story is a frequently-used template that incorporates the dramatic curve:

1　Call to adventure

a) The ordinary world

b) The call to adventure

c) Refusal

2　The ordeal

a) Mentor helper

b) Crossing the threshold

c) Test, allies and enemies

3　Unification and transformation

a) Approach

b) Ordeal

c) Reward

4　Road back and hero's return

a) Road back

b) Atonement

c) Return

Think about a popular fairy tale – like Aladdin – and you can start to see all of these components within the story – an ordinary boy, finding a genie in a ring, coaxed by Jafar to enter the cave, the genie in the lamp who helps him, his wife accepting the 'new lamps for old' and the loss of all his riches before his final success.

Think about both the content of the story and its delivery. The words you use are important. Remember in Part 1 we talked about NLP? There I mentioned that people have different sensory preferences and that you can detect these by their choice of words. So visual people use words like see, look and perspective, whereas auditory people might use hear, listen and sounds. Incorporate words from all senses to ensure that you connect with those you are addressing.

You might also consider what words the people you are talking to use a lot – in many organizations there will be favoured words and phrases that reflect the culture. Try to use those words to strengthen your connection with people – adapt to the language of the people you are talking to. Writing expert Joe Vitale argues that some writers use certain words and repetition to put their readers into an hypnotic state.

Use the journalist's inverted pyramid to think about the content as a one-sentence story. Be clear about the aims of your story – how you want people to feel and what you want them to think and do as a result. Use words that paint strong mental images. Use powerful words that evoke emotion.

A hook grabs people's attention. A bridge acts as a connection between something that the listener already knows and what you are trying to explain. The Celtic cross is a good example of a bridge. The people of Ireland were originally pagans – they regarded the sun as an all-powerful force. The early Christians linked their story to that of the sun, which is why the Celtic cross combines the circle shape of the sun and the cross. We also use analogies and metaphors to connect new information to ideas that people already understand. We connect to their existing frameworks of knowledge in their mental map of the world.

Non-verbal communication (NVC) – particularly your voice – will have a big impact on the way you deliver your story. Use it to good effect and allow your emotion to show in your face, your voice and your gestures. You will appear sincere and authentic if your non-verbal communication is congruent with the words of the story.

As Maya Angelou said, 'I've learned that people will forget what you said, people will forget what you did, but people will never forget how you made them feel.'

12

Public speaking and presenting

Sometimes in business you have to make a presentation. Presentations can be informal – such as being asked to describe something briefly in a meeting – or formal – such as preparing a pitch for a customer.

You will feel more confident and provide a better presentation if you prepare. The first step is to plan the presentation. Whilst most people plan and prepare their content, they often spend insufficient time planning their delivery, the subsequent interaction and follow-up.

The Ebbinghaus **forgetting curve** suggests that people forget 30 per cent of what they are told after just three hours and 90 per cent is forgotten after three days, so if you want people to remember things you will have to work hard in both preparation and delivery.

When we recall the most impressive presentations we have ever seen or heard, it is the emotional impact made by the speaker and the feeling that the speaker evoked rather than the rational information presented that we recall. Emotions embed memories more strongly.

Prepare the presentation content

Plan and prepare the presentation content

Aims – What do you want to achieve with your presentation? What are the three key messages that you wish to convey? How do you want the audience to feel afterwards? What do you want them to do as a result of your presentation? What impression do you want to make of yourself, your team and your firm? How will you know if the presentation is successful? You may want to set specific objectives in terms of support received, feedback ratings, connections made afterwards or even enquiries and referrals.

Audience – Think about the audience. What is their existing level of knowledge? What do they want to hear from you? What are their expectations? What value will they obtain from your presentation? Do some research if you don't know. Take care if you have a mixed audience (some with technical knowledge and some without) to ensure that you address their different needs. It often helps to rehearse your presentation to a 'friendly' audience – who can indicate where they think changes might assist comprehension or flow.

Content – Most presentations include too much information. Less is more. Consider the aims and (no more than three) key messages as well as the needs of the audience. Plan what needs to be covered – possibly using a mind map which might also help structure the information.

Simplify – Simplify complex ideas – break them down, start at the lowest level and add layers of details if required. Your job as presenter is to act as a translator or interpreter of ideas. Additional information can be provided as a handout – it doesn't all need to be included in the presentation. Furthermore, if there is more detail available this presents an excellent opportunity for follow-up contact after the presentation.

Images – Think beyond words and bullet-point lists: 'A picture is worth a thousand words.' Use photos, quotes, diagrams, charts, tables, newspaper clippings, maps, infographics, music and videos. Make sure that everything is big enough to see. Try to have just one item (text or image) on each slide so things don't get cluttered. Videos can be useful to explain complicated ideas, add humour or evoke emotion – but keep them short. Props – for example different hats to identify different perspectives – could also be used.

Signposting – Help the audience know where you are going and where you are at present. Navigate for them. Tell them what you are going to cover at the start and remind them what you have covered at the end. This helps reinforcement and retention by using the primacy and recency effects.

Specificity – Avoid general lists of things. Try to be as specific as possible – provide names, dates and numbers. It is easier for people to remember specific points and actual examples.

Storytelling – Stories, as we saw above, are one of the most effective ways to communicate ideas, as people become emotionally involved when they can identify with or relate to one of the characters. People like surprising endings too.

Structure – Use a three points approach to structure presentations. Plan your greeting and a hook (the benefits of your talk) and then present your first message (story, evidence, other information) and then the second and third message before your conclusion and interaction. Avoid starting with an apology and take care with humour. You need a strong start and a positive finish.

Timing – Most people attempt to include too much material in their presentations for the time available. The presenter is not there to simply offload a huge amount of information – he or she has extract the key points, or offers different perspective so that the presentation adds more value than simply listing information. Have a timing device at the edge of your vision or ask someone to warn you when you are nearing your time limit.

Prepare the presentation delivery

Whilst most people invest time in preparing their presentation content, there is often little evidence of preparation of delivery. Rehearsing – alone and with team members and to be familiar with the environment and equipment used – will improve confidence. Rehearsing is also the only way to be sure that you will stick to the allocated time.

Empathy – This is a core skill in emotional intelligence (EQ – see p. 7). You need to put yourself in the audience's shoes and see the presentation from their perspective. You are not there just to tell them all that you know – you are there to help them understand the key points that are of value to them.

Audio visuals – A combination of verbal and visual material has been shown to deliver 85 per cent recollection after three hours and 65 per cent after three days, so use visual aids. If you are using presentation software, avoid looking at the screen (and therefore losing eye contact with the audience) – either refer to notes (don't hold them – if you have to have something in your hand then make it a small deck of cards showing key points) or position the laptop screen so that you can see it whilst still facing the audience. The slides are not there to support the speaker – they are there to provide a signpost, a different perspective or additional information to the audience. Research shows that retention is aided with both auditory and visual senses involved. And some people prefer visual information whereas others prefer auditory information. Focus on one key point per slide. Use images and charts rather than lists of words. Complex charts might be offered as a handout instead of appearing as a slide. Think about different ways to convey your ideas rather than just bullet-pointing what you are saying (although if your presentation is being translated into other languages then it might help to have the key points listed, but you can provide a script to translators). Avoid transition effects – the only one recommended is dissolve as the others can be too distracting. Use of upper- and lower-case letters makes text easier to read than using all upper case. Dark letters on a white/light background are easiest to read. Use the notes slide layout option so that additional information about the content of the slide can be seen in handouts but not on the screen.

Body language (non-verbal communication – see above) – The most critical non-verbal communication during a presentation is eye contact and 'lighthousing' to connect to all members of the audience. Avoid looking at notes or the screen too much as this reduces eye contact. Gestures help highlight key points but they need to be authentic and congruent. Don't forget how important it is to smile – remember the audience really wants you to succeed. Don't stand stock still, as this can seem impersonal and stilted. But don't allow yourself to move too much as this can be distracting and may convey nervousness.

Hands – If you naturally use your hands to make gestures then that is great if it amplifies your verbal message. But make sure your gestures are authentic and congruent with what you are saying – and that they don't get out of control and convey nervousness. Also be careful that you don't clutch your hands, the remote control or notes and inadvertently convey nervousness.

Confidence – Even if you don't feel confident, you can project confidence through your non-verbal communication. Planning and practice builds confidence. You will avoid 'uumms' and other verbal tics if you rehearse.

Emotion – Communicate emotion with emphasis in your speech and also with your hand gestures. You need to convey genuine interest in what you are talking about. Be measured and animated but not fidgety.

Interaction – Ideally, your presentation should prompt interaction. Asking questions, requesting a show of hands or asking audience members to undertake some activity are ways to do this. We fear questions that we may not know how to answer. We fear a lack of control. We fear embarrassment and damage to our reputation. Anticipation and preparation for questions will build confidence.

Lectern – While a lectern is helpful for a screen or your notes, it acts as a barrier between you and the audience. And there is a danger that if you are nervous you will hold on to it. Move out from behind the lectern to create a better connection with your audience.

Questions – Anticipate what questions you might be asked. In sales training, you can learn how to analyse, classify and respond to **objections**. Never be tempted to provide an answer when you don't know it. Showing a little vulnerability by saying it's a good question and that you will come back to the questioner later is OK. You could also bounce the question back to others in the audience.

Rehearse – Rehearsing alone and with team members and to be familiar with the kit and visuals used will improve confidence. But be ready to divert from your plan if the audience wants you to move in a different direction. If there is more than one presenter, ensure that handovers are smooth. Bouncing back and forth between two speakers can be effective – but practise and don't overdo it as the audience can get dizzy. Refer to those speaking before and after you so that you are integrated and 'joined up'. Control your behaviour while others are speaking – look at the person speaking or their slides. Show interest in them and occasionally look out to the audience. Even though someone else might be speaking, the audience may be looking at you.

Script or notes? – Avoid reading from a script. However, you might want to write a script to help you rehearse and to extract the key points for bullet-point notes. If you memorize your script, remember to retain some emotion and inflection as you speak. Whilst you don't have to memorize the entire presentation, it will help your confidence if you memorize the first two or three minutes whilst you are concentrating on creating a connection with the audience.

Timing – It is vital that you stick to your allotted time – particularly in some cultures such as the monochromatic British. Often people overrun because they either try to cover too much content or they have failed to rehearse enough. Allocate sufficient time for questions, audience participation and interaction.

Words – 'Don't think about elephants' – so now you are thinking about elephants! Be careful you do not **prime** your audience with the wrong words. Take care with words such as 'complex', 'bore', 'panic' or 'difficult'. And if you use a technical word or jargon provide an explanation. The audience will not pay attention after hearing a word that they do not understand.

Dealing with nerves (visualization, etc.)

Many people are nervous about making presentations. The fear of public speaking – **glossophobia** – is experienced by three-quarters of people, so you are not alone if you feel anxious about presenting. Some nervousness ensures a good presentation – even experienced actors say so!

We learned earlier that our fight, fright or freeze response creates changes in our physiology and makes it more difficult for us to speak in a calm manner. It can make our pulse race and our breathing change and it can make our mouth dry and our hands shake.

Planning, preparation, practice and rehearsal will help build confidence and alleviate anxiety. However, if you are experiencing too much anxiety you should use techniques (counting, deep breathing, exercise, etc.) to help you.

There are techniques in Neuro-Linguistic Programming (NLP) to help with nerves. For example, you can visualize a positive situation (such as a circle of confidence) and trick your mind into experiencing all the things you visualize for real. A simple visualization exercise (ask someone to read the instructions while you concentrate on them) is:

1   Prepare

- Find somewhere quiet
- Calm yourself and clear your mind
- Close your eyes
- Breathe slowly and deeply

2   Focus on your goal or desired state

- Visualize yourself having achieved the goal or desired state – spend at least five minutes exploring your vision
- How do you know you have achieved your goal or desired state?
- What have you done or achieved?
- What does it look like? Colours? Shapes? Images?
- What does it sound like? Voices? Words? Other sounds?
- What can you smell?
- What are you saying? What are others saying?
- What does it feel like? What emotions do you feel? What are the physical effects?
- What are the most pleasant aspects?
- What is different? What is happening around you?

3   Capture the state

- What are the most significant aspects of your vision?
- Fix five key positive points and most powerful images, sounds or feelings in your mind
- What would you do to recreate this state?

And remember that you might feel very nervous inside, but the audience is unlikely to be aware of it! There is a great TED video by psychologist Amy Cuddy called *Fake it 'til you make it* which shows that holding one of five 'power poses' for just two minutes can change your physiology (e.g. raising the amount of testosterone in your bloodstream) and actually make you feel more confident.

13

Written communication: emails, blogs, social media and reports

Don't worry if you missed out on learning about language structure, writing and grammar at school, as there are books that can help you learn the basics (see the 'Further reading' section).

When communicating face-to-face or on the telephone, the communication is two-way. We can ask questions and we respond to the non-verbal communication, perhaps adjusting what we say or how we say it or repeating points and asking questions if we detect uncertainty.

However, when we write we have to anticipate how the reader will feel and how he or she will react – and that may be affected by their mood or their situation as well as the host of potential personal differences we learned about in Part 1. We also have to think about how we are going to capture and retain their attention – whether it is a short informal email or a long formal report.

I will address four aspects of writing – the essentials of good writing, email communications, social media and report writing – as these are the most likely to be of value to you in forming better business relationships.

The essentials of good writing

Be clear about your aims and key messages – Plan your writing. Decide why you are writing – what you want to achieve. Identify the key points – ideally no more than three – you want to convey. Consider what you want the reader to think and feel when they read.

Focus on the reader – Use empathy to imagine what the reader will be thinking. How much knowledge of the topic do they already have? Are they likely to be positive or negative towards your ideas? What do they want from reading your material? How can you anticipate their needs and respond to their questions and concerns?

Choose the right structure – At school we often learn to have a beginning, a middle and an end or conclusion. But in business we must get the message across at the start – to tell the whole story in the first sentence. There are various structures we can adopt, depending on the purpose and audience of the document.

Be brief and keep it simple – Less is more. Why say something with four words when you can say it in one? It is quicker to provide a list of bullet-points than to write sentences. The **Flesch formula**, which measures readability, looks for short words (with few syllables) in short sentences and short paragraphs. Only provide as much detail as required – if in doubt, then leave it out. You can always provide links to further information or appendices if required.

Adopt the right tone of voice – For formal communications you may want an impersonal and perhaps authoritative and cool voice. Some organizations have guidance on how to write in the appropriate tone for their brand. For informal communications you may let your personality shine through.

Use images – A picture is worth a thousand words. Sometimes it is better to include a chart, table, diagram or picture. Infographics are effective at conveying facts and figures in an attractive format which visually-oriented and younger people may prefer.

Make it scannable – Use subheadings to make it easy for people to scan through and gain the general meaning. Avoid large chunks of text which look unappealing on both paper and screen.

Check it – Once you have written something, put it aside for a while and come back to review it when you are fresh. Check the spelling and grammar and take particular care with people's names. When it is an important document or you are new to writing, you might ask a colleague to read it for you to make suggestions for improvement.

Writing emails

People receive hundreds of emails a day. So if you want to win their attention when there is so much competition then you need to craft your email well. Most people agree that we send and receive too many emails – so always consider whether it is better to pick up the phone or talk to someone.

If you need to convey a lot of (technical) information, reach a number of people and leave a record of your communication then email is a good choice. And emails are not intrusive – they don't interrupt the recipient. But if you need to establish or build a relationship, share sensitive information, obtain an immediate response or the nature of the communication is more interactive then a telephone call might be better.

You can control what you say in an email and you have time to consider what you write whereas in a telephone call it is possible for the conversation to move in directions you didn't anticipate. It seems that the older generation prefer telephone calls, while younger people prefer emails.

If you receive a short, informal email from a colleague it is best to respond in a similar style. However, if you are writing to someone you don't know or have a longer request or explanation that may be circulated to several people then you should adopt a more formal style.

In today's fast-paced life, it is tempting to simply write out everything you feel you need to say without giving it much thought. But plan your emails – and structure them carefully – for maximum impact. Always review what you have written before hitting the send button. If you have an international audience, remove any cultural or colloquial references that they may not understand.

Avoid the use of cc (which stands for 'carbon copy' from the typewriter days) unless people really need to see it. If you do not want everyone to see who is on the circulation list – and privacy is increasingly important – then use bcc ('blind carbon copy'). Only use 'reply all' when absolutely necessary.

Provide an accurate summary and any action required in the subject line – so people can scan their inbox and get a feel for the content and urgency of your email. Be clear what you want people to do – sometimes this is called a 'Call to action' – in the subject line. Avoid using capital letters as it can make the email look like spam or 'SHOUTY'.

Start your email with a suitable greeting. Then use the journalists' **inverted pyramid** by including a short summary of the entire email in your first sentence. You can inject some personality and tell stories to make the email more interesting and to stand out but keep in mind the need to keep emails short. Ideally, the main content should be viewable above the review line so that it doesn't have to be opened to be understood.

Where your email contains information that might be difficult to convey or receive, some people suggest a '**comfort sandwich**' approach. Start with something positive, then include the 'meat' of your message before ending on a positive note. Be polite – use 'please' and 'thank you'. Thanking people in advance for their help has been shown to increase the chance of a response.

Avoid using emoticons, jargon, abbreviations (unless you know that they will be understood by the recipient) and slang. And in all business communications you should try to be legal, honest, decent and truthful and avoid swearing and comments that could be considered defamatory or discriminatory.

Remember that emails can be seen by and forwarded to other people – so resist including sensitive or confidential content. Some organizations have rules about the sharing of sensitive information – especially relating to colleagues and clients – so check your internal policies. And if you are forwarding an email to someone else, read through all of the material in the thread in case you inadvertently share confidential information.

Don't attach large files – use one of the systems like DropBox if you need to, or, better still, upload to a secure collaborative shared space – otherwise your email may not get through to people. And if you are attaching several documents, ensure that the titles make clear what they contain and in which order they should be read.

Most organizations will have a pre-set 'signature' for emails – showing your name, title and department as well as details of your organization and contact details. Many will also have legal information such as company registration number and disclaimers. If your direct dial telephone number and/or mobile phone number are not included in the signature you may want to add these.

When you are away from your PC, make sure that you update your 'out of office' message so that people know when you are able to respond or from whom else they can obtain help in an emergency. And be sparing with read receipt requests (where the reader must confirm they have received the email) and high importance indicators (which are flagged differently in inboxes).

In Part 1 we explored emotions. Never email or respond to an email when you are angry. Give yourself time to calm down and reflect on the best course of action. It is often better to deal with difficult or sensitive topics face-to-face or on the telephone – there is less chance of misunderstanding or of getting into conflict (see Part 4). And you don't want any keyboard warriors to be provoked.

Writing blogs and using social media

You no doubt use social media in your personal life but you should be careful when you produce blogs or use social media in the business environment.

First you should check to see whether your organization has a social media policy – there may be restrictions on what you can say and share even on your personal accounts. You should also be careful if you use social media to keep track of and stay in touch with your business relationships – it may be that there are guidelines and rules about how you conduct these relationships in social media. For example, some organizations may not allow you to disclose your location or client names for security and confidentiality reasons. There may be restrictions on your giving and receiving endorsements and recommendations too.

However, you may be asked to contribute to or write blogs for your organization to help with its promotion to the wider community of customers, clients, suppliers, internal colleagues and potential recruits. These blogs may appear on your organization's website, on the website of other organizations or even on your own profile (e.g. in the Pulse publishing platform on LinkedIn your articles become attached to your profile).

Some organizations may have style guides that provide advice on what to say and how to phrase things – so adhere to your organization's tone of voice. There may be approval procedures too where you need to check content before sharing it publicly.

Whether your blog is public or for a restricted audience, be aware that it may be seen by many people including those you do not know, and that once something is on social media it is almost impossible to remove it – even after you delete it. Whatever you say on a blog or social media will be there for everyone to see forever. Inappropriate material could damage your reputation (and career prospects) as well as that of your organization. The media is full of examples of people's careers and lives being destroyed as a result of long-forgotten social media posts and tweets. Recruitment and human resources professionals may check personal social media accounts so take care what settings you have and what content (especially photos) you and your contacts post.

Blogs and social media are an important way to establish and maintain business relationships and this is explored further in Part 6 (see p. 271).

Typically social media is more informal writing where people expect your personality and own voice to be more apparent. Avoid being overly formal and distant. You might want to share your views or a report on something that you have done or attended. The essentials of good writing discussed above will still be important – consider what will be of interest to your target audience, be clear about your key messages and keep things short and simple.

Blogs are typically between 300 and 600 words long. Posts on platforms such as Twitter are limited to 280 characters – although the previous limit of 140 characters is still preferred by many. Use link shorteners to make most use of the available characters. You can post updates onto your LinkedIn profile and have them simultaneously appear in your Twitter feed. Proofread carefully so that there are no spelling or grammatical errors.

Include key words and phrases as this is important for search engine optimization (SEO) as well as conveying your key messages. So, for example, if you want your blog post to turn up in Google searches for particular words and phrases then these need to appear in the title, first paragraph and subheading of your blog. You need to be specific. Use the correct method to mention other people and organizations (for example, + in LinkedIn and @ in Twitter). When you do this they will be alerted to your presence and this can initiate a dialogue and generate gratitude for the exposure.

Remember the importance of the word 'social' as an integral part of social media. It shouldn't be viewed as a broadcast medium. Don't just push out information you want to share – like, comment upon and share other people's content and engage in the conversation. As a rule of thumb, post 30 per cent of your own material and 70 per cent of other people's material in your feeds. Take a role in curating – selecting and editing – others' material that you think might be of interest to your connections and followers. If people trust you, they will value your choices, and sharing other people's content is a good way to show them that you appreciate their content. It may even prompt some reciprocity.

Writing reports

You may be asked to prepare a report for your colleagues internally or for external clients. Or you may be part of a team that is tasked with producing a report. While many organizations make more use of presentations, videos and other interactive and collaborative formats, reports are still a common requirement in many business situations.

Typically, reports are more formal in tone than other communications and they usually follow a particular structure. For example:

- Title, date and author (and intended audience)

- Executive summary

- Introduction

- Brief (purpose of the report) and background

- Sections on each of the main topics

- Conclusion and next steps

- Appendices containing more detailed information

It can be difficult to know how much information to include in a report – you want to share everything that you know or have researched, but you don't want to overwhelm the reader. For this reason, reports have appendices (or hyperlinks) where the reader can see more detailed information if they choose.

You may have readers with different interests and levels of knowledge so you will need to bear this in mind when you write a report – use empathy to try to get inside the minds of the readers, appreciate their level of knowledge, consider their views and anticipate any questions they may have.

The most important section of any report is the executive summary. It's like a synopsis or abstract of the report which people can read quickly to gain an understanding before they read the rest of the report. It provides them with a framework and helps them navigate through the material. Imagine if you had just two minutes to tell them about the report – that's what you should cover in the executive summary.

Most people write the executive summary when they have finished writing the whole report so that it provides an overview of all the key points. Others might write a draft executive summary first – so that it acts as a guide as to what to include in the rest of the report.

Executive summaries should be produced when a report is more than five pages and should be about five per cent of the size of the entire report. Only information in the report should appear in the executive summary although you may alter the emphasis.

Whether you are writing the report alone or as part of a team it is important that you allow yourself time to review, edit and proofread. With multiple authors it can be difficult to present the same style and tone and the danger is the report feels disjointed. Ask someone else to read it to gain input on how to improve it further.

14

Influence and persuasion

Whether you are talking to people, making a presentation or writing a report, you are likely to be trying to influence and persuade them. At the simplest level you want people to like you so that you can build a relationship (see p. 127). But usually you are trying to influence or persuade them to accept your ideas or to take some action – for example, to complete a task, to gain management support or to buy the products and services of your organization.

As we saw in Part 1, there are two ways we think. When it comes to persuasion there is a central route – which requires a thought process to occur, so the content of the message is important. And there is a peripheral route which does not require much thought as the brain makes the connection for making simple decisions.

What makes people say 'Yes'? Primarily, you have to match their principles and values, beliefs and opinions and needs and wants. You have to develop your understanding of their view of the world and answer the question 'What's in it for me?'

Here's another way to think about persuasion:

- You say it – they doubt it

- You argue it – they defend it

- You prove it – they diminish it

- They say it – they believe it

You need to ask the right questions to allow the other person to come to their own conclusions. This is one of the main principles in coaching (see

Part 5 on p. 234) – helping people to make their own assessment of the options and choices. Another approach is to ask a doubter to present or argue a case that they don't support to move their attitude. It's hard to persuade others without believing something yourself.

Philip Zimbardo suggests that to be persuaded we need to understand:

- Who the communicator is
- What the message is
- Who the audience is
- The effect or desired outcome

There are many ideas and approaches to help you increase your influence and persuasion – from behavioural science and sales techniques – but I only have space to consider a few here.

Develop your credibility and confidence

Your **credibility** as a communicator rests partly on how expert and trustworthy you are perceived by other people (Hovland and Weiss). The amount of attitude change you create is directly related to your degree of attractiveness (Percy Tannenbaum). The '**Sleeper effect**' is where the person remembers the message but has forgotten the source. So you must consider how other people perceive you before you can attempt to influence and persuade them.

Your credibility can depend on many things – qualifications, experience, knowledge, track record, confidence, reputation, presence, authority, impact, reliability and trustworthiness. If you are experiencing problems influencing or persuading people then you may have to take steps to assess and improve your credibility based on how others perceive you.

Interestingly, there is often an inverse relationship between influence and power. So the more power you have the less likely you are to influence people and the less power you have the more you are likely to influence people.

Later we will explore confidence (Part 6) and trust (Part 1).

Use opinion leaders

Where your credibility is not high, you might harness opinion leaders to act as influencers for you. The idea here is that if you can persuade those seen as having high credibility and trust then they will have a big impact on other people.

Opinion formers are those known to be knowledgeable about a subject and whose advice is credible. Opinion leaders are those who reinforce messages sent and to whom others look to for information and advice.

Persuade experts, leaders, champions, sponsors, influencers and role models to your way of thinking and then allow them to persuade everyone else. This is an effective method of '**word of mouth**' communication that is widely used in marketing and selling. In the digital world, it has received much interest because of the viral nature of communications through social media channels where influencers have thousands (sometimes millions) of connections and followers and have a massive impact when they share information or endorse something.

Establish rapport and trust

Before you can influence and persuade people, you need to have a degree of **rapport** with them and they need to trust you.

Rapport is one of the most important characteristics of unconscious human interaction. It is a commonality of perspective, being in 'sync' with or on the same 'wavelength' as the person with whom you are talking. The topic is discussed further in Part 6.

Most people know about sensible (rational) trust which is about experts demonstrating knowledge and intelligence, doing what they say they'll do and knowing their stuff. But there is also sensitive (emotional) trust which is based on empathy and social intelligence (see p. 10).

Use reason, respect and emotion

Whereas you need to convey credibility, confidence and trust in order to persuade, you need to think about respect, reason and emotion for the person(s) you are trying to persuade.

Aristotle talked about ethos (respect), logos (reason) and pathos (emotion), and argued that if you used all three you are likely to achieve a result. You can tap into various emotions to influence and persuade people – greed, envy, pride, fear, pity, guilt, anger, happiness and hope. But be careful not to use too many negative emotions as people can switch off.

Help everyone to understand – stakeholder mapping

Sometimes there are misunderstandings or a lack of knowledge. These can be revealed – and then dealt with – by asking questions which challenge limitations: for example, 'What are your views on this?', 'What would happen if we didn't take some action?' or 'What would have to happen to make it possible?'

A simple way to increase your influence is to build on other people's ideas rather than ignore or dispute them. You can do this simply by saying 'AND' rather than 'BUT'.

In marketing, we use segmentation techniques to break down a large heterogeneous market into smaller homogenous segments. We can do a similar exercise with those we wish to influence and persuade by mapping out the different **stakeholders** – and the degree of impact the change will have on them and their influence. Then we can tailor the message and our approach to influencing and persuading depending on the interests and needs of the different segments or groups.

Provide options

There is evidence that sometimes it is better to provide a one-sided argument rather than a two-sided argument. More educated people are trained to resist a one-sided argument, so present both sides of the story to them so that they can make up their own minds.

When people feel they are being told or forced to do something, it is likely that they will push back or resist. We want to avoid **resistance** if we can. It can help with persuasion if you outline information relating to the situation and the possible options going forward. If people feel that they are involved in the decision and that their views are heard (and validated), they are more likely to be committed to a course of action that they have helped to choose.

In decision theory (see Part 6, p. 289), the number of options presented can also change the way people decide. Experiments show that there are different results when people are offered two or three options. People tend to avoid extremes (or outliers) and opt for the middle road. There are often decoys in pricing to encourage people to select the cheapest but one option.

The order in which you present options is important too. People tend to remember the first option (the primacy effect) and the last option (the recency effect) more than the others. In some situations, for example with estate agents, they may present two awful options first so that people more readily accept the third and least bad option. We will consider cognitive bias in more detail in Part 6 (see p. 291).

Emphasize the benefits

To increase your ability to persuade, you must see things from other people's perspectives and try to understand both their concerns and fears and consider their response to 'What's in it for me?' This requires you to use empathy (see p. 10) and ask questions so that you have all of the relevant information and understand their hopes and fears.

Value is in the eye of the beholder. So what is important to you may not be important to other people. To persuade people you have to understand how and why they should be interested in and supportive of your idea.

In sales and selling situations we talk about converting **features and advantages into benefits**. Persuasion occurs when a benefit balance sheet shows that the upside outweighs the costs/doubts. So, for example, instead of saying 'We will introduce a new system to increase efficiency in accounts', you translate it into something that is relevant and valuable to them: 'You will find it quicker and easier to receive your expenses when we introduce a new system.' Notice the subtle but important difference in shifting the conversation from 'we' (internal, self-centred view) to 'you' (external, reader-focused view).

Recognize influencing styles

People often show a preference in their influencing style. These can be summarized (and you will see that they are similar to the negotiating styles we consider later – see p. 173) as:

- Autocratic, push approach – imposing decisions on others by telling them what to do
- Collaborative, pull approach – working together to make decisions
- Logical approach – using data and making a rational argument
- Emotional approach – using emotions
- Assertive approach – being direct and articulate
- Passive approach – waiting for the actions and decisions of others
- Sales approach – stressing the benefits and finding solutions
- Bargaining approach – trading concessions (for example, 'If you do x, I will do y')

The difference between a 'tell' or push approach and an 'ask' or pull approach was mentioned previously when we considered learning and change management. The same rule applies with influencing.

Use the psychology of persuasion

One of my favourite books was written by psychologist Robert B. Cialdini. In *Influence: The Psychology of Persuasion*, Cialdini provides a great deal of psychological evidence to show the underlying science of persuasion. For example, he shows that we have automatic responses to single trigger features or words: so when, for example, we hear the word 'because' we are more likely to comply – even if the words that follow are not particularly persuasive. This compliance process makes humans efficient and economic. Cialdini explores six key methods to influence people:

- Scarcity – The rule of the few

  - Opportunities seem more valuable to us when they are less available

  - We all know how a retail sale makes us keen to find a bargain

  - We are more tempted to respond when someone says 'only a few places left'

  - There's a tendency for us to fear missing out (**FOMO** – fear of missing out – is often cited in social media)

- Reciprocation – Give and take

  - Palaeontologist Richard Leakey said that the urge to reciprocate is so deeply rooted, it's the essence of what it means to be _human

  - If someone makes a big request and we reject it, we are more likely to accept a subsequent smaller request

- Commitment and consistency – Hobgoblins of the mind
  - ○ Once we make a choice, we will encounter personal and interpersonal pressures to behave consistently with that commitment
  - ○ Cognitive dissonance occurs when we try to hold two conflicting beliefs
  - ○ Small commitments lead to a big commitment – so if we say 'Yes' once, we are likely to continue to say 'Yes'
  - ○ To position yourself as an expert, tell people something that they already agree with
  - ○ This is sometimes called the 'foot in the door' technique
- Social proof – Truths are us
  - ○ We view a behaviour as correct in a given situation to the degree that we see others performing it (especially where there is uncertainty)
  - ○ There are links to group behaviour – we will emulate others in the group to secure our identity and membership
  - ○ Conformity was confirmed with a famous experiment by Solomon Asch when people started to agree with the incorrect view of the rest of the group
- Liking – The friendly thief
  - ○ We prefer to say yes to the requests of people that we know and like
- Authority – Directed deference
  - ○ We have a deep-seated sense of duty to authority
  - ○ Many cultures and personality types will want to comply with rules and regulations given by those in authority

Research shows that sometimes repetition alone can make a message more believable. This is called the **Mere-Exposure** effect – Robert Zajonc found that people rated false statements as true if they were made to read them a week before. A similar idea is the 'broken record' approach mentioned in the assertiveness section.

Align goals

Each person and each group of people will have **goals**. Sometimes our goals – even in the same organization – are not aligned. We may have a great idea or project but we have to persuade people to give us their time and attention when they are busy working towards their own goals.

People may have many, complex and contradictory goals (e.g. 'I want to help but I am busy doing something else now') and their goals might be changeable. Some goals may be unconscious or emotional – for example, relating to our need to be heard, recognized or valued as an individual. Sometimes we are not clear about our goals.

What is a goal? Wilmot and Hocler define a goal as the answer to the question 'What do I want?' Answers fall into four types:

1 Topic goal – the surface issue which is often the easiest to identify

2 Relational goal – this relates to how we want to be treated in the relationship: we may want equality

3 Identity goal – how we want to be perceived and how we perceive ourselves

4 Process goal – how we want to tackle the challenge

Identifying and clarifying goals is an important part of influencing and persuasion and a first step in any negotiation (see p. 169). I am sure you can remember occasions when you were working at cross-purposes with someone where, for example, you focused on the surface issue but discovered that some aspect of the person's emotion or personality was the real issue.

Further material on influence and persuasion is found in the section on selling (see p. 283).

SECTION SUMMARY

THIS SECTION HAS CONSIDERED the elements and process of effective communication and considered some of the commonly encountered problems. Etiquette – particularly with regard to formal and informal styles – was addressed with regard to different business relationships and situations.

The power of face-to-face communication – particularly non-verbal communication – was considered before we looked at telephone communication. The principles of storytelling were set out, as the emotional connection gives them more impact than facts and figures alone.

A discussion on public speaking and presentations took us through the processes required to prepare and deliver great content. We also looked at some techniques to overcome nervousness.

The fundamentals of good writing were summarized and we looked in detail at writing emails, blogs, social media posts and reports. There was a final section on influence and persuasion, describing techniques from selling as well as psychology.

PART FOUR

RELATIONSHIP FORMATION AND CONFLICT MANAGEMENT

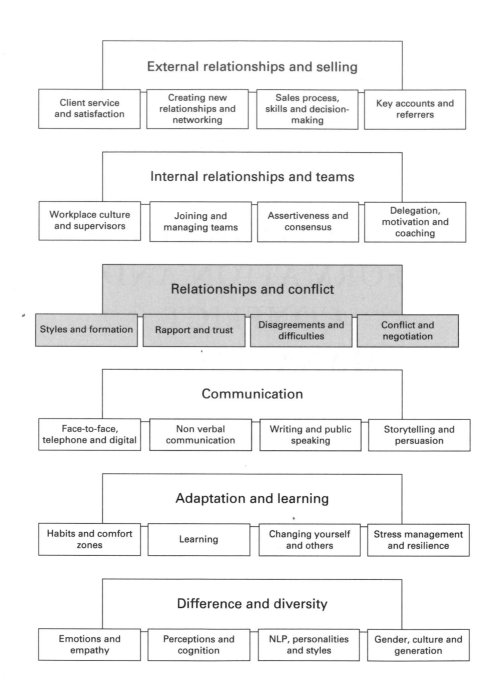

External relationships and selling

| Client service and satisfaction | Creating new relationships and networking | Sales process, skills and decision-making | Key accounts and referrers |

Internal relationships and teams

| Workplace culture and supervisors | Joining and managing teams | Assertiveness and consensus | Delegation, motivation and coaching |

Relationships and conflict

| Styles and formation | Rapport and trust | Disagreements and difficulties | Conflict and negotiation |

Communication

| Face-to-face, telephone and digital | Non verbal communication | Writing and public speaking | Storytelling and persuasion |

Adaptation and learning

| Habits and comfort zones | Learning | Changing yourself and others | Stress management and resilience |

Difference and diversity

| Emotions and empathy | Perceptions and cognition | NLP, personalities and styles | Gender, culture and generation |

15

Relationship competencies and formation

We have seen how people are different (Part 1) and how we learn to adapt to get on with different types of people and behaviour (Part 2). We considered ideas about communication – face-to-face, telephone and writing – which is fundamental to all business relationships. Now we can blend these ingredients together to understand how relationships are formed, developed and maintained. Common problems in relationships are explored before we consider how to deal with challenging behaviour and conflict when it arises – as it inevitably does – so that business relationships can be preserved.

There are various **relationship management competencies**; some focus on ourselves and some on other people. For ourselves:

- Self-awareness – Knowing our emotions and styles and the related strengths and weaknesses (Part 1)

- Communication (Part 3)

- Assertiveness – The ability to articulate what we need in clear terms (Part 5)

- Honesty and integrity

For others:

- Awareness of others and how they are feeling (empathy and emotional intelligence in Part 1)

- Ability to respond to and manage other people's feelings
- Respect (a feeling that someone is good, valuable or important)
- Ability to create rapport (see below)
- Questioning and listening (Part 6)

Daniel Goldman, an early pioneer of Neuro-Linguistic Programming (NLP – see p. 14) suggested that the six core elements of relationship management are:

- Inspire
- Influence (Part 3)
- Develop (Part 5)
- Initiate change (Part 2)
- Establish team work and collaboration (Part 5)
- Manage conflict (see below)

To **inspire** someone means that you have the ability to fill someone with the urge to feel or do something. Effective leaders inspire or motivate their people to change, to take on big challenges and to go above and beyond the call of duty. Sometimes you can inspire others through your own beliefs and behaviours – by being enthusiastic or passionate, really good at what you do, standing up for what you believe in, utterly focused on an aspirational goal or by overcoming adversity. You can inspire others by believing in them and encouraging them to succeed; or by making them feel involved, valued and recognizing their contribution and importance.

Influence is the ability to build agreement and consensus and win people's support by being able to focus on what is important to them. We looked at influence and persuasion in Part 3, and the host of things that you can do to encourage others to think or act in a way that you wish.

Developing people means helping them to learn and grow. Coaching skills (see p. 234) are important here – supporting people as they try to find answers for themselves rather than being told what to feel or think.

Initiating and promoting change was addressed in Part 2, where we considered the challenges of change management, habits and resistance and looked at methods to drive change in individuals, teams and organizations.

Establishing team work and collaboration – getting people to work together – is considered in Part 5 on internal relationships, and managing conflict is dealt with below.

The stages of relationship formation

There are various models illustrating the stages of relationship formation.

Evidence shows that humans are motivated both to form bonds with one another (to receive affection and a sense of belonging) and to carve out space for themselves (to achieve an individual identity and freedom). Leslie Baxter, a researcher, developed a model of these opposite motivations which create relational dialectics. People manage these by moving closer and further away at different times in a relationship and we are rarely in sync, which causes conflict.

Martin Knapp put forward the idea of relationship stages:

1 Initiation

2 Experimentation

3 Intensification

4 Integration

5 Bonding

Not all relationships reach bonding, and bonding isn't permanent as even in long-term relationships, both parties need some space. People also go through stages in moving apart:

1 Differentiation

2 Circumscribing (communicating less)

3   Stagnation

4   Avoidance

5   Termination

You could consider the strength of the relationship as a progression:

1   Formation – getting to know each other

2   Divergence – having differing opinions, with doubt and disagreement (moving apart)

3   Convergence – reconciliation, acceptance and agreement (coming together)

4   Association – working together co-operatively or collaboratively

Another model offers the following stages of a business relationship:

1   Honeymoon stage

    Where each party sees the best in the other and sees the potential of the relationship. Shortcomings, differences and potential issues may be overlooked.

2   Power struggle stage

    Each party starts to see 'faults' in the other and is sometimes shocked when those issues start to appear in the relationship. There may be conflict and dissent, with each party needing to be right. Each party is fighting to have their voice heard and their needs met.

3   Dead zone stage

    Both parties tend to withdraw to 'lick their wounds' and think about things. They don't want the relationship to end but either they don't see they are in this position so it becomes 'business as usual but less productive than it could be' or they realize that there is a problem but don't know what to do about it. Or they see that there is a problem and, whether they are aware of the solution or not, decline to move forward.

4   Partnership stage

>   With the earlier problems resolved, the relationship becomes about 'us' rather than 'them' and 'us'. It is productive.

5   Leadership stage

>   Once two people can make the relationship about 'us', they can make it about the other person. Typically, people are able to make the other person more important than them – but not making themselves inferior or weaker or a victim.

What is interesting about these models is that there are usually problems when a new relationship is established. Most people shy away from difference, disagreement and conflict, so many relationships can be lost at an early stage. If you recognize that there will be teething problems and are prepared to work through them, you stand a better chance of creating and maintaining more business relationships. That's why conflict management is one of the core relationship management competencies.

16

Types of relationship

Not all relationships are the same. Dwayne D Gremler identified the following types:

- Personal – based on the knowledge each party has of each other
- Formal – based on roles occupied by individuals (e.g. accounts assistant and finance director)
- Communal – based on the concern for the welfare of others (e.g. what you might feel for members of the same team)
- Exchange – based on the giving and receiving of benefits (e.g. between a salesperson and a customer)

The way you approach the creation and maintenance of these different types of relationship will depend on their nature and the situation. Naturally, there will be occasions where people have multiple relationships with the same person, for example, when you become friends (social) with your boss (formal), who is also a work colleague (communal). Where there are multiple types of relationships between the same people there can be difficulties – for example, how you shift your approach at a social occasion with a work colleague.

Commitment and loyalty

Some believe that commitment and loyalty are the hallmarks of a strong and enduring relationship.

Morgan and Hunt explored the variables that impact on commitment and trust in a relationship:

- Communication – the openness and honesty of conversations
- Shared values – similarity and alignment in beliefs
- Relationship benefits – what each partner gets out of the relationship
- Acquiescence – the reluctant acceptance of something without protest (suggesting that one party is dominant and the other is sacrificing their views or needs)
- Propensity to leave – how likely someone is to leave the relationship
- Uncertainty – the level of certainty about each other in the relationship
- Co-operation – how people work together
- Opportunistic behaviour – the extent to which mutual opportunities are seized
- Termination costs – how difficult or costly it is to leave the relationship (some refer to this as 'lock in' costs)
- Functional conflict – how people resolve differences

In another model, where there is a focus on client relationships, you might see a relationship pyramid like this:

- Awareness – where the parties know about each other
- Trust – where trust exists between the parties
- Transaction – where the first piece of business between the two parties take place
- Satisfaction – where there is satisfaction with what is provided
- Commitment – where there is a level of commitment or loyalty
- Advocacy – where clients provide positive recommendations and referrals

A similar model considers the stages of a client relationship using the metaphor of personal relationships. Many businesses use this approach to classify their most critical client relationships as part of a **Key Account Management** (KAM) programme:

1   Transactional (using one product or service)

2   Multi-service (using multiple products and services) (Dating/courtship)

3   Loyal

4   Trusted (Engagement)

5   Partnership

6   Flagship (Marriage)

7   Broken (Divorce)

Dick and Basu characterized loyalty as follows:

1   No loyalty – low levels of behaviour (e.g. a one-off interaction)

2   Spurious loyalty – low relative attitude but frequent interactions due to convenience

3   Latent loyalty – high relative attitude but low interactions due to the situation

4   Loyalty – regular interactions due to strong preferences

But loyalty could be towards you as an individual or to your organization or brand. It is likely that there will be a degree of both – and you will inevitably be seen as an ambassador for your organization – but you are in a position to influence and improve the personal relationship component.

Some businesses use something called the **Net Promoter Score** (NPS) to assess the loyalty and likelihood of recommending their organization. They ask the question 'On a scale of 1 to 10, where 1 is low and 10 is high – how likely would you be to recommend us?' Those scoring 1 to 6 are seen as detractors, those scoring 7 to 8 seen as passive supporters, and those scoring 9 and 10 as promoters or advocates.

Online and digital relationships

In these digital times it is possible to create and maintain a business relationship online without ever meeting the person in real life (IRL). This is particularly so for those people who rely heavily on social media or work in international roles or global organizations. Social media presents the opportunity to have many more relationships and a much greater reach than ever before amongst those people you do and don't know.

But social media is sometimes used inappropriately by businesses and individuals to simply broadcast information about themselves or their businesses to others in the online space. But this is missing the 'social' element of social media. Social media's roots – in things like Friends Reunited and Facebook – were all about informal, social relationships amongst friends, families and former school or college colleagues. It is relatively recently that platforms such as LinkedIn and Twitter have been adopted by business people to find, create, develop and sustain business relationships online. Although **social selling** has seen phenomenal growth in some sectors, it is still in its infancy in others – with many using it simply as another PR channel.

Social media communications tend to be more personal and less formal – yet they are shared publicly or amongst a large number of your connections, even if you have only 'met' them online or briefly in person.

You might use LinkedIn to connect with someone after you have met them in person at a networking event. You can then learn about them from their profile and posts, perhaps liking, sharing or commenting on their content to show that you are aware of and approve of their material. If the online interaction continues and mutual understanding and appreciation grow, then social media helps identify opportunities and reasons to meet in person again.

However, you might exchange comments with someone in a LinkedIn group (an online community where there is a shared professional or business or geographic interest) without meeting them in person and then make the connection. So social media is a way to reach and connect with other people with similar interests.

On Twitter or Instagram, you might follow someone you don't know so that you see their tweets or photos. You might then retweet or comment upon their tweets and photos so they become aware of your interest. They may then follow you back and this enables you to message each other privately. But you only know as much about these people as they allow you to know – their profile and posts may depict just one aspect of themselves or even a different person to reality.

And, of course, while you may share posts, links and photos, the conversation in social media is largely written. Unless you use live options such as Periscope on Twitter, you are not actually speaking to people. You write your comments. And others write back. And, as we saw above, the lack of immediacy and the written word means that there is a greater chance of misunderstanding. And any misunderstandings are in the public domain and potentially damaging beyond just the two of you. Social media brings reputational risk.

Some people are open and informal on social media, balancing information about their worklife with stories from their personal lives. Others maintain a formal stance. Some show humour, but some people may not always share your view on what is funny. So it can be hard to decide what you want to convey and share.

There's also the possibility that you will be judged on the number and type of your connections. And even if you say that sharing others' information is not necessarily an endorsement, the reputation and quality of the material you share – and who created it – will have an impact on how people perceive you. There's a need these days to apply some critical thinking skills and ensure that you don't share factually incorrect information and become inadvertently responsible for 'fake news'.

It's worth thinking about and planning how you intend to use social media. Some people select certain platforms for different aspects of their lives – for example, Facebook for family and friends, LinkedIn and Twitter for business. Others might opt to have personal accounts and business accounts. Some people will decide to focus on just a few key themes (a content management plan), so that all of their social media activity reinforces key messages which support the development of a personal or organizational brand.

But as well as being a way to communicate with people, social media provides a valuable source of information that helps you develop your understanding of people and organizations and provides reasons to pick up the phone or email people for more personal interactions.

Being digital, you can measure your relationships in social media – how many you have, how many new ones are created, how many likes or endorsements, how many views, how many interactions and how much engagement. So you get immediate feedback on what appears to be popular.

There are also tools to measure your social media reputation. For example, Klout and PeerIndex provide a rating of the strength of your online presence and highlight those topics for which you are known or considered an expert. There are some business people who choose to only interact with those who have a similarly strong social media presence.

Social media is a quick, efficient and unobtrusive way to stay on the radar by sharing information on a regular basis so that you consistently pop up on people's feeds and remain front of mind. But remember that these interactions are public. Others can see what you share and exchange. There are situations where people may perceive you to be showing others greater preference – or that there are conflicts or competitive issues.

So while there is clearly a role for social media in creating, maintaining and developing business relationships, you must be careful – particularly with important relationships such as those with your work colleagues, customers and clients. Most organizations have a social media policy which you should read to ensure that you don't inadvertently break any company rules. Many organizations provide training in the use of social media so that you can see how to safely integrate social media into your overall business relationship management. Other organizations may use social media management systems (e.g. Hootsuite) so that any material is checked in advance by communications professionals before it is released into the public domain.

How many relationships?

Social media allows you to create thousands of digital relationships, but is it realistic to expect to manage all those business relationships?

Psychology theory suggests that the cognitive limit to the number of people you can maintain a stable social relationship with is 150. The number was first proposed by British anthropologist Robin Dunbar, who found a correlation between primate brain size and average social group size (tribe). He extrapolated from human brain size that humans can comfortably maintain only 150 stable relationships.

Other researchers have put the number between 100 and 290 and identified long-term memory size as a factor. Social grooming may not be something we consider relevant to today's business relationships, but it is worth considering what is feasible for a busy business person who has to complete a significant amount of technical work as well as various administrative, supervision, training, financial and business development duties whilst maintaining a family/social life as well as nurturing existing and prospective business relationships such as client and referrer relationships.

Modern digital marketing methods make it possible for people to remain in touch with an almost infinite number of colleagues, clients, referrers and contacts. So whilst there may be a limit on how many personal relationships you can manage, at least you can stay in digital touch with a somewhat larger number of your digital tribe now. Interestingly, recent studies have indicated that Dunbar's number is applicable to online social networks and communication networks. Have a think about who is in your priority 150 business relationships.

17

Why relationships go wrong

We saw above that most relationships will go through a period of difference, divergence or disagreement. But why do relationships go wrong? Some of the reasons are:

- Misunderstanding
  Many things can get in the way of clear communication – the language you use, your non-verbal communication, your personal style, your understanding of the other person's knowledge and needs, a mismatch in personality and even culture. To avoid misunderstandings you need to have empathy skills and understand the other person. You should check their understanding by asking questions and listening carefully to their responses.

- Being let down
  People have expectations of what the other person in a relationship will do. If those expectations are not met then they will be disappointed and feel let down. Often, they will not talk about their feelings. To avoid this you must manage their expectations – say what you will do and do it. Reliability leads to trust. Sometimes people are so keen to form a relationship that they overpromise and then underdeliver. Be realistic in what you offer.

- Loss of trust
  If someone lets us down then we may cease to trust them. But there may be other reasons why trust is lost. Someone might break a confidence or take someone else's side – showing loyalty elsewhere. Someone may make a commitment and promise and then break it.

Where there are repeated disappointments, let downs and broken promises then trust will be lost.

- Loss of respect

  If someone lets us down we may lose respect for them. Similarly, if they behave in a way that we weren't expecting or disapprove of we may lose respect. There are many things that might make us lose respect – they may have negative views or make inappropriate remarks or act in a way that isn't decent, fair or professional. They may treat us unfairly or badly. Once we lose respect for someone it is very difficult for it to be regained – once bitten, twice shy.

- Arrogance

  Arrogance is a form of false self-confidence. Sometimes people misinterpret personal styles as arrogance (for example, someone who is emotionally detached and focuses on the task rather than people issues could be considered aloof, distant and arrogant by some). But if someone perceives another as arrogant they will believe that the person sees themselves as superior. Someone perceived as arrogant needs to be less directive and controlling and seek and listen to the views of others.

- Judgemental

  This is similar to the arrogance issue – where one party is perceived to consider themselves above the other. If someone is judgemental – making assumptions about the other person and conveying their disapproval – it is unlikely that a productive relationship can continue. We need to recognize that people are different for many reasons (Part 1) and to celebrate rather than resist and reject diversity.

- One-way traffic

  We learned in the persuasion section that reciprocity is important. We also know that relationships need to be equal. If someone feels that they are making all the effort and contribution and the other party is doing nothing then they may switch off and direct their attention to another, more equal, relationship.

- Envy and jealousy

  Envy is a reaction to lacking something. Jealousy is a reaction to the threat of losing something or someone. Jealousy is a common human emotion. People may be jealous of someone's appearance, background, education, privilege or role. If someone is very jealous then they will not want to help, support or even communicate with the person who evokes their jealousy.

- Conflict of interest

  This is where someone is committed to two people or organizations that are perceived to be in competition or where their interests are seen as contradictory. Conflicts of interest are carefully managed in the professions – for example, you wouldn't expect a lawyer to be acting for both the landlord and the tenant in the same dispute.

Disagreements

You can prevent disagreements spiralling into conflict and relationship breakdown by adopting some simple steps:

- Avoid verbal attacks, bad language and continually criticizing someone

- Stay on topic and keep the conversation on the current problem rather than resorting to the past and other issues

- Calm your emotions and articulate the issues rather than shouting or clamming up

- Avoid threats and terrorizing – value people, ask for their views and open discussion

- Don't interrupt – let people finish what they are saying

- Use 'I' statements to own your feelings

- Accept that there will be differences of opinion

Remember that disagreements, arguments and conflict can damage relationships. When there is a rupture in a relationship, you need to make an effort and repair it afterwards (see 'apologies' below).

Disruptions in close relationships

Roger Fisher and Scott Brown, authors of *Getting Together: Building Relationships as We Negotiate*, offer suggestions for building strong, supportive personal relationships that create a good context for conflict resolution. The principles can be applied to close business relationships – for example, between business partners.

1   Balance emotion with reason

2   Develop an interest in your partner's viewpoints

3   Always consult before deciding on anything that might affect your partner and listen to their feedback

4   Be wholly trustworthy but not wholly trusting

5   Never coerce your partner – negotiate as equals

6   Practise acceptance of your partner and when you have differences, deal with them seriously

Other suggestions include giving at least 80 per cent positive feedback. This is positive reinforcement of good behaviour and also puts negative feedback in context. The work on appreciative environments by Nancy Kline is examined further in the next section. Couples counselling adopts a useful approach for all relationships – each person is given time to talk while the other party practises active listening, and questions may be asked but not challenged.

A critical communication context is where a disruptive event creates a situation in which effective communication becomes simultaneously more important and more difficult. Such destabilizing events can change the self-concepts of the parties, alter individuals' ability to perform, change the demands of established roles and threaten the identities of the parties. Whilst emotions may run high, there is a greater need for communication to perhaps renegotiate elements of the relationship, to deal with the conflict and move on.

John Gottman identified the Four Horsemen of the Apocalypse (signals for the end of a relationship) in personal relationships:

1 Complaining and criticizing

2 Showing contempt

3 Becoming defensive

4 Stonewalling (delaying or obstructing by refusing to answer questions or by being evasive)

If you have a relationship that appears to be going wrong, it might be worth considering the causes of the problem – from both your perspective and that of the other person. You will need to use your empathy skills here although there is no substitute for actually asking someone 'What went wrong and how can we fix it?' Take a look at the material on dealing with difficult behaviour (see p. 158) and on conflict management below.

As an aside, Don Miguel Ruiz, in his book *The Four Agreements*, suggested that we can avoid self-limiting beliefs by following four simple rules: be impeccable with your word, don't take anything personally, don't make assumptions and always do your best. They seem like good rules to follow when developing business relationships too.

Psychology of problematic relationships

There are some models in psychology that help us take a different view of problems in relationships. And with a different view, we can adopt an alternative approach that may help problematic business relationships.

The **drama triangle** is where three or more people adopt particular roles that are dysfunctional. The roles in the drama triangle are:

- Persecutor – The problem dominates their thinking and action and they blame the victim and keep him or her down

- Victim – The person feels powerless, persecuted and sorry for themselves

- Rescuer – The person tries to relieve the pain of the victim because they themselves fear not being needed

The unhealthy drama triangle causes problems. Not least in that it stops the victim taking responsibility for themselves and standing up to the persecutor. **Triangulation** – where two people are set against a third – is discussed further when we consider negotiation below.

Eric Berne, a psychologist, developed a framework for **Transactional Analysis** (**TA**). In his book *I'm OK, you're OK* he said that ideally in a relationship we need to establish and reinforce the position that recognizes the value and worth of every person. He suggested that this happens through units of interpersonal interaction called strokes, which everyone needs in order to survive and thrive. You may have heard people talking about '**ego strokes**' – these are positive statements that we make about others to make them feel good.

Berne suggested that there are three ego states – Parent, Adult and Child (sometimes called the **PAC model**) – and that we can all slip between these states. There can be problems in relationships when there are dysfunctional behaviour patterns or cross-state communications.

Parent – These are behaviours, thoughts and feelings that are copied from parents and parent figures. They relate to rules, judgements, decisions, advice, care and punishment. On the positive side, these behaviours are there to nurture, support, calm and keep others safe. On the negative side, these behaviours can be controlling, critical, patronizing and finger-pointing.

Child – These are behaviours, thoughts and feelings replayed from childhood. They are creative, playful and self-expressive in nature but can either be compliant and obedient or rebellious. On the positive side this behaviour is curious, spontaneous and creative but on the negative side they might involve insecurity, rebellion and even tantrums.

Adult – Thoughts, feelings and behaviours which are direct responses to the current situation – the 'here and now'. They are based on sensory information, perceptions and facts rather than emotions. Generally, adult behaviour is reasonable, logical, rational and non-threatening.

In a business relationship we would expect people to be in their adult states. However, if someone moves to a parental state then it is likely to make the other person move to their child state and vice versa. So the relationship will experience difficulties not to do with the rational current situation but to do with past thoughts, behaviours and experiences from the individuals involved. There is more information about this in the material on the psychodynamic approach (see p. 50).

18

Creating rapport and trust

Perhaps we are getting ahead of ourselves. To start a business or any other type of relationship we need to have rapport with the other person.

Rapport is a connection. It is usually an unconscious process alongside communication. Some describe rapport as having a close and harmonious relationship where people understand each other's feelings and ideas and communicate well.

Some describe rapport as a common perspective or being in 'sync' or being 'on the same wavelength'. The word rapport comes from the French word meaning to 'bring back' – almost as if we are bringing back the feelings of the other person to ourselves.

Some people seem to find it easy to 'click' or connect with other people – they seem to do it naturally. They get to a position of trust and mutual understanding within a few minutes. And whilst it is true that some personality types find it easier to approach and talk to other people, these skills can be learned and practised by everyone. Research suggests that most people achieve rapport naturally with between 10–30 per cent of people, and with training most people can double their starting percentage.

In his book *The Elusive Obvious*, Michael Grinder claimed that there are two broad types of people – dogs and cats. Dogs are the 'pleasers' and high on rapport. Their voice, pace and energy, hand gestures, head movements, facial expressions and body posture are much more animated than the 'cats', who are independent and high on credibility.

According to researchers Linda Tickle-Degnen and Robert Rosenthal, when you have a rapport with someone, you share the following qualities:

- Mutual attentiveness – you're both interested in what the other person is feeling, saying or doing

- Positive – you're both friendly and upbeat and show care and concern for each another

- Co-ordination – you are 'in sync' with one another, share a common understanding and have similar energy levels, tone of voice and body language

When you have rapport with someone, you're better placed to influence, learn from them and teach them. Rapport is similar to trust. You can build trust and rapport simultaneously. However, rapport focuses more on establishing a bond or connection, whereas trust relies more on creating a reputation for reliability, consistency and keeping your promises.

Earlier in the book I talked about Neuro-Linguistic Programming (NLP), which can help with forming relationships. But be careful when using the techniques as you should always be honest, sincere and authentic – otherwise people may think that you are trying to be manipulative.

To help develop rapport:

1 Align your appearance
First impressions count (see Part 6) and your appearance should help you to connect with people, not create a barrier. Psychologists suggest that you should dress just a little 'better' than the people you're about to meet. Others suggest that you should aim to be as similar as possible to the people you are meeting – so if everyone is in a suit and you are in jeans you may inadvertently create an unconscious barrier. There is a theory about '**in group bias**' – people feel more comfortable with people they consider to be similar to them and in their group.

2 Remember the basics of good communication
Communication is considered in detail in Part 3. Be culturally appropriate – in many cultures this will involve smiling and having eye contact. Always ask people's names – and remember them and use

them and introduce yourself clearly and confidently. Ask questions to
show interest and listen to the responses carefully and keep the
information-exchange equal.

3   Find common ground
    Most conversations start with 'small talk' – about the weather, the
    journey, topical news events or the reasons for meeting. This is where
    you start to explore where there is some common interest or ground.
    Most people like talking about themselves, and if you show genuine
    interest in them, they are more likely to relax and 'open up'.

    Use open-ended questions and listen carefully and show that you
    are doing so, perhaps by asking further questions on what they have
    said or repeating what you have heard or offering your views on a
    similar issue.

4   Create shared experiences
    Rapport can't grow without human interaction, and a great way to
    interact is to create new, shared experiences. Shared experiences can be
    as simple as attending the same conference session together and
    exchanging views on the venue or speakers.

5   Use empathy (see Part 1)
    Try to understand how the other person is feeling and thinking – put
    yourself in their shoes and see things from their perspective.

6   Mirror and match style and behaviour
    Research shows that we prefer people we perceive to be just like
    ourselves. We subconsciously adapt our style of speaking and behaving
    when we meet people. **Mirroring and matching** are techniques for
    building rapport by making yourself more like the other person by
    having similar non-verbal communication. So if the person is sitting
    forwards, you do the same. If they are holding a glass in their left hand,
    you do the same. And so on. But you must be discreet – otherwise they
    will notice you copying them. If someone's NVC mirrors your own
    then it is an indication that they feel a degree of rapport with you. You

can 'test' other people's feelings by changing your stance or position and see if they follow suit (unconsciously). Alex Pentland drew attention to the mirror neuron system in our brains – when people mimic each other's gestures it is correlated with feelings of trust and empathy.

How to be liked

While it isn't necessary to be liked in all business relationships (for example you don't have to be liked to be a supervisor), it certainly helps when you try to build that initial connection. Often in business that common ground is the fact that you work in the same organization or industry or have similar goals – but not always. For this reason it helps if you are similar in some way – sharing social or educational backgrounds, being of a similar age, class or nationality or having the same interests such as a particular sport. You might have acquaintances, friends or associates in common or a similar knowledge of a topical issue.

Relationships are about people. So before you can get onto business matters it helps if you get on as people. So how do you encourage people to like you? How do you increase your likeability? Some people call this being personable. Naturally, it is important to be authentic – to be the real you – as people can detect when you are being fake or insincere.

Rather than being totally absorbed in yourself, people will like you if you show an interest in them – asking them questions and taking the time to get to know them. This questioning – which should be balanced, otherwise it feels like being interrogated – should involve sharing an equal amount of information about yourself. You will need to reveal some of yourself if you want others to open up to you. But be careful, since in some cultures – for example in Japan – it is not socially acceptable to ask people about their personal lives too early in the relationship.

In Dale Carnegie's great book *How to Win Friends and Influence People*, he famously said that 'You can win more business in two months by being interested in other people than in two years trying to be interesting.' Another thing that helps with being liked is to ask for or give help. In the persuasion section we saw that one of the six ways to persuade people mentioned by Robert Cialdini is to be a 'friendly thief'.

Keep things positive. No one wants to spend time around a negative, critical or moany person. Keep initial conversations upbeat and light – look for the positive in any situation. Smile and laugh – others usually join in and it creates a bond. Emotional contagion was discussed earlier (see p. 9).

Creating trust

Trust is the firm belief in the reliability, truth or ability of someone or something. But we need to understand more about trust to help us create it in our business relationships.

Diago Gambetta said that 'Trust is a means of reducing uncertainty in order that effective relationships can develop.' Cousins and Stanwix suggested that trust refers to ideas concerning risk, power and dependency. Paul A Pavlou argued that there are three outcomes from trust: satisfaction, perceived risk and continuity. Morrison and Firmstone have contended that there are several elements to trust: reputation, familiarity/closeness, performance and accountability. Young and Wilkinson claim that trust is influenced by the duration of the relationship, relative power, the presence of co-operation and environmental factors.

Between businesses, trust might be based on reputation (knowledge of past actions) and brand (a future promise). These ideas are supported by another model of trust which sees various levels of trust. There is inter-firm trust – for example, we may trust brands and organizations that we have heard about. Then there is interpersonal trust – which is reliant on an individual. This is broken down into two parts: sensible, rational trust is based on the knowledge and expertise that you demonstrate ('knowing your stuff') and doing what you say you will do when you said you would do it (reliability); but there is also sensitive or emotional trust which is based on your empathy and social intelligence.

There was some interesting work done on the elements of trust by management consultants David Maister and Charles H Green. Their formula is as follows:

$$T = \frac{C + R + I}{S}$$

T stands for trustworthiness, C is credibility, R is reliability, I is intimacy and S is self-orientation. The key to trust is to minimize your self-interest and concentrate on being credible, reliable and learning about and getting close to the other person. **Integrity** is also important for establishing trust – being honest and having strong moral principles.

Tsedal Neeley talks about **swift trust** (where team members learn to swiftly trust one another from the first interaction) and **passable trust** (linked to online behaviour where trust is deduced by studying interactions with others).

When thinking about customer or client service, Roy J. Lewicki differentiates between **Calculus Based Trust (CBT)** – which occurs in the early stages of a relationship, where an individual calculates how the other party is likely to behave in a given situation and extends their trust only as far as necessary to achieve a positive outcome – and **Identification Based Trust (IBT)** – which occurs when there is a deeper understanding of each other from repeated interactions, and each party identifies with the goals and objectives of the other party. This is a more emotionally driven bond which is harder to break and the foundation of loyalty.

Trust is contextual too – and varies depending on the situation and circumstances. Engel's and other studies have found that people are more trustworthy if they are: elderly, female, face-to-face and if they believe you are deserving. They found that people are less trustworthy if they can conceal their dishonesty; have to work hard to achieve something to be shared; are amongst people talking tough; make decisions in a group and are asked repeatedly to be benevolent.

Build trust through communication, commitment and competence:

- Communicate
  - Have regular and open conversations
  - Listen and reflect back – check understanding
  - Tackle difficulties early and assertively
- Connect
  - Express emotion
  - Show your vulnerabilities
  - Find things in common and mirror behaviour and feelings
- Be honest
  - Tell the truth
  - Be sincere and your authentic self
  - Admit errors and mistakes quickly
- Curiosity
  - Show interest
  - Ask questions
  - Request feedback
- Be respectful
  - Be polite
  - Respect their views if they are different
  - Value and thank them for their time
- Be reliable
  - Set realistic deadlines (underpromise and overdeliver)
  - Say what you are going to do and do what you say
  - Take responsibility and never let them down

- Have integrity
  - Have strong morals and principles and stick to them
  - Always do the right thing
  - Decline to do something if it's not within your expertise
- Care
  - Understand how they feel
  - Show appreciation and that you care
  - Focus on their needs rather than your own
- Be consistent
  - Remain the same each time you meet
  - Manage expectations
  - Avoid erratic behaviour that is unpredictable
- Trust others
  - Demonstrate that you trust other people
  - Be positive and encourage people to trust
  - Be flexible, patient, generous and forgiving
- Focus on the long-term success rather than short-term gains
  - Initiate and reciprocate favours
  - Give without expecting anything in return
  - Forgo a short-term win if it jeopardizes the long-term relationship

19

Conflict and dealing with difficult behaviour

What is conflict?

Conflict can be defined in many ways. Some see it simply as 'a discomforting difference'. Others define conflict as 'an expressed struggle between at least two independent parties who perceive incompatible goals, scarce resources and interference from others in achieving their goals' (William Wilmot and Joyce Hocker).

There are five elements to conflict:

1   Interdependence (the behaviour of one party has an effect on the other)

2   Difference

3   Opposition

4   Expression

5   Emotion

We must manage conflict because we want to avoid the harm that can result and we want to receive the benefits of resolving conflict. Conflict management is an essential relationship management competence, as all relationships experience some conflict.

There are four unpleasant truths about conflict:

1   Conflict WILL occur – it is inherent in human interaction

2   Conflict always involves some risks and costs

3   Damage from conflict results from dysfunctional strategies

4   Some of the damage that occurs in conflict is irreversible

Conflict management research spans psychology, sociology, communication and organizational management. Much of the way we manage conflict is learnt from our families, schools and other members of our culture.

Is all conflict bad?

There is evidence that a lack of conflict is not necessarily a good thing.

For example, a lack of conflict can lead to '**Group Think**' (Irving Janis). This is where a group of people who have a strong desire for harmony or conformity results in irrational or dysfunctional decision-making. Group members try to minimize conflict and reach a consensus decision without critical evaluation of alternative viewpoints by actively suppressing dissenting viewpoints and by isolating themselves from outside influences. Loyalty to the group requires individuals to avoid raising controversial issues or alternative solutions, and there is subsequently a loss of individual creativity and independent thinking.

The dysfunctional group dynamics of the 'in-group' (see pp. 49 and 215) produces an 'illusion of invulnerability'. The 'in-group' overrates its own abilities in decision-making and underrates the abilities of its opponents (the 'out-group'). A study found that 85 per cent of US/European executives are afraid to raise concerns and issues that might cause conflict.

Some conflict is needed for good organizational performance – too little and there is complacency and no adaptation, change or innovation; and too much causes too much disruption. Stephen Robbins and Mary Coulter distinguish between functional conflict (which sweeps stagnation away and allows creativity to flow) and dysfunctional conflict (which explodes out of control and destroys creativity).

Historical perspectives on conflict management

History plays an important part in how we deal with conflict. The adversary system was used by the ancient Greeks to resolve conflicts instead of resorting to war. It uses reasoning and the principle of non-contradiction – exemplified by Aristotle's view that 'a thing cannot be and not be at the same time'. This led to 'black and white' thinking. Plato and Socrates objected to this approach on the grounds that it positioned winning as more important than finding the truth. Fundamentally, it is competitive – there are winners and losers.

To be effective at argument you must:

a) Understand forensic reasoning – the process of comparing the facts against a general principle such as the law

b) Learn to recognize the issue and the starting-point for the argument (Richard Whately did this by 'presumption in favour of the status quo' – this is why we assume someone is innocent unless guilt can be proved)

c) Have credible evidence

d) Check your own logic

e) Examine your opponent's logic and evidence

f) Seek professional help when required

Dealing with 'difficult' behaviour

Before conflict there is often a perception of 'difficult' behaviour. What you perceive as difficult behaviour might be a clash of personality or style (see Part 1, p. 14). You should also take care not to attach a **label** to someone, as this can have an impact on how you perceive their future behaviour – this topic and the idea of reframing is also covered in Part 1 (see p. 17).

Talking about difficult behaviour, it's probably worth mentioning the **dark triad**. These are three negative personality attributes – narcissism (excessive focus on self), psychopathy (mental illness or disorder) and Machiavellianism (dishonesty and manipulation). Despite people with these traits being unpleasant and causing distress to others, long-term studies have shown that they succeed in moving up the career ladder. This means that you cannot assume that those in positions of seniority and authority will act with integrity. Some common types of 'difficult' behaviour in business relationships – bullying, stubbornness and micro-managing ('control freaks') – are explored in Part 5 (see p. 205).

The table on pages 160–5 categorizes different types of 'difficult' behaviour, explaining what the behaviour involves and possible reasons for it, how it makes us feel, our typical responses and some alternative approaches. This is based on the work of Robert Bramson in his book *Coping with Difficult Bosses*:

Changing your perspective

One method to avoid conflict is to see things from the other person's perspective. 'To go to the balcony' means mentally removing yourself from the conflict situation and looking down on it as if you were on a balcony.

Another technique is to imagine that there is a 'third person' watching the situation – what would they notice and suggest if they were watching the interaction from a distance? Wilmot and Hocker suggested you imagine using a lens to consider:

- Your perspective
- Their perspective
- Where you focus
- Where they focus

Type	What do they do?	Why are they like this?	How do they make us feel?	What behaviours should we avoid?	Potential strategies
Ogre (Shrek)	Hostile and aggressive Shout and insult Overwhelm us by evoking buried childhood fears	Rapid and confident decision-makers Need to feel powerful – perhaps they have a little unconscious self-doubt	Silent confusion Speechless rage	Silent acquiescence Righteous complaining Appeasement Angry rebellion Any sign of weakness	Simultaneously show your own strength but that you are not a threat Watch your posture and projection Humanize – use their name Don't argue – disagree Use interruptions If you can't talk, write (informally) Keep them posted Acknowledge their strengths
Fire-eater (Volcano)	Irritable and moody Hot tempered and explosive Sudden rages	Feeling personally threatened while at the same time under pressure to take some sort of action	Surprised and shocked Confused	Arguing back Defending	Leave them to calm down Make neutral statements to stop the tirade Repair the threat (use terms that reinforce their seniority) Break off the interaction – allow them to be alone for a short while Understand mood patterns and triggers Help them understand the effects of their outbursts Humour: 'Glad I got you on a good day'

| Expert know-it-all (Bulldozer) | Closed to other ideas Lecturing mode Superior Acts like a teacher Always right Aggressive Unforgiving | They are very good at their job and are intolerant of anyone who doesn't reach their high standards | Irritated Inferior Worthless Stupid | Do not wish they were different or try to change them Do not challenge their standing as experts Do not say 'Maybe' – be clear in your recommendations Don't confront | View them as a source of great knowledge and an opportunity to grow/deal (see reframing on p.17) Show respect for their knowledge Prepare and methodically plan as well as you can Provide as much concrete analysis as you can Select tasks that are of little interest to him/her and with clearly defined responsibilities that can be measured Use questions to point out problems – 'Explain it to me' and 'Describe how it might work in other areas' Help them save face if things go wrong Cost/benefit analysis You may have to give up! |

(continued)

Type	What do they do?	Why are they like this?	How do they make us feel?	What behaviours should we avoid?	Potential strategies
Artful Dodger (Invisible Man)	Stallers Wafflers Super-delegators Abdicate leadership Avoid confrontation Avoid anyone feeling bad Fail to explain their expectations 'Dump' on you Too many sidelines taking their time and energy No supervision	Co-dependents (want everyone and everything to be OK)	Unclear about how we are doing Don't know what the goals are Overburdened In the dark Lied to Suspicious Frustrated Impatient	Going to their boss Going it alone Questioning their honesty Accepting a dependent role	**Stallers** Ask their thoughts on how to improve Be positive about any negative feedback you receive Don't reveal you are upset at feedback Ask them to make conflicts explicit Act like a problem-solving consultant Give verbal support to the right behaviours (agree) Emphasize quality and service, not your own advancement Take decisions for them – 'Here's what I plan to do' Watch for signs that you are pushing too hard **Wafflers** Be personal and ask them about themselves Don't fight but compromise – find a win–win

Type	What they do	Causes	How it feels	Outcomes	Strategies
					Incremental small steps forward **Superdelegators** Let them know how you want to be supervised Negotiate your level of authority Coax out guidelines Schedule regular short meetings Agree turnaround times
Powerclutchers, Paranoids and perfectionists (Ceasar and Marvin)	Too much supervision Detailed instructions Check everything you do Micro-manage	Need to be certain Lack of confidence and trust Irrational search for perfection Over-strong wish to be in charge Fear of failure	Stifled Stupid Untrusted Deskilled	Making mistakes Insufficient attention to detail	Uncover any hidden doubts they have about your abilities or trustworthiness Acknowledge their concern and show how you plan to avoid it in future Communicate in his/her style (see thinking styles) Build trust by accepting fears and suspicions Welcome frequent check-ups Probe for clues to fear points Emphasize contingency planning Verbal support for risky decisions Try subtle teaching

(continued)

Type	What do they do?	Why are they like this?	How do they make us feel?	What behaviours should we avoid?	Potential strategies
Scallywags, schemers and skunks (Devil)	Scallywags – prey on others for own self-gain Schemers – focus on own gain without considering the firm Skunks – knowingly upset others	Unscrupulous or offensive Aberrant set of values Fearful of others (need to strike first) Lack of empathy and inability to feel for others (sociopaths)	Violated Offended Shocked Cheated Misrepresented Dishonest Angry Frightened Disgusted	Impulsive accusations Doing nothing	Assess the situation – distinguish bad guys from smart asses and simpletons (honesty may show good guys are unaware of the offence they cause) Clarify what you are up against – illegal or unethical, others feel the same, support for behaviour from above, your own goals, costs if you take action Disengage, if practical (resign – with a record of your achievements in tact) Protect yourself – resist, express your feelings, consider counselling, document everything Blow the whistle – attempt collective security, attack the problem not the person
Hurt friends (Angry child)	Crossed expectations Behaviour blindness Interaction accidents	Failed to communicate properly Misunderstanding Unaware their behaviour caused upset	Resentment Distrust Confused Shut out in the cold	Bringing up past disappointments Accusations Brash confidence	*Expectations* Confirm your understanding of what you are expected to do/responsibilities in an informal note

Reacted badly to something negative you said

Hurt feelings

Avoid RASP (Reciprocal Attack Spiralling Phenomenon)

Recommend rather than assert

Confirm with them before proceeding

Behaviour

Make a formal appointment to give unpleasant feedback

Show that you recognize ambiguity – your interpretation may not be the correct one

Help save face – focus on what needs to be changed

Describe the difficult behaviour (be specific and descriptive)

Restate assumption that they are unaware, watch for acknowledgement and provide support

Interaction

Assess – abrupt change for the worse, precipitating event, good relationship with others, own emotions are extreme

Make a short-notice appointment late in the afternoon, set the stage, comment on state of relationship, prepare to be dumped on, convey understanding without excuse or apology, state your intentions, move to problem-solving (focus on the future)

Managing emotions in conflict situations

We explored emotions earlier (see p. 7). Our emotions are multiple, complex and changeable. Emotions are internal facts – they are generated by real neurological, physical and chemical processes. Different people have different abilities to manage their emotions. In conflict, the most common emotion is anger. Emotions occur in reaction to stimuli – which are the perception of events. Remember that two people might react completely differently to the same stimuli.

There are two central elements of emotion: a) the feeling itself, which may be positive or negative; and b) the strength of the emotion. We can feel a variety of emotions at the same time and some emotions may mask others. Men, for example, tend to mask fear with anger.

In a conflict situation, remember that an emotion is not a behaviour. Being angry is not the same as acting angrily. Telling someone that you are angry does not require you to scream. You don't need to apologize for emotions either – they are an internal fact. You can mishandle emotions – by faking, hiding or by acting out. It is better to calmly express your emotion and offer a suggestion for moving forward.

In a conflict, you should:

a) Report you emotions to the other party

b) Remember that an emotion is not a judgement about the other party – it is your reaction

It's hard to listen to another party expressing negative emotions without defending yourself or interrupting with your own points and responses. But listening doesn't mean you should tolerate verbal abuse. Keep things level – don't allow your emotions to spiral upwards into hostility. And don't spread information that the other party has shared with you about their emotions.

Alternative approaches to conflict avoidance and management

There are many approaches to dealing with conflict, depending on its severity and where it takes place. For example:

Alternative dispute resolution (ADR)	Ombudsmen, expert evaluation, etc.
Arbitration	Where an objective third party with power is involved
Avoidance/inaction	Do nothing, wait and see
Capitulation	Give in
Domination	Abuse, bullying
Litigation	Legal process and court
Mediation	A third party with no power helps
Negotiation	Two parties try to reach agreement – seeking common ground and trading concessions
Referral up the chain of command	Let seniors take care of it
Unilateral power play	Physical violence (illegal and not recommended in business relationships!)
Withdrawal	Leave or avoid

In the world of project management, conflict is considered in terms of people, priorities or problems and whether they are negative or meaningful. The first action is to scope the issue and assess:

- Do I have enough information?

- Do I have the required diplomatic skills?

- Is it self-terminating?

- Will it work itself out with a meeting?

When the conflict revolves around people issues, you need to determine whether they are:

- Intrapersonal (relating to an individual's feelings)

- Interpersonal (between two people)

- Intragroup (amongst those in a group)

- Intergroup (between groups)

De-escalating and exiting the conflict spiral

Conflicts don't appear out of nowhere – they can often start as a small problem and then things escalate into a full-blown row. To prevent a full-blown conflict, you can help yourself and others exit the spiral by taking the following actions:

Spiral phase	Critical reaction
Covert resistance	Challenge gossip, non-co-operation, sabotage
Overt resistance	Challenge nagging, whining, complaining, anger
Critical incidents	Challenge unthinkingly negative interpretation
Selective perception	Challenge filtering and distorting perceptions
Enlisting others	Resist recruitment to unthinking in-group – check motives
Issue linkage	Challenge whether issues are really linked
Ritual/hot button words	Challenge unthinking use of words and labels
Threats	Challenge use of intimidation, pressure and bullying
Action	Encourage healthy actions and monitor
Provocation	Challenge interpretation – resist or ignore
Retaliation	Refuse or at a less intense level
Violence	Refuse and seek help from authorities

De-escalation can be achieved by opening a new channel of communication; changing the rhetoric to describe the conflict situation; suspending or altering a ban, limitation or sanction; changing leaders or role holders; publicly acknowledging some responsibility; recognizing the adversary and right of representation; modifying or abandoning aspects of the ideology; or permitting or participating in informal discussions.

If apology is sometimes seen as a strategy of weakness, then forgiveness is usually seen as a strategy of strength.

20

Achieving win–win and negotiating styles

During the eighteenth century ('the Age of Reason') there was more religious tolerance and this resulted in more negotiations between nations. In the twentieth century, the psychologists Kurt Lewin and Morton Deutsch developed a theory of human behaviour and motivation in groups called **field theory**. We see ourselves in a field and our motivation is movement across that field and other people can help or hinder us in that journey. How we interact with people depends on whether we see them as allies or obstacles.

Deutsch defined conflict as 'a condition that exists when Person A makes a move that makes it harder for Person B to reach his or her goal.' But he noted in task-oriented groups with shared goals that most conflict arose over how to achieve the goals. Findings from game theory (the branch of mathematics analysing strategies for dealing with competitive situations) suggest that people tend to compete rather than co-operate in conflict situations. Deutsch defined two kinds of conflict:

1 Competitive conflict – a situation that requires one party to lose in order for the other to win

2 Pure conflict – a situation where both parties can win. He found that most conflicts were of this kind.

Therefore, he argued that the possible outcomes in conflict are:

1 Win–Lose (competitive)

2 No Win–No Lose (compromise/tie but still competitive)

3   Lose–Lose

4   Win–Win

The reality is more complex – people's views about goals and solutions may differ and people may have multiple, complex goals, some of which may be unconscious and some of which may be contradictory. Also, it is sometimes possible to increase the size of the 'pie' – increasing the range of things being used as part of the negotiation.

Perception and punctuation

Perception is the cognitive activity where we assign meaning to the things people say or do or the things we see. In a conflict situation, the parties usually have different perceptions about what is happening. So a key skill is using empathy to be able to appreciate the other person's perspective.

Punctuation refers to the timing that parties assign to events. In conflict situations, there are often different views as to the start of the problem and therefore different views of the causes and reactions. For example, a junior person may be annoyed that a more senior person is not giving them time to explain a task, whereas the senior person may feel that they have already explained the task and the junior person didn't pay attention or take notes.

Wilmot and Hocker, in *Interpersonal Conflict*, suggest a tool called the lens model of conflict interaction. This means looking at the conflict as if through a lens – from different angles, with zooms and from the other person's perspective. However, according to the fundamental attribution error model, almost all of us attribute mistakes or failings on our part to external events and we also tend to attribute the behaviour of others to their own character or emotions. This often means that the other party feels that you are attacking their personality (which they can't change) rather than their behaviour (which they can change).

The key is to use person-centred communication instead of position-centred (taking a stand and defending it) or rule-centred (focus on asserting the facts) communication.

Power – how much do we need and how to use it?

Every conflict involves a power struggle. Power can be defined as 'the ability to cause or influence an outcome'. It is not the same as control, which is always limited and often an illusion. Power takes us back to the idea of interdependence.

There are three basic kinds of power:

1   Personal power – talents, skills and knowledge

2   Relational power – from the nature of the relationship between the parties

3   Situational power – the conditions of the conflict that give power to one party or one issue more than another

There is no set amount of power available – one person having power doesn't take it away from the other party. A lack of power is not a moral weakness either. We often give away power in a situation – to be liked or to be promoted.

John French and Bertram Raven identified five bases of power (**power currencies**):

1   Reward power – what we get from our ability to give reward

2   Coercive power – the ability to punish

3   Legitimate power – explicit given cultural roles (e.g. Managing Director, Police authorities)

4   Referent power – from people we are associated with

5   Expert power – based on expertise or knowledge

In a conflict you do not need more power than the other party in order to meet your needs and resolve the conflict. What you need is sufficient interdependence. Your leverage is the other party's stake in your satisfaction with the solution.

Research has shown that the more equal the conflicting parties are in power, the better the chances are of working out a win–win resolution. If you have more power in a conflict, you should exercise restraint and explicitly recognize the interdependence ('Look, we both want to find a solution to this problem').

Successful managers know that they must treat their employees as having power and importance of their own. If you have less power in a conflict, you must stay engaged and keep speaking up. Research shows that if you do, your power will grow and the other person will begin to listen to you more. You can also gain power by seeking allies or by building your knowledge or increasing your personal skills.

Here are some ideas about the sources of power and leverage:

Power source	Rationale	Example
Strength in numbers	Individuals band together – united we stand	Workers in a union against a boss Independent retailers against wholesalers – for discounts
Asymmetrical resistance	Less powerful apply leverage to more powerful ones by turning weakness into strength	Weak nations using guerrilla military tactics Young child blackmails older sister by threatening to report to parents if she doesn't get a sweet Office worker warns a senior person will be involved if no action is taken
Mosquito clout	Less powerful apply leverage by ploys of irritation and concentration	Blustering, delaying and exercising their veto and temporarily walking out Weaker, smaller parties have more focused concerns and single-mindedness
Pain avoidance	Make it less desirable to confront or negotiate with them	Create a reputation for prickliness or a fearsome temper
Publicity	Pressure on each other in the public domain	Acting up in public – causing a scene Protests Releasing information to the media

Carrots not sticks	Try to change behaviour through inducements and rewards	Pay rises to avoid strike action
Divide and rule	Attempt to drive a wedge through solidarity on the other side	Boss offers to settle with one group that is part of a union Offers salary rises to key workers to cross a picket line
Expertise	Impress with knowledge, credibility or status	Content (issue) or process (negotiation) knowledge Employers bring in an economist to union negotiations Firm uses a consultant to explain solutions
Charisma	Personal magnetism, charm (referent power)	Charismatic leader uses influence Lawyer from TV acts for one side Actor or celebrity endorses a cause
The boss	Power from legitimate position of authority	CEO/MD as part of team but without negotiating
Emotional blackmail	Interpersonal dynamics	Secretaries refusing to talk to bosses
Perception manipulation	Perception rather than reality of power	Illusions and bluffing
Great and powerful friends	Presence of powerful party in a negotiation appears to redress power balance	'Once the game becomes the one known as negotiation, the rules change and everyone becomes empowered by this transformed reality' (Rubin and Zartman, 1995)
Thinking makes it so	Self-perpetuating beliefs	Self-belief leads to self-confidence
Éminence grise	Exercises power unseen or unofficially	Wife may appear weaker, but has power to withhold children
BATNA	Best Alternative to a Negotiated Agreement	The stronger the BATNA the more power that negotiator has in a negotiation

Conflict and negotiating styles

Most people fall back on one or two key strategies ('**conflict styles**') for resolving conflict, so try to develop other strategies rather than always relying on the same approach.

Kenneth Thomas and Ralph Kilmann applied the early theory of management styles to managing conflict. They identified five conflict strategies and arranged them in a model depending on the degree to which each reflected 'concern for self' and 'concern for the other person' and the amount to which each represented co-operativeness.

1 Avoidance – Acting as if the conflict isn't present (Lose–Lose)

2 Competition (duelling) – One party trying to get what they want at the other's expense (Win–Lose)

3 Compromise – Both parties give something up (No Win–No Lose)

4 Accommodation (benevolent) – One party gives something up but doesn't get anything in return (Lose–Win)

5 Collaboration (engaging) – Working together (Win–Win)

There is no right style. There are occasions when each style might be appropriate:

Style	When to use
Competing	• Quick decisive action needed – emergencies • Important issues where unpopular action is needed • Vital to personal or organization welfare • Against people who take advantage of non-competitive behaviour
Collaborating	• Need to find an integrative solution • When the objective is to learn • Merge insights from people with different perspectives • Gain commitment to a consensus • Work through feelings that interfered with a relationship
Compromising	• Goals are important but not worth the effort of more assertive modes • Opponents with equal power committed to mutually exclusive goals • Temporary settlements to complex issues • Expedient solutions under time pressure • Back-up when collaboration or competition is unsuccessful
Avoiding	• Trivial issues or more important issues are pressing • No chance of satisfying your concerns • Potential disruption outweighs benefits of resolution • Let people cool down and regain perspective • Gathering information • Others can resolve conflict more effectively • Issues are tangential or symptomatic of other issues

Accommodating
- When you are wrong – to show your reasonableness
- Issues more important to others than yourself
- Build social credit for other issues (see reciprocity)
- Minimize losses when outmatched and losing
- Harmony and stability are especially important
- Allow subordinates to develop learning by mistakes

Warner had a different way of thinking about different styles of negotiating considering empathy and energy and pointed out the pros and cons of each:

Style	Pros	Cons
Pushy bullying	• Loudly commands attention • Draws negotiations to rapid close	• May adopt 'take it or leave it' attitude • Often insensitive and miss subtle points
Quietly manipulating	• Quickly draws attention to real threats • Can subtly focus a debate	• May distort information • Exploits other party's weaknesses openly
Confident promoting	• Quickly focuses on major issue • Wins people over with enthusiasm • Usually adapts flexibly to reach a deal	• Can be too aggressive • Can fail to listen fully
Carefully suggesting	• Keeps negotiation calm • Good at drawing attention to deeper issues	• Can fail to commit to convincing the other side • May enjoy the negotiation process more than reaching the outcome

Aronoff and Wilson identified eleven different personality variables that had an impact on negotiating styles:

	Co-operative	Competitive
Revealing	Affiliation Achievement Nurturance Style: INTEGRATIVE	Dominance Recognition Style: ADVERSARIAL
Concealing	Dependency Approval Order Style: INGRATIATING	Abasement Authoritarianism Machiavellianism Style: EXPLOITATIVE

John Gottman, a psychologist, developed a framework of bids and responses. One party communicates with the other, seeking a response – perhaps to negotiate a compromise or to collaborate. The three types of responses are:

1   Turning towards (acknowledges and validates the bid – moves towards closeness in the relationship)

2   Turning away (indifferent response and creates distance between the parties)

3   Turning against (acknowledges the bid but rejects its validity which creates hostility)

Sometimes compromise can be a problem as it often involves 'splitting the difference', so people will ask for much more than they would do normally – mainly because they expect the outcome to be about halfway towards their goal. Seasoned negotiators will offer only very small movements or concessions.

Dysfunctional conflict strategies

When Aristotle listed his seven causes of human happiness, he put revenge on the list. Some of the strategies mentioned above have harmful side effects on business relationships.

Avoidance – Ignoring a problem doesn't make it go away. It often makes it worse. It can also result in losing one's credibility for dealing with problems by allowing the problem to become embedded. Sometimes it is a useful strategy – for example, if the other person has more power and will impose an unwanted solution.

Withdrawal – This is where one party reduces interaction to avoid addressing the problem or to punish the other person. It can involve avoiding eye contact or talking in a flat emotional tone. The other party may feel hurt as a result and the relationship is damaged. Sometimes it is a good strategy if you or the other party needs to calm down.

Imposition – One party imposes a resolution. This may cause the other party to counter with a greater exercise of power and escalate the conflict. It may cause resentment and decrease morale. But it may be necessary when immediate action is required, such as in an emergency.

Triangulation – This is complaining to a third party instead of addressing the conflict directly with the other party involved. Sometimes it appears in the guise of asking for advice or presenting yourself as the victim. Sometimes it is to vent and sometimes it is to gain an ally and power. Research shows that **venting** can actually make you madder instead of calming you down.

Manipulation – This is where you use indirect means to achieve a goal without letting the other party know and without regard to their interests. It might include planting information or masking true motives. It can be harmful to credibility and trustworthiness.

Absolute framing – This sets the conflict in absolute black-and-white terms. It is sometimes known as drawing a line in the sand and daring the other party to cross it. It tends to lead to escalation.

Payback/revenge – This is doing harm to or withholding good from the other person. Perceptions of the harm done tend to cause escalation and have a detrimental effect on the future relationship.

Compromise – Should only be used where we have tried and failed to achieve a win–win.

21

The negotiating process

You will need to understand some of the theories and practices in negotiation. There are three phases to a negotiation:

1 Pre-negotiation – preparation and planning

2 Negotiation – the beginning, the 'muddle' (sometimes things get complex and confused) and the end

3 Post-negotiation – implementing the agreement

Harry A Mills used the RESPÉCT acronym to remember a more detailed breakdown:

- Ready yourself
- Explore each party's needs
- Signal for movement
- Probe with proposals
- Exchange concessions
- Close the deal
- Tie up loose ends

Principled negotiation

Roger Fisher and William Ury, two researchers in the Harvard Negotiation Project, developed four principles for win–win negotiations:

a) Separate people from the problem – focus on events and behaviours rather than the parties

b) Focus on interests, not positions – interests are the reasons for the position someone might adopt and position is someone's stand on an issue. Imagine an iceberg: there is but a small part of the top showing – this is the position. The larger area below represents the interests – these needs must be revealed and explored

c) Generate options for mutual gain – brainstorm multiple options, keeping in mind mutual gain

d) Base choice on some kind of objective criteria – try to find measureable ways to assess the value of suggestions

Fisher and Ury developed the idea of **BATNA** – Best Alternative To a Negotiated Arrangement. In any negotiation, identify your bottom line and your power bases relative to the issue, and consider your best alternative if you don't negotiate a good arrangement with the other party. They use the idea of negotiation jujitsu – in negotiations don't meet force with force; instead draw the other party in and use his or her force. Try to discover the other party's interests, then present your own interests and make suggestions for mutual gain.

Integrative bargaining – from positions to interests

Distributive bargaining is a negotiating process in which the two sides try to concede as little as possible and to gain as much as they can, using a zero-sum model. Integrative modelling means moving beyond a least-worst outcome for one or both sides.

The reason we need to understand the interests rather than positions is shown in the following table:

Position	Interest	Mutually satisfactory solution (win–win)	Interest	Position
I want ...	Because ...	Common ground	Because ...	I want ...
The orange	I want juice	One gets peel, the other gets juice	I want peel	The orange
Window open	I want fresh air	Open window in adjacent room	Papers will get blown away	Windows closed
Access to river	I want irrigation water	One gets irrigation run-off, one gets fishing spot	I want fish	Access to river
The corner office	I like the view	One gets office, one gets new title/ responsibilities	I need prestige	The corner office

However, the positions versus interests approach has been criticized by Geert Hofstede. He argued that the theory is uniquely American and contained hidden cultural assumptions.

Prepare to negotiate

There's a seven-step process for applying the four principles of negotiation. There are two conditions that must be present to use the process:

a) You must be able to define the issue in terms of voluntary behaviour from the present moment forward

b) The other party must be willing and able to negotiate

You also need to be calm enough to do the intellectual work or thinking of negotiation. If the issue relates to the past, consider what you want – an apology, no repetition, compensation? If the issue can't be defined in voluntary behaviour then you can't negotiate – your options are then to accept the situation; escalate the conflict; impose consequences; get an ally; or exit the relationship.

1 *Define the conflict issue*

   a. State the issue that's bothering you and identify why it's bothering you.

   b. State the issue in terms of the other party's voluntary behaviour – not in terms of emotions, attitudes or character or the past. Try writing the issue down.

      i. Personal relationships – XYZ formula 'In situation X, when you do Y, I feel Z'

      ii. Professional relationships – 'You are (behaving in this way), and that's a problem for me because . . .'

2 *Identify and evaluate your goals*

   a. Remember the four types of goal above (topic, relationship, identity and process) and the focus on interests.

   b. Ask yourself questions such as 'Why do I want to resolve this conflict?', 'What is a good resolution for me?', 'How important is it to me that I reach a resolution?' and 'How do I want to be viewed by the other party?'

3 *Decide whether you want to resolve the issue by negotiating*

   a. Consider the degree of interdependence, your leverage, the context, the relationship, the risks of introducing the issue and BATNA.

   b. Don't delay – it's a form of avoidance.

   c. You may want to negotiate a minor issue in order to practise your negotiation skills.

   d. Once you've decided, take responsibility and credit if the negotiation goes well.

Research positions and concessions

A key part of your preparation will be research. This means thinking through your own position as well as that of the other side (TOS). Identify, for both parties:

- The ideal scenario and targets

- What concessions can be traded

- Unacceptable outcomes

- Disaster or 'worst case' scenario

This should help you to identify the zone or range of agreement. As you think these things through, you might also prepare a matrix or grid to map out what information you know and what you don't know and what the other side knows and what it doesn't know. This helps you work out what questions to ask and also to identify what possible concessions you and they might be able to make.

You should be aware that people differ in their bargaining stance (firm vs yielding) and also in their techniques for using information (rigid vs flexible).

You can prepare a matrix that shows what concessions are cheap/easy and expensive/difficult for you and the same for the other side. As you will see from the integrative bargaining example above, sometimes things that are of little value or cost to us might be highly valued by the other side.

Arrange to negotiate

4   *Arrange a meeting with the other party to negotiate*

   a. Remember you've prepared but the other party might not
       have.

   b. Approach the person directly and privately and label the conflict as
       a problem and state the issue exactly as you defined it in step 1
       above. Tell them that you'd like to find a solution that will satisfy
       both of you and ask when would be a good time to meet, providing
       a specific time frame.

   c. If they raise other issues, agree to address them after the initial
       problem has been solved.

You should be aware that there are considerable pros and cons to holding a negotiation on your territory, on their territory or on neutral ground.

Negotiate conflict resolutions

5   *Conduct the meeting*

   a.   Arrive at the meeting prepared to explain your point of view and offer suggestions but don't be overly committed to them.

   b.   Be prepared to listen to their views, feelings and suggestions.

   c.   Start the meeting by thanking them for their time and willingness to listen.

   d.   Restate the issue and purpose of the meeting – to find a solution that works for both parties.

   e.   Ask the other person how he/she wants to proceed.

   f.   If they try to raise other issues, explain that these will be addressed after the issue you have raised is resolved.

   g.   During the meeting, do not allow discussions of feelings or explanations to become repetitive – focus on the interests and goals.

6   *Make a contract*

   a.   Make a contract or agreement about what each of you will do to solve the conflict – the voluntary behaviour going forward. During negotiations, verbalize the agreement and check he or she agrees.

   b.   You may specify a time when you will check back that the agreement is working.

   c.   If you can't reach a win–win, try a compromise. If that fails you may decide to escalate or exit the relationship.

7   *Follow through on the contract*

   a.   Do what you agreed to do.

   b.   If the other party complies with their side, you should express your appreciation – this is positive feedback to reinforce the new/good behaviour.

c. If the other party is not adhering to the agreement, arrange another meeting to adjust the original agreement.

d. If they fail repeatedly, you may consider escalation, giving up or exiting the relationship.

Negotiating tactics

There are many negotiating tactics. The tactics reveal something about the other person, and your reaction to them reveals information about you, your style and sometimes the real issues. It is helpful if you can anticipate and identify their tactics and consider how you will respond. Some of the most common tactics include:

- Ambit claim – Open with an extreme position, expecting that some aspects will be rejected

- Deadline – Create a timeframe to add pressure

- Divide and conquer – Try to split the other side by appealing to some interests

- Good guy, bad guy – One person aggressive and the other soothing and civilized

- No authority – Say you are not empowered to make deals

- One cuts, the other chooses – Incentive to divide physical resources equally

- Playing to the gallery – Grand and extreme statements to impress people

- Red herring – Distract with irrelevancies

Signals during negotiation

During a conflict, the other side may indicate a desire or propensity to change their position or make concessions by making signals. Some of these signals may be non-verbal.

Signal type	Example	Meaning	Possible response
Qualifier	• We don't normally give discounts • We can't consider that at this time	• Change it slightly and we might • Show me a more interesting agreement	• If you give us an idea of what you are looking for • Let's discuss which paragraphs are causing an issue and I'll discuss it
Grandstanding	• It's a board policy	• Like-to-have not must-have objective	• Sure the board will be pleased with other elements
Concealed appeal	• If only you'd listened to us last week	• We want some ritual apology	• Yes, we made an error of judgement but we can repair
Hypothetical	• Let's assume for the sake of argument	• We're interested but we don't want to be seen committing	• Just for the sake of argument, we'd be looking for . . .
False refusal	• I won't negotiate under duress • We won't be agreeing today	• There's still a chance – try harder	• Thanks for telling me • If we change . . .
Emphasis prompt	• Our major concern is that	• Change your focus	• We understand
Cornering	• We consider our offer fair and reasonable	• If you reject this, you will be unfair and unreasonable	• Much of life is unfair, let's look at the merits

Sometimes you meet an impasse or **stalemate**. Accept them as normal and don't presume fault. Explore the reasons and others' perceptions of what has happened and why. Let the parties find their own way through. However, the threat of impasse may force people to see conflict more realistically.

Manage conflict's aftermath (apologies)

The aftermath of conflict is often marked by emotional residues, damaged trust and relational distances. Sometimes differences can't be bridged, leading to resentment and new conflicts. So take action to return to a healthy relationship by acceptance, apology, amends, forgiveness, reconciliation and healing.

Apologies have five parts:

1   Specific definition of the offending behaviour

2   Acknowledgement that the behaviour caused harm

3   Statement of responsibility for the behaviour and harm

4   Statement of regret

5   Commitment to avoid repeating the behaviour

Making amends is about fixing what has been broken. Forgiveness means letting go of emotional residues and may take time. Reconciliation is an interactive process that requires co-operative effort. It requires new behaviour to be noticed and positive feedback.

How management theories affect conflict

A study by the American Management Association estimated that about 25 per cent of their work time is dealing with conflict. Poorly managed conflict makes work life unpleasant and affects how organizations function.

The costs and consequences of organizational conflict stem from how conflict is handled. Costs to the individual include:

- Wasted time and effort

- Increased stress

- Reduced performance and motivation

- Delayed career development

- Loss of employment

Costs to organizations include:

- Impaired communication and function

- Damaged relationships and rapport

- Reduced morale and productivity

- Increased absenteeism and turnover

- Litigation

One of the issues concerns how we think of an organization establishing rules, control and relationships:

- *Classical management* – German sociologist Max Weber based his model on a hierarchical, bureaucratic structure where there is an ordered chain of command, with communication and decisions flowing from the top down. This embodies power and status differences that impede direct negotiation in conflicts.

- *Human relations management* – This model took hold around 1930. Developed by Elton Mayo, it suggested that productivity can be improved by treating employees as individuals and interacting with them on a friendly basis. The metaphor he used was an organization as a family.

- *Human resources management* – This model developed between 1940 and 1980. A key assumption is that the primary resource of any organization is its people, so motivation is likely to be vital to increase productivity. Motivation is achieved by matching or aligning the individual's goals to those of the organization. The metaphor for this model is the organization as a team, with employees participating in the decision-making.

- *Systems management* – This emerged around 1980 and the assumption is that organizations are like living organisms, constantly moving, changing and interacting. A change in one element changes others. The challenge is to maintain stability while adapting to change and solving problems as they arise. It recognizes that some parts of the system operate informally and unofficially.

SECTION SUMMARY

WE STARTED BY CONSIDERING relationship management competencies and how relationships are formed. We looked at different types of relationship, including digital relationships and ideas such as commitment and loyalty. We explored where relationships can go wrong, different types of 'difficult' behaviour and how to deal with them and some problematic relationships. The drama triangle and the Parent–Adult–Child model from Transactional Analysis were explored. We considered what makes people like us and how to create rapport and trust.

As conflict is endemic in all relationships – and conflict management is one of the core competencies of relationship management –significant space was devoted to understanding conflict, including changing perspectives, managing emotions, the win–win approach, bargaining, perception, punctuation and power. Different negotiating styles – including dysfunctional ones – were considered, as well as when it is best to use them. Then we navigated through the stages in a negotiation and considered various negotiating tactics and signals.

PART FIVE

INTERNAL RELATIONSHIPS

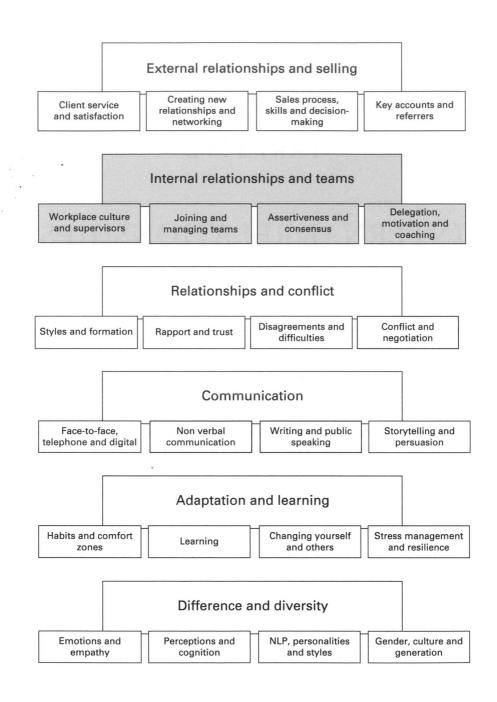

External relationships and selling

| Client service and satisfaction | Creating new relationships and networking | Sales process, skills and decision-making | Key accounts and referrers |

Internal relationships and teams

| Workplace culture and supervisors | Joining and managing teams | Assertiveness and consensus | Delegation, motivation and coaching |

Relationships and conflict

| Styles and formation | Rapport and trust | Disagreements and difficulties | Conflict and negotiation |

Communication

| Face-to-face, telephone and digital | Non verbal communication | Writing and public speaking | Storytelling and persuasion |

Adaptation and learning

| Habits and comfort zones | Learning | Changing yourself and others | Stress management and resilience |

Difference and diversity

| Emotions and empathy | Perceptions and cognition | NLP, personalities and styles | Gender, culture and generation |

Before we consider business relationships with people external to your organization, we are going to spend some time considering internal relationships. These are the relationships you form with your manager and senior people, your teammates and peers, those who work for you and people in other departments or offices. Some of these relationships will be formal, distant and dependent on your role and others will be informal, close, and social – perhaps some may even be friendships.

The main difference between internal and external business relationships is that you will have something in common with those in internal relationships – your organization. Typically, you will share the same aims (e.g. to make the organization successful) and values.

It is likely that you will work as part of a team – perhaps with senior and junior people working alongside you on activities or projects. Relationships with the team overall and team members individually will need to be forged and negotiated. People may behave differently when they are part of a group or team than they do as individuals.

You will need to form different types of business relationships internally and sometimes it won't be plain sailing. Whilst you share an employer, you may have competing goals or priorities which can lead to conflict (see Part 4). And there may be a lack of mutual understanding, rivalries or even personality clashes that may get in the way. In some organizations, you will need to understand the office politics (behaviour involving competition for status or power) that drive many interactions.

22

Adapting to workplace cultures and internal politics

Working with your boss (line manager)

One of the first people you will need to form a business relationship with is your boss. You may have met him or her as part of the recruitment process – or as you go through a formal or informal induction when you join the organization. Sometimes you don't meet your boss until you start your job. In some large, global organizations you may find that your boss is in another office or country or that you have multiple bosses depending on what projects you are working on.

The relationship with your boss is different to other relationships as there is power inequality. You are an employee of the organization and your boss has the authority to tell you what to do and to reprimand you if you get things wrong.

Some bosses are controlling and directive whereas others are more supportive and consultative – they like to engage their people and listen to their views. There's more about this in the section on leadership (see p. 245). Your boss's style will dictate how you form and conduct the relationship. Whatever his or her style, it will take you a while to figure him or her out and understand how to conduct this business relationship and whether an informal relationship is also possible or desirable.

You should have a job description that outlines what you must do. There may also be criteria or objectives (in some organizations these are called **Key**

Performance Indicators – KPIs) that enable your boss and the organization to measure your performance.

In many organizations, you will also have a Personal Development Plan, which outlines what you and the organization must do to help you improve, develop and progress. Your boss – and the **Human Resources (HR)** Department – will have responsibility for working with you on your development: identifying opportunities for learning, practice to gain experience and in providing feedback.

There may also be a formal **appraisal** for a discussion about your strengths and development needs once or twice a year. This may or may not be linked to your pay and rewards. In smaller organizations, though, there may not be a job description, development plan or appraisal process, which means you have an additional challenge in managing the relationship.

Adapting to the workplace culture

Each organization has its own **corporate or workplace culture** and this will have a bearing on how you form and maintain your relationships with your boss and other people in the organization. It influences the external relations of the organization as well as the internal relationships of the employees. It's hard to define corporate culture. Simply, it is 'how we do things around here'. Various management experts have described corporate culture as:

- 'Norms for acceptable behaviour' (Lin Hai)
- 'It reinforces ideas and feelings that are consistent with the corporation's beliefs' (Charles Hampden-Turner)
- 'Behaviours that new employees are encouraged to follow' (John Kotter and James L. Heskett)

Some have described corporate culture as 'the invisible hand' that guides the behaviour in an organization. Gerry Johnson and Kevan Scholes suggested that there were various components of corporate culture such as symbols, governance, organizational structures, leadership and role modelling, systems and processes, customs and stories which all contribute to a shared mental model. Part of the recruitment process will involve the employer and the potential employee trying to figure out whether there is sufficient 'fit' between the organizational culture and that of the individual.

The **organizational culture** is captured within the **employer brand**. This is a term commonly used to describe an organization's reputation as an employer and its value proposition (what it offers) to its employees as opposed to its more general corporate brand reputation and offer for customers or clients. Usually it is expressed as a key message, core values, the personality of the organization, what it says about the organization and how it makes members feel.

We saw in Part 2 that change management (see p. 46) was difficult and it is perhaps even more so when people attempt to change corporate culture. To do so requires any change to link to the organization's vision, mission and objectives, a sense of urgency for the need to change, addressing stakeholder issues (i.e. those of owners, employees and clients of an organization), generating enabling mechanisms (such as reward systems) and leaders who act as **role models.**

Gary Hamel, in his book *The Facebook Generation*, suggested that in order to attract, retain and engage with Generation F (some people call these folk Millennials or Digital Natives or Born Digitals) there are twelve crucial elements which are largely due to the 'corporate culture' (see p. 25).

Whatever the organizational culture, there will be unwritten, implicit rules about how to go about forming and developing internal business relationships.

Internal politics

In some workplace cultures, there can be internal, office or organizational politics. This is where power and social networking are used to benefit the organization, teams or individuals within it. Sometimes, individuals use their influence to serve personal interests without regard to the effect on the organization or others within it.

There are models which attempt to categorize different styles of political behaviour. In one scenario there is an axis of 'plays games' with 'acts with integrity' and another axis of political awareness and unawareness. So the following types emerge:

- Clever fox (plays games, politically aware)

- Wise owl (acts with integrity, politically aware)

- Innocent sheep (acts with integrity, politically unaware)

- Inept donkey (plays games, politically unaware)

Another model suggests the following types:

- Rising star

  - Rapidly progressing up through the ranks

  - Supported by a mentor

  - Trusted by the 'top guns'

  - Gets information quickly

- Fallen star

  - Around for old time's sake

  - Promoted to incompetence level (i.e. progressed up through the ranks until they reached a level where they failed to succeed)

  - Limited influence

  - Bypassed on decisions

- Fox

  - Sly and moves quickly

  - Hard to identify as acts covertly

  - Well connected, with lots of contacts

- ○ Acts in his or her own interests

- ○ Rarely trustworthy

- Foot soldier

  - ○ One of many ordinary workers

  - ○ May be aspiring to progress and promotion

Whether or not you use these models to identify different types of political behaviour, remember that people will have different motivations, power, influence and awareness of internal politics. The different types of political 'creature' will have an impact on which business relationships you form – and how. Some people will seek out those who are powerful, rising stars so that they can 'hook onto' their success. Others may prefer to stick with the foot soldiers and ignore the political undertones.

Jean Hartley, Professor of Public Leadership in the Open University, suggested that you can manage the personality and chemistry issues by developing **political astuteness**. She saw this as comprising the following qualities – many of which are encapsulated in emotional intelligence (see Part 1):

1 Personal skills

- Be self-aware and have self-control. Be curious about people and proactive – take the initiative.

2 Interpersonal skills

- Make others feel valued, build relationships with a variety of people, encourage people to talk to you, develop soft skills and tough skills such as negotiating and dealing with conflict.

3 Reading people and situations

- Get people together to address issues below the surface, understand the power that people have, recognize when you might be perceived as a threat, use analytical and intuitive skills.

4 Build alignment and alliances

- Reach out to people to build collaboration, decide who to include and exclude, go beyond the immediate and obvious partners, work across competing interests.

5 Strategic direction and scanning

- Understand your purpose and what you want to achieve, anticipate and time things correctly.

23

Assertiveness

Sometimes you may be intimidated by your boss. This may be because you lack confidence – which is natural when you start working with new people – or because his or her behaviour makes you feel uncomfortable. You may find yourself unable to express yourself or that your requests are overlooked. In extreme cases this can be considered bullying (see p. 205) and is not acceptable, so you may need help from the Human Resources professionals in your organization. Similarly, you may find that you are reluctant to speak up at meetings. You need to develop your confidence and learn to be more assertive.

Being assertive means that you have self-confidence in conversations. It means you have a self-assured, open and confident manner and approach. You need to have self-respect to be assertive – to value yourself and your right to be heard and for your needs to be met (see the material on self-esteem on p. 266). Assertive people express negative thoughts in a healthy and positive manner and confront challenges and issues without getting personal. Assertive people convey their ideas clearly and enthusiastically.

Assertive people are also considerate to others and accept that people are responsible for their own behaviour. Assertive people are regarded as firm and fair. You may need to adjust your thoughts and actions as a result of understanding the other person's position.

Assertive people ask for time to think about and complete tasks properly – they are not pushed into accepting unrealistic deadlines. Assertive people welcome feedback and accept criticism and compliments positively.

Being assertive – balancing needs

A passive person allows others' needs to dominate (I lose–You win: see negotiation on p. 169). An aggressive person insists on meeting their own needs (I win–You lose). An assertive person seeks to balance their own and other people's needs (I win–You win or, more simply, **Win–Win**).

Passive and aggressive behaviour

Often the way we behave has roots in how we were treated when we were young and how we learned to cope. Established and habitual behaviour can be changed with knowledge, effort and practice (see Part 2).

Aggressive behaviour

Aggressive people get angry or lose their temper. They have no consideration for others, and may even bully them – by demanding compliance and being threatening. Aggression is dangerous as it is harmful to relationships and reputation. Aggression creates fear or prompts others to become aggressive too. Forcing your opinion and will on others isn't conducive to good team spirit and morale.

Passive behaviour

At the other end of the spectrum, a passive person does not express their feelings. They accept requests and defeat so the other person gets their way or wins. If you passively accept everything without stating your views and needs you are likely to bottle things up and become frustrated and resentful. Sometimes, young or inexperienced people passively accept tasks that they would not be given if they explained their reasons or consequences. Sometimes this means they are given more and more inappropriate tasks or unmanageable workloads, simply because they haven't helped others understand the situation.

Passive-aggressive behaviour

Sometimes people are passive-aggressive. This means that while they appear on the surface to be passive and compliant, there is an aggressive undertone. For example, someone might say 'Yes I'll do it', but with an angry tone of voice and non-verbal communication such as a frown or crossed arms that show the spoken words are incongruent with their true feelings.

Everyone has some basic rights – to be treated with respect and to be able to express their views and to have their needs met. You also have the right to request more information if you don't understand something. You have the right to change your mind and even to make mistakes. More importantly perhaps, you also have the right to decline responsibility for other people's problems.

Start with clear goals and focus. Assertive people know what they want – and what they don't want. So you should be clear about your aims, goals and priorities. If you and those around you are aware of your goals – and they are SMART (Specific Measureable Achievable Realistic and Time-specific) – it is easier to decline or negotiate on other tasks. Clarity on Key Performance Indicators (KPIs) can also help. If you are unable to articulate clearly what you are supposed to be doing, it is easier for others to persuade you to do the things that they want you to do.

Techniques for being more assertive

There are several techniques for being more assertive. For example:

Understand their needs – Use empathy to see the other person's point of view. Ask questions and listen carefully so that you understand their perspective and needs. At the very least, this gives you more information on which to base your decision and response. But by asking questions you are showing respect for their views and entering into a mature dialogue to resolve the matter.

Probe – Ask more detailed questions to understand the nature of the situation and request. During the questions you might reveal other approaches and solutions to the person's problem or request.

Acknowledge – Acknowledging means that once you have listened to the other person, you acknowledge their views. It's called **validation**. Your response might be 'I understand that you are worried and stressed about your client's project.' It is particularly effective if you reflect back the words that the other person has used.

Prepare yourself – If you are afraid that you will cave in when confronted by a dominant person, spend some time preparing yourself. Make a note of your aims and priorities, the reasons why you are unable to comply or what you need in order to do so. Prepare yourself mentally too – and request that the discussion happens at a time and in a place where you will feel calm and confident.

Consider a conditional agreement – Agree to a request but qualify it with conditions. So, for example, you might say 'I understand that you need your project completed urgently. I will be able to help you but please speak to my manager to check that it is alright.'

Use the three-part sentence – This follows the approach of a) listening carefully; b) saying what you think and feel; and c) saying what you want to happen. Your three-part sentence might be 'I understand that you are worried about your client project. I would like to be able to help you but at the moment I am working on something urgent for John. Please ask Maria for help but come back to me later this afternoon if you still need assistance.'

Practise saying 'No' – Saying 'No' can be challenging – especially if you are in a reactive, service-providing role or the person asking you to do something is more senior. There is always the fear that saying 'No' will lead to argument and conflict. Some people worry that saying 'No' means that others will perceive them as unhelpful or uncommitted.

Developing the confidence to state your views and say 'No' appropriately is important. Aim to be polite but firm. Sometimes you might explain the reasons. Sometimes you may need to seek help from your line manager. It might help to provide an alternative solution to the person by directing them to another source of help.

Avoid childlike responses – Transactional Analysis (TA – see p. 146) suggests that while we generally behave in a rational and adult way, sometimes others behave in a parental or childlike way that triggers us to mirror or react to that behaviour and act inappropriately. Keep your manner adult and rational.

Play a broken record – Repeat your views when the person continues to put pressure on you. For example, you might say 'I understand that you are in a difficult position, I would like to help but at the moment I have been asked to complete another task.' And when they explain further why you should assist, you should firmly but politely repeat the same sentence.

Point out discrepancies – This is a way to deal with contradictory behaviour. Imagine where a boss says that you are to focus on one particular project but then keeps asking you to do other things. Calmly point out the discrepancy. 'You stressed at the start of the month that my top priority was to complete Project X. But since then you have given me many other things to do. I understand that you are really busy. I am working very hard and trying to do as you say. However, you are giving me contradictory instructions. Please explain whether you want me to focus on Project X or whether you want me to complete the other tasks.'

Explain consequences – Calmly explain the consequences of the requested action. You might say 'I know this report is urgent and important. However, if I do this work for you then I will be letting down Jane and Henry on their urgent work. Are you OK with me letting down Jane and Henry?'

Understand cultural differences – While in the UK we are generally open and egalitarian, other cultures are different. This means that there is a danger that behaviour and communication can be misunderstood. For example, in cultures where there are more hierarchical structures (see Part 1, p. 27), those higher in status give orders to those lower in status who will not challenge such instructions. This doesn't mean that the people are being aggressive – they operate to different social rules and you must guard against judging that behaviour with your values.

24

Bullies, control freaks and stubbornness

In the previous section, we considered how to identify and deal with different types of difficult behaviour (see p. 158). There are three types of difficult behaviour that you might experience with your boss. I mentioned before that you should not label people as 'difficult' as this will affect the way you perceive any future behaviour and may make the problem worse.

Bullying

Bullying can be devastating and can make people feel frightened, angry, isolated, worthless, depressed, undermined and even suicidal. If bullied, physical health is likely to suffer and there is a greater risk of developing mental health problems such as depression, anxiety, low self-esteem or adult onset PTSD (post-traumatic stress disorder). People who are bullied are more likely to miss or skip work to avoid being bullied. Bullying should never be underestimated or tolerated.

Bullying is repeated aggressive behaviour that can be physical, verbal, online or relational. There are **gender differences** involved – men frequently bully using physical threats and actions, while women are more likely to engage in verbal or relationship bullying. Increasingly, mobiles and social media are being used to shame and bully people (online and cyber-bullying). **Sexual harassment** is a form of bullying, where someone abuses their seniority or position to make inappropriate sexual comments or actions – this behaviour should be reported to your human resources team or senior management.

Bullies are usually trying to remove power from a colleague and retain the power for themselves. They do this by trying to limit the behavioural choices at the time of attack. The bully wants the target to feel so anxious that they don't fight back.

There are five contexts for bullying:

1   The bully starts to fear that they are failing at their job. The bully targets a successful or popular colleague in a mistaken attempt to take the spotlight off their own shortcomings.

2   The bully chooses to work with people who have similar values. They feel contempt for anyone who doesn't present themselves as able, active and confident (see in-group bias, pp. 149 and 215).

3   The bully becomes jealous of the success of a colleague so they attempt to undermine that colleague.

4   The bully fears that their role may be under threat from a talented colleague. The bully targets the colleague in an attempt to eliminate the competition.

5   The bully is envious of the work of a colleague and makes them doubt their competence.

Bullies want to demonstrate how weak others are and thus feel more powerful and buttress their own strengths and control. Bullying often causes others to react in very specific ways.

The target of bullying must recognize that they have a choice in how to respond to a bully's activities, and that what they say and do will either interrupt or sustain the bullying dynamic. In essence, this means that the person being bullied must react in a way that is not anticipated by the bully.

If you are being bullied, remember:

•   Don't blame yourself. It is not your fault. You should not be ashamed of who you are or what you feel.

- Be proud of who you are. Despite what anyone says, there are many good things about you. Keep those in mind instead of the negative messages you hear from others.

- Get help. Talk to a colleague, another manager or the human resources department. Bullying in the workplace is serious and there are laws to prevent it and protect you. As well as dealing with the bully, you may need to take care of yourself – seeing a counsellor does not mean there is something wrong with you.

- Learn to deal with stress and build your **resilience** (see p. 70).

There is no single solution to bullying or a best way to handle a bully. It may take experimentation with a variety of different responses to find the strategy that works best for you. Things you can try include the following:

- Bullies want to know they have control over your emotions, so don't react with anger or retaliate with physical force. If you walk away, ignore them or calmly and assertively tell them you're not interested in what they have to say, you're demonstrating that they don't have control over you.

- Protect yourself. If you can't walk away and are being physically hurt, protect yourself so you can get away. Your safety is top priority. Report the bullying to the authorities. If you don't report threats and assaults, a bully may see this as 'permission' to bully and may become more aggressive.

- Change your attitude towards bullying so that you can regain a sense of control. Try to view bullying from a different perspective. For example, see the bully as an unhappy, frustrated person who wants to have control over your feelings. They may be bullied themselves. They may need to bully others to feel better about themselves. They may be insecure. Don't give them the satisfaction of letting them see that they have upset you.

- Look at the big picture. Bullying can be extremely painful, but try asking yourself how important it will seem to you in the long run. Will it matter in a year? Is it worth getting so upset over? If the answer is no, focus your time and energy elsewhere.

- Focus on the positive. Reflect on all the things that you appreciate in your life, including your own positive qualities and gifts. Make a list and refer to it whenever you feel down.

- Don't try to control the uncontrollable. Many things in life are beyond our control – including the behaviour of other people. Focus on the things you *can* control, such as the way you choose to react to bullies.

- Reach out to connect with family and close friends or explore ways of making new friends or other relationships at work. Consider a transfer to another team or office.

- Boost your confidence. Exercise is a great way to help you feel good about yourself, as well as to reduce stress. Punch a mattress or take a kick-boxing class to work off your anger. Don't beat yourself up. Don't make a bullying incident worse by dwelling on it or replaying it in your head. Deal with it or get others to deal with it and focus on positive experiences you've had.

Control freaks

Sometimes you may regard your boss as a control freak – who micromanages everything you do. This leaves you with little opportunity to take the initiative or try out your own ideas. And when someone spends too much time telling you what to do and how to do it then you may feel untrusted, de-skilled and frustrated.

There are both good and bad reasons why bosses can oversupervise. On the positive side, if you are learning a new task then they may feel that you need the support and guidance. They are providing on-the-job training. If you are new to them, they may need to gain a better grasp of your strengths and abilities. It may be that what you are doing is a critical function or that there are policies and regulations governing how the work must be completed. They are likely to have more experience and may be aware of pitfalls and problems that you don't know and they want to prevent you from failing.

On the negative side, they may feel vulnerable in their position, threatened by you or lack faith in your abilities. They may have a personality that seeks perfection or is overanxious. Ideally, as you will see in the section on **delegation** (p. 239), your boss should adapt their level of supervision and feedback as you become more experienced. When you are experienced, they should delegate the outcome or results that are needed rather than the detailed process to get there.

When dealing with overcontrolling behaviour, you need to observe and assess whether you are underestimating the complexity of the task or whether your boss is unaware of your skills and abilities. Either way, communication is the way forward – whether this is to reassure your boss by agreeing in advance what you will do and when you will check-in or whether it is to ask your boss at what stage they will feel comfortable about allowing you more freedom.

Stubbornness

Someone is stubborn when they refuse to change their mind about an idea or action and also refuse to give a clear explanation or reason for their resistance. They may be stubborn because they are ignorant or arrogant (overconfident). They may be defending an idea that is important to them or they may feel taken for granted. They may be busy, tired or afraid. People are often afraid of change. Edgar Schein found that people may suffer from **learning anxiety** (fear of learning something new) or **survival anxiety** (the pressure to change). They may be afraid of temporary incompetence, punishment for incompetence or loss of personal identity or group membership.

There are many ways to tackle someone who is stubborn – use empathy to develop rapport and trust, communicate, explore their reasons for resistance, focus on their needs, listen and be flexible, find a common ground, identify a motivator, describe the consequences, try different timing, explain things in a different way, use data and logic, build on their ideas (use 'and' rather than 'but'), enlist allies, compromise, negotiate or escalate to someone more senior.

25

Buy-in and consensus

Sometimes you will need people to support you in completing a piece of work. This may be just part of your regular duties that require others to contribute or it may be that you want to get people to back you up on an idea or project you are leading. It may be that they are directly involved or it may be that they are a stakeholder with some other interest.

Buy-in is where people believe in and accept an idea, concept, system or project. Consensus is where a group of people reach the same opinion or agreement. **Stakeholders** are those who have a share or interest.

The material in the persuasion section (see p. 116) will be useful when trying to achieve buy-in and consensus. But there are some other things that you can do to achieve buy-in.

I have been developing a 7P toolbox of techniques for buy-in and **stakeholder management** – drawing on material from two decades of practice in psychology, selling, communications and change management:

- People – Understand the people involved – their natures, styles, preferences, experience, attitudes and motivations. Understand that they may have different aims and interests to you – and a different perspective (Part 1). Communication – both speaking and listening – is vital in engaging people. Your own credibility – expertise, role, authority, assertiveness, track record and reputation – will also have an impact (Part 2).

- Psychology – There are all sorts of psychological tools that can help us develop our relationships with people and achieve their support and buy-in – whether this is empathy, emotional intelligence, personality assessment, perception (of yourself and those you are trying to influence), communication approaches, learning styles, Neuro-Linguistic Programming (NLP), Transactional Analysis (TA), motivation and group dynamics.

- Process and Precision – There are processes to guide communication, education, consultation, negotiation and change. You may need data, information, benchmarks and research – tailored to the different stakeholders – to support your case and to set out your aims, rational arguments, proposed strategies and expected results.

- Plan – Most things are better when you have a plan. A plan forces you to think in advance about what you want to achieve, what you need to do and what the stages might be – and the timing. Planning requires you to consider alternative options and scenarios so that you are ready for the unexpected. It guides you through a process that makes sure nothing is forgotten and that things stay on the right track. Often, you will have others review, refine and support your plan, which provides added confidence and authority.

- Persuasion – Techniques for influence and persuasion can be found in Part 3. Selling skills – covered in Part 6 – may also be useful to you.

- Pressure – You can use the power of more senior people to exert direct control or you can enlist the support of advocates, champions, sponsors and key influencers to support your cause. Recognize that there may be **objections** and resistance to deal with, so you should anticipate that and have some responses and strategies ready. There may be a need to deal with conflict here too (see p. 156).

- Patience – Change takes time – and so can winning people over. You need to find ways to manage your own frustration and motivation. Sometimes you have to be patient – but persistent. And celebrate each small victory along the way.

Another way of looking at this subject draws on some of the ideas in change management (see p. 46). I use a model with the metaphor of dancing with oranges and elephants.

Oranges – segment the internal audience/stakeholders

Not all people are the same. And not everyone needs to be central to the buy-in campaign. In marketing there is an idea called **segmentation** where we break up a big market into smaller parts or segments which are different from each other but where those in the segment share some characteristics, interests or needs. We adapt our message and approach to the various people or stakeholder groups that we need buy-in from – some may be senior people who we need to sponsor and support us, others may need to be consulted on particular aspects, and others simply need to be kept informed. Part of the segmentation approach is to align our plans to their differing goals, needs and motivations. The **impact-influence matrix** might also be used for this purpose.

Elephants – understand the role of emotion

We know that emotions are important. Even if what you want to do is logical and rational, we still need to accommodate people's different styles, opinions and needs. They don't always act in a rational and logical way. They may be contradictory or even argumentative. We need to find a way to connect with them emotionally and engage their interest and motivation for our project. The reference to emotional elephants comes from the great book by Chip and Dan Heath called *How to change when change is hard*.

Dancing – make the specific steps clear

You wouldn't expect people to dance without providing a step-by-step guide as to exactly what they need them to do and when, and allowing them plenty of safe practice time. It's the same with buy-in. If you want people to do something different then you need to show them exactly what you want them to do and why and to keep it simple. You must provide the necessary information and training, allow them to practise, encourage them when they succeed and reassure them if they fail. The journey of 1,000 miles starts with a single step.

26

Working as part of a team and finding a mentor

It is likely that within your organization you will be a member of a variety of different groups and teams. Some of these will be formal and permanent teams such as your department or office, and some may be temporary, informal and even virtual – such as project and social groups. You will need to forge business relationships with the members.

We saw before that teams can be defined in a number of ways:

- 'A team is a small group of individuals who share responsibility for outcomes for their organisation' (Eric Sundstrom)

- 'A team is a distinguishable set of two or more individuals who interact interdependently and adaptively to achieve specified, shared and value objectives' (Ben Morgan)

- 'A team is a collection of individuals who are interdependent in their tasks, who share responsibility for outcomes, who see themselves and who are seen by others as an intact social entity embedded in one or more larger social systems and who manage their relationships across organisational boundaries' (S. Cohen and D. Bailey)

Whereas there is usually clarity in your role – it is outlined in your job description – and your line manager(s) will likely have set you some personal goals or KPIs – it is possible that there no targets for your team. Or your goals may conflict with those of your team and other teams.

It is possible that you may have several bosses – the **line manager** you report to on a day-to-day basis and a variety of other people who are responsible for your work in different teams or projects. This can be confusing – especially when you are receiving conflicting instructions, being pulled in different directions or overloaded with work.

Some people learn time management and assertiveness skills to help them. Others rely on regular communication with their line manager and try to maintain a dialogue with several bosses themselves. Communication is important and if the pressures become too much you should seek help from the human resources department, a colleague or a mentor.

Working as part of a team (Ambassador)

When you work as part of a team your behaviour will have an impact on the reputation of the team – and all of its members – as well as on your own. So you are effectively an '**Ambassador**' for your team whenever you interact with people in other parts of the business or externally.

We saw above that organizations have their own culture and that when you join a business you need to be aware of the unwritten rules about behaviour. The same can apply to a department, group or team – it may have a slightly different culture to other teams within the same organization. Therefore, your first task is to settle into the team and learn how they see and do things. Then you can be a good Ambassador for the team and your team mates will trust you, and others in the firm will see that you are an integral part of the team.

As well as you having an impact on the team, the team will also have an effect on you – and it may be positive or negative. A confident team sees a challenge positively – as an opportunity to learn and a chance to shine. A team lacking confidence will see challenge as a criticism or threat – a reason to blame others or something to avoid.

Integrating into the team – in-groups and out-groups

People find it frustrating and confusing when someone agrees to something on a one-to-one basis and then does a volte-face when they are with others. People's behaviour changes when they are in a group. In order to integrate into a team, we have to adopt the same attitudes and behave similarly. There's a natural tendency for people to conform to group norms (typical behaviour). There's a famous psychology experiment where twelve people say that 'black is white' and eventually the thirteenth person starts to doubt themselves and believe the others.

As social creatures, we derive part of our sense of identity from our peers or those in our group. Think how people originally lived in **tribes**. Our sense of belonging can be enhanced by making comparisons with out-groups. Researcher Glynis Breakwell studied teenage soccer fans, some of whom went to most games, whilst others did not go to games. Those who did not go to games were the most vehement about their loyalty and showed most in-group bias, presumably as they had a greater need to prove themselves as fans. Another example is that when abroad, especially in countries which have particularly different languages and cultures, we feel our nationality far more keenly than when we are at home.

If we believe that someone else is in a group to which we belong, we will have positive views of them and give them preferential treatment because we build our **self-esteem** through belonging. The opposite of in-group bias is out-group bias where, by inference, out-group people are viewed negatively and given worse treatment. Out-group people are described in abstract terms (which depersonalizes them) when they conform to the out-group stereotype. Out-group people will be referred to in more specific, concrete terms when they act in an unexpected way.

Henri Tajfel divided people into random groups who rapidly found in-group people preferable to out-group people, even finding rational arguments for how unpleasant and immoral the out-group people were.

Sometimes people model their behaviour on other people whom they admire (**role models** are very powerful), and resist involvement with those outside the group. A common example is when someone becomes a manager and behaves like other managers – even to the detriment of previous relationships with other colleagues. Make yourself and the other person feel part of the same group, and they will be biased towards you.

Finding a mentor (or a coach)

The European Mentoring Centre defines **mentoring** as 'off-line help by one person to another in making significant transitions in knowledge, work or thinking'. Other definitions include the following:

- 'A wise and trusted counsellor or teacher' (Greek mythology)

- 'A mentor is a more experienced individual willing to share their knowledge with someone less experienced in a relationship of trust. A mixture of parent and peer, the mentor's primary function is to be a transitional figure in an individual's development. Mentoring includes coaching, facilitating, counselling and networking' (David Clutterbuck)

- 'In the modern business context, mentoring is always at least one stage removed from direct line management responsibility and is concerned with the longer term acquisition and application of skills in a developing career by a form of advising and counselling' (Eric Parsloe)

Each organization may have a different view of the role of mentors, so you should probably explore what is usual within yours to help manage your expectations and get the relationship off to a good start. There is usually a special type of business relationship with your mentor.

Many organizations allocate mentors or 'buddies' – someone who may be older or wiser or more senior or someone who has been with the organization or in the job for a long time and 'knows the ropes'. Part of the internal mentor's role is to help you adapt to the new environment and the organization's culture so that you fit in quickly.

Often, the mentor will not be someone you work with directly – they may be in a different part of the organization. Sometimes, mentors work outside the organization so that they can provide an objective view.

As well as providing another channel of communication (that is, in addition to your boss), a mentor is someone to whom you can ask questions, express your opinions and 'reality check' your perceptions and reactions to others in a safe and confidential environment. Mentors are likely to be able to offer advice or guidance or point you in the right direction for more help.

If your organization does not have a mentoring scheme then you can always find a mentor yourself. A mentor doesn't need to know the exact nature of your job or a lot about your organization – and sometimes their lack of inside knowledge enables you to see things more clearly.

A coach is different. Eric Parsloe defined coaching as 'a process that helps and supports people manage their own learning in order to maximise their potential, develop their skills, improve their performance and become the person they want to be'. Usually, coaches are specially trained and qualified to help you help yourself. Whereas mentors often give their time and advice for free, organizations usually pay for coaches – who are sometimes external consultants. Coaches are trained to help you find your own answer rather than give you advice. Being given a coach is a great privilege and often means that the organization has identified you as a potential high performer or has put you on 'the fast track' to promotion.

The coaching process is dealt with in more detail later in this section (see p. 234).

27

Team roles and how teams form

In addition to the specific technical or functional role within a group, people will have a preference for and adopt a particular role within a team. Their role will determine the way in which they relate to other people and therefore on the nature of the business relationships they form.

Fiona Elsa Dent did some work on analysing working-relationship types. She recognized that there were relationships that were based on work teams, functional relationships with other teams and social relationships. She observed that there were different levels of intimacy between team members too – from acquaintances to colleagues to 'inner circle':

	High	Transactional	Mutually dependent
Work need	Low	**Casual**	**Social**
		Low	High
	Sociability need		

She also analysed styles of behaviour on two axes – people focus versus task focus and reserved personality versus an outgoing style (see the diagram on page 31).

Sometimes there is conflict in a group and it doesn't perform well, possibly as a result of a clash of relationship styles between people. Forceful people may press on to get the job done – perhaps without listening to what others have to say. Harmonizers may be so focused on keeping the peace that they don't express their opinions.

There's an interesting situation, which Irving Janis called '**Group Think**', where a group is so focused on maintaining harmony and consensus that everyone – on the surface at least – agrees. This can then lead to bad decisions.

Elias Porter developed a theory of relationship awareness based on four premises:

1 Behaviour is driven by motivation

2 Motivation changes in conflict

3 Personal weaknesses are overdone strengths

4 Personal filters influence perception

He identified seven styles of relating to others when things are going well:

1 Altruistic – nurturing

2 Assertive – directing

3 Analytical – autonomizing

4 Flexible – cohering

5 Assertive – nurturing

6 Judicious – competing

7 Cautious – supporting

There are psychometric tools that assess and classify people's behaviour in groups – the typical roles they adopt. A good example of this is the **Belbin Team Roles** assessment. Through completing a questionnaire, people can determine the extent to which they have a preference for different roles when working in a team. Often, there will be a distinct preference for more than one role.

Team role name	Team role
Shaper	Task focus
Co-ordinator (earlier versions called this Chair)	Leads
Plant	Has ideas
Resource Instigator	Gets things
Monitor Evaluator	Checks and asks questions
Team Worker	Promotes harmony
Implementer	Systematic
Completer Finisher	Does the job
Specialist	Expert knowledge

However, the situation and group dynamics may mean that you adopt a different role in some teams. And it is possible for you to learn to adopt different roles – remember that your brain is 'plastic' and can learn new ways of thinking and behaving.

This is a useful tool when there is a problem in a team – such as a clash of personalities or a lack of performance. It could be that the team has too many plants ('people with ideas') and that there is a lot of talking but no real action. Or it could be that there are too many completer-finishers and no one generating ideas or leading everyone. If you are in a position to create your team, you might want to check that you have members from each of the different styles.

How teams form

Just as it takes time for a business relationship to form between two people, so it takes time for the relationships within a team to form. And because there are multiple one-to-one relationships within a group or team – that may be new or existing – these may need to be reviewed and renegotiated as they settle into a new group.

There is the added dynamic of having those one-to-one relationships possibly changed by the different group dynamics and the potential creation of new dyads (two people) and triads (three people). Therefore, it's no surprise that it can take a while for a new team to become effective. In 1965, Dr Bruce Tuckman proposed that teams move through a process as they form – this was mentioned in Part 1 (see p. 32).

It is not possible to gauge how long the team-forming process will take due to the number of variables involved, such as whether people have been placed in the team or volunteered themselves, the urgency and nature of the work to be done, whether the team members have worked together before and whether the team has complementary or conflicting views and roles. So be patient when a new team is formed – or when new members are introduced.

Some organizations – for example management consultancies and real estate advisers – work almost entirely on projects. So in addition to people being members of a specific department or work group, where they report to a line manager who manages their performance, appraisals and development, they are also members of a variety of different project groups. Within this **matrix style** of organization, people become used to having multiple bosses and conflicting priorities – although they usually have good support networks and human resource professionals to help them navigate the trickiest situations. They also become skilled at joining new groups and forming new teams quickly.

Rollin and Christine Glaser (1992) suggested that to enhance a team's effectiveness, the following five criteria are needed:

1 Clarity on the team's mission, goals and plan

2 Team member roles and responsibilities specified

3 Clear operating processes – what needs to happen at each meeting and between meetings

4 Sound interpersonal relationships between team members

5 Good inter-team relations – how the team communicates and collaborates with other teams

When a team is formed there should be a brief on what is to be achieved and by when as well as terms of reference specifying the range of work to be done as well as the boundaries or constraints to be observed. Often there are no such guidelines and the team has to work these out while it is forming. So that's why sometimes the storming stage can be prolonged and even painful to those within and beyond the team.

Alexander Pentland, a leading researcher into 'honest signals' and non-verbal communication, suggests that the three most important factors for team productivity and cohesion are:

- Energy

- Engagement

- Exploration

This suggests that all the team members should be engaged – contributing to discussions and supportive of the team's goals and work. There needs to be positive energy to make things happen and complete the necessary work. There also has to be a desire to explore and search for ideas and different approaches – for members to be curious and creative.

28

Managing teams, virtual teams and giving feedback

In many organizations, there are all manner of permanent teams, such as departments and divisions and offices and a variety of temporary project and campaign groups, cross-departmental teams and even virtual teams where the members rarely meet. Sometimes the team members are dispersed geographically and usually they are psychologically distant as they typically belong to different departments or exist within a matrix structure.

Some of the key things to consider when managing a team include:

1 Provide clarity in goals and roles

Fundamental to the success of any team is clarity of goals (What are we trying to achieve? Is it worth the effort? Is it strategically important? How does it align with the organization's goals? How will we be measured and rewarded? Are there SMART objectives?). And along with goals for the team it is important to clarify the targets, role and responsibilities for each team member.

There are many teams who are not given a clear brief or terms of reference and thus spend too much time in off-agenda discussions, focusing on the wrong things or dealing with the detail rather than the big picture. Objectives, KPIs (Key Performance Indicators) and milestones and timescales are needed to avoid scope creep.

Social loafing is a tendency for people to put less effort into a task when they are in a group than when they are alone. It can drain a team's performance. Social loafing happens when no one is personally accountable, so measure each person on their personal contribution.

2   Review the team structure

Sometimes, the structure and skills of an established team lose alignment with the strategy and needs of the business or project. This means going back to basics, considering the firm's (or project's) goals and redesigning or reshaping the team. Sometimes the addition of new members to an established team can bring new thinking and a fresh impetus.

3   Appreciate that team members are different

Team leaders and members need to understand that everyone – in addition to having different technical skill sets and practical experience – will have different personalities, relationship approaches, learning preferences, communication styles and motivations. These differences are described in Part 1. Helping team members to recognize differences and appreciate alternative strengths, weaknesses and approaches – rather than fight against them – is a good starting point.

4   Understand team dynamics

There are numerous tools to help teams appreciate other members' strengths and weaknesses and to explore ways to work together as a team more effectively from old favourites such as Belbin to more recent methodologies such as Talent Dynamics.

A team leader needs to deploy considerable emotional intelligence – particularly empathy – to identify the underlying emotions and dynamics between group members and to facilitate interactions that are productive and healthy. A little pressure and stress is a good thing; too much is dangerous.

5   Allow time for team formation

We read above that teams need time to settle into working together effectively – the forming, storming, norming and performing phases. Time needs to be allocated for people to get to know each other and establish trust – either through some social interaction or by a preliminary teamworking activity. Even on a teleconference for a virtual team it is important to allow a little time at the start of discussions for social chit-chat so that team members can form relationships at a distance.

Psychology can also help with insights from **social identity theory** and in-group bias research allowing groups to meld. Social identity theory suggests that when we belong to a group, we are likely to derive our sense of identity, at least in part, from that group. We also enhance the sense of identity by making comparisons with out-groups. Social identity is different from personal identity which is derived from personal characteristics and individual relationships.

More recent models also look at phases of team convergence (coming together) and divergence (moving apart). Be alert that once the team is established there is a risk of Group Think, where everyone agrees in order to preserve team harmony.

6   Use face time and technology

Face-to-face time is vital to enable relationships to become established. But with a virtual team this is often a luxury that is not available. The team leader at least should make an effort to get out and see people in their own environments at least once at the outset. Sometimes, the location of the host of the meeting can be rotated so at least some team members visit others in their offices.

Tools such as Skype, GoTo Meetings and Google+ Hangouts mean that at least some semblance of face-to-face contact can be achieved online. Larger firms have teleconferencing or telepresence facilities in their meeting rooms, allowing people from various locations to appear as if they are in the room.

7   Create a thinking environment

Psychologist Nancy Kline did some interesting work on creating a **thinking environment** – where everyone is empowered to make a contribution. Her ten indicators of a thinking environment comprise listen; ask incisive questions; establish equality; appreciate; be at ease; encourage; feel; supply accurate information; humanize the place; and create diversity (see p. 3). She also had some interesting insights into how to build appreciative relationships with her research on the 5:1 positive to negative interactions.

There's also interesting neuroscience research by Naomi Eisenberger into how different people react to **feedback** – while some personalities (and generations) welcome feedback and appear to be 'thick-skinned', others experience critical feedback almost as severely as physical pain.

8   Deploy leadership skills and motivate people

One of my favourite leadership models is that of John Adair. He sees both strategic and operational leadership success depending on the balance of three things: the task, the team and the individual. This ensures that one member of the team – whether over- or underachieving – does not divert attention from the task nor put the entire team at risk. Underperformance by an individual cannot be tolerated as it will have an impact on the motivation and effectiveness of the rest of the team.

9   Manage from a distance (virtual teams)

Once there is clarity of the team's aims, purpose, roles and communication methods, there needs to be regular communication to ensure that everyone feels involved, issues can be addressed and the work stays on track. Obviously, if budgets permit, it is valuable for remote workers to get on a plane, train or into a car and meet with other team members at least once.

Virtual meetings are an important method for virtual teams to stay connected. Each virtual meeting should focus on relationships, be properly prepared so that everyone can be present and productive, and balance completing the agenda with gaining broad participation.

Try to mix it up a bit, because if every meeting follows the same pattern, people can become disengaged. Activities that allow all team members to explore their similarities and differences (such as individual and team assessments mentioned above) or providing time for people to get to know each other socially will help.

According to Patrick Lencioni, one of the most important aspects to work on here is psychological trust to support those who may feel vulnerable if they are at a physical (and cultural) distance. His tips for building trust within a team include have the leader go first; seek first to understand; create a circle of safety (treating people like people); talk straight; right wrongs; keep commitments; and share an experience together. According to US studies, nine out of ten US employees believe that their boss trusts them to get their work done – regardless of where they are.

The leader should call individuals before group teleconferences to ensure that they know what is happening and why and are able to mention views that they may want to raise themselves or anonymously. Similarly, a short call to individuals after the group call will also convey support and generate feelings of inclusion.

Leaders may adjust the agenda to allow different remote workers to take centre stage – people need to be able to express themselves – on particular issues or make a point of asking for their views during the teleconference.

At the close of each virtual meeting there should be checks for closure. Has everything been completed? Is everyone in agreement? Are the next steps clear? Has everyone something of value to take from the meeting? Has everyone been acknowledged and/or contributed?

Team leaders need to be available between meetings and at regular checkpoints if team members have questions or issues they wish to raise. Leaders should take the initiative in calling at unexpected times to provide informal feedback – especially positive feedback – and seek views from members.

10 Communicate. Communicate. Communicate.

I meet plenty of team leaders who despair when their team members complain that they have inadequate information or don't feel that they are up to speed. The leaders sometimes forget that because they have been heavily involved in a topic they have a lot of knowledge and underestimate the time required by others to understand and/or keep up.

Another issue is the need to repeat or return to key issues – people may forget things that are raised once, they may only assimilate some of the information when it is first presented and may need reminders of the key points or documents that have been previously circulated.

Asking team members to outline their recollection of the key facts – and asking others to provide additional points or updates – can make the process more interactive. Reinforce key points regularly.

11 Coach rather than control

A good leader will understand when and how to delegate (see p. 239) and will alter the amount of support provided to those given unfamiliar tasks – delegating the outcome rather than the process to experienced team members. Using coaching skills (see p. 234) to develop team members and build their confidence is a vital leadership activity.

12 Deal with conflict

Small disagreements or tension between people can quickly escalate into destructive conflicts. And sometimes the damage from conflict is irreparable. Therefore, you need to be alert to conflicts and whether they are within or between individuals or between the team and others and take early action. You need to ensure that you are not inadvertently drawn into taking sides in triangulation. There is more on conflict management in Part 4 (p. 156).

13 Be aware of multicultural needs

Cultural awareness and sensitivity is a significant topic in itself (see Part 1, p. 27).

A summary of the main components needed for team performance:

- Vision – There needs to be a clear sense of purpose and an understanding of what success looks like

- Rules of engagement – There should be a document – ideally produced by the team – describing how the team will work together and the scope of the work for which they are responsible

- Stakeholder management – The team must understand who the stakeholders are, what they require and how to engage effectively with them

- Right members – The team needs people with the relevant skills, experience, authority and influence. It also needs clarity on roles and a leader

- Accountability – The team must recognize that they are responsible collectively for their results

Appreciation and a safe, positive team environment

Hopefully, the culture of your firm will enable the team leader or line manager to create a happy, safe and positive environment in which the team members can be fully productive.

Psychologist Nancy Kline in her book *Time to Think* found that a five-to-one ratio of appreciation to criticism helps people think for themselves. She said that change takes place best in the context of genuine praise. Kline argued that society teaches us that to be positive is to be naïve and vulnerable, whereas to be critical is to appear informed, buttressed and sophisticated. So there is a cultural bias to being negative which isn't helpful.

Kline argued that there are ten components to a thinking environment:

Thinking environment	Male conditioning (in many Western societies)
Listen	Take over and talk
Ask incisive questions	Know everything
Establish equality	Assume superiority
Appreciate	Criticize
Be at ease	Control
Encourage	Compete
Feel	Toughen
Supply accurate information	Lie
Humanize the place	Conquer the place
Create diversity	Deride differences

Barbara Fredrickson found that there were many benefits to having a positive environment – teams create more insight, produce more creativity and perform to a higher standard. Jessica Payne noted that a high-performance environment required the following things:

1 A degree of stress to perform. If there is too little stress then people become complacent and lethargic and too much makes the pre-frontal cortex of the brain shut down causing forgetfulness and panic.

2 A positive mood. This aids learning, memory, insight and executive brain function. It also enables understanding of a broader perspective and it is easier to make connections and solve problems more creatively.

3 Sufficient sleep. This is essential for consolidation of memory and helps the brain make connections and improves decision-making.

However, there are dangers for a group or team that is really close. Group Think was mentioned earlier. Dan Ariely talked about the 'Ikea effect', which is when a team creates something they buy into it but lose objectivity and think it is better than it might be.

Team members need to be engaged with the organization's goals and activities and they need to be empowered to take the necessary action on their own initiative (within the relevant constraints). Bowen and Lawler said that to achieve **empowerment**, there are four organizational ingredients that must be shared with frontline employees:

1   Information about the organization's performance

2   Rewards based on the organization's performance

3   Knowledge that enables employees to understand and contribute to organizational performance

4   Power to make decisions that influence organizational direction and performance

The organization has to be committed to regular, two-way and open communications and must align its goals to the performance management and rewards systems. This is an area where the Human Resources or Internal Communications teams can play an important role, but ultimately it is up to the line managers to **cascade** information down from the top and to provide feedback back up the line to ensure the senior management and frontline staff are connected. Programmes such as **Investors in People** help an organization link its strategic business aims to the goals of every employee.

Giving feedback

Effective feedback 'means paying attention and giving high-quality feedback from an empathic place, stepping into the other person's shoes, appreciating his or her experience, and helping to move that person into a learning mode' (Kate Ludeman).

We can minimize stress and conflict by giving feedback on performance in a positive way. It should be seen as a way to increase self-awareness, offer options and encourage learning rather than being judgemental and critical.

Feedback is important for motivation too (see below). The Progress Principle study found that there were three types of feedback:

- Nourishing events that were uplifting – such as praise or emotional support

- Catalytic events that helped work tasks – such as training or resources being provided

- Progress events – receiving feedback on progress in meaningful work

The study found that employees' 'best' days involved progress events.

The content of your feedback should be information-specific (i.e. provide examples), issue-focused and based on observation. Your manner will be important too – you need to be direct and sincere and 'own' the feedback. You should comment on the behaviour (which can be changed) and NOT the person or personality (which cannot be changed).

Some people talk about a feedback sandwich – with positive layers wrapping up the more critical material. So start with a positive comment and appreciation for effort or work done well. Then mention the areas requiring change and improvement. Keep language descriptive rather than evaluative. Ask for explanations and offer alternatives. Always leave them with a choice. Be careful on the timing of your feedback – as soon as possible, but pick your moment. Ideally, feedback should be given on a regular basis.

Research by Naomi Eisenberger has shown that the brain treats social pain much like physical pain. Positive feedback can activate reward centres the same or more than financial windfalls. There appears to be five social rewards and threats that are deeply important to the brain: status, certainty, autonomy, relatedness and fairness. People can experience feedback as an attack on their 'status', which to the brain is perceived as a physical attack.

Geoffrey James offers ten rules for giving feedback:

1   Make negative feedback unusual
2   Don't stockpile negative feedback

3   Never use feedback to vent

4   Don't email negative feedback

5   Start with an honest compliment

6   Uncover the root of the problem

7   Listen before you speak (most people can't learn unless they first feel that they've been heard)

8   Ask questions that drive self-evaluation

9   Coach the behaviours you would like to see

10 Be willing to accept feedback too

29

Developing and coaching people

As well as getting the team to fulfil its task effectively and efficiently, the team leader is responsible for recruiting, assessing, training and developing team members. There are formal processes here such as interviewing and appraisals which will be supported by the human resources (HR) people. But a team leader also needs to coach people.

Unlike mentoring, where the mentor often imparts his or her wisdom and knowledge, coaching is a process designed to help people think for themselves and find their own ideas and solutions. Coaching is a distinct discipline with its own professional guidelines and qualifications, although all managers can learn the basic principles and apply them in their day-to-day dealings with team members.

Coaching requires many different skills – most of which are covered elsewhere in this book:

- Listening
- Paying attention
- Offering perspective
- Exploring for information
- Problem-solving
- Creating solutions
- Managing performance

- Providing feedback

- Motivating

- Developing people

- Teaching and guiding

A simple, well-known coaching framework was developed by John Whitmore. His **GROW model** (Goals – Reality – Options – Will to act) is a series of questions designed to help a person reach their own conclusions about what they want and need to do. The individual builds self-confidence from deciding what they need to do – rather than being told – so it is important for delegation (see below) and developing team members.

As people are often unclear about their goals when they start coaching, it helps to begin with questions about their current situation or reality. This enables the team leader to obtain relevant background about the person and their work and also to start thinking about what sorts of goals they are likely to need. It also helps establish a relationship of openness, interest and trust.

Reality testing – understanding the current situation

With coaching, questions are used to lead people to explore their values, views, options and actions in a structured way and to help them reality-test their goals and plans.

We know from the latest research on insight selling that people are more likely to be persuaded when a person asks insightful questions, provides additional ideas and information with those questions, educates and challenges them and creates an impact by asking the right questions.

In coaching we need to help people break out of their old ways of thinking and behaving. Human beings are creatures of habit – doing things the way that we have done them in the past is safe and relatively low-risk. To try something new is risky – both to our reputation and to relationships. See the material on learning and change in Part 2.

By asking questions, we allow people to explore their inner world. And we can also begin to understand their perspective and mental model. People need to reflect on what has happened in the past, what worked and what didn't work and how they would like things to be different in the future.

Questions also encourage people to think about other people's perspectives which may be different to their own. It can help them develop empathy with colleagues and clients. Just as in selling, we use questions to explore afflictions (from which people want to move away) and aspirations (towards which people want to move). Questions help us understand the motivations for a particular individual.

We use questions to build a compelling view of the past and to think about the future. We use questions to help the individual consider the downsides of not acting and the upsides of changing. The firm's culture and formal and informal reward systems will have a bearing on this too.

Goal setting

With coaching, we are providing a safe environment where people can express their views, questions and even fears in confidence. In coaching, we are providing a supportive environment in which the person can explore what they want and need to do in their own way.

In coaching, people need to think about their goals. These may be short-, medium- and long-term. They may focus on the current work activities or tasks, on their personal life or on their career. Once people are clear about their goals, it is easier to identify strategies and options for achieving those goals. Once there is a goal it is possible to measure progress.

If we tell people to do something, we are likely to meet resistance. And if people are told to do something, they are less likely to be committed to doing it than if they had come up with the idea themselves. People need to set their own goals – although they may need help in aligning these goals with the organization's or team's goals.

Aims might be general. But goals or objectives are better if they are SMART. Sometimes goals need to be broken down into bite-sized pieces. A **stepping stones** approach may help people – if their goal is ambitious and in the far future, you can help them break the goal down into what must be achieved each year to ensure that they reach their future goal.

Dr Gail Matthews in California found that written goals were 42% more likely to be achieved.

Option development

People are often stuck because they can only see one route forward and for some reason this is not a palatable or feasible route.

Coaching questions help people to think through what else they might do – to think about other options. There might be questions about what has worked for them in the past and about what they could do differently in the future. There might be questions about what other people have found successful, or questions about what people they admire might do under similar circumstances.

Questions will also help to explore any **limiting assumptions** that may be preventing someone from setting or attempting to achieve a goal. If someone lacks self-confidence, questions might help them reflect on their past successes and strengths to prevent those limiting assumptions.

Questions can help the person to consider the pros and cons of different options and to choose the most appropriate course of action.

Commitment to act

Questions can help people think through out loud what they need to do and when. We use questions to test what might be involved and to ensure that the person has considered all of the possible steps that they need to take and barriers to overcome to achieve their goals. We might ask questions about what they need to do to take the first step, what they need to do to maintain momentum and to anticipate what might get in the way of them making progress.

And in the final stage of coaching we have to consider whether the person is really in a place where they can make progress towards his or her goal(s). This might involve questions about what can be reasonably achieved in the short term – bite-sized and manageable chunks of activities that can be completed before the next coaching session.

30

Delegation and supervision

Supervision and delegation are not the same thing. Supervision is about professional responsibility to manage risk and ensure quality. It helps with adherence to procedures and the sharing of best practice. Professional bodies usually have specific requirements for supervising trainees.

Delegation is the act of empowering another to act and assigning responsibilities. It is likely that you would want to heavily supervise those to whom you are delegating for the first time. Both have a role to play in training and development. Typically though, there is a more directive approach in supervision (for juniors) and a more consultative style to delegation (for seniors).

Supervision and delegation skills

Supervisors will need excellent technical knowledge as this is one of the main things that they are sharing and assessing. However, it is possible to delegate tasks where technical knowledge might not be paramount and other skills are required.

Communication and feedback skills are required for both supervision and delegation. It is important that an appreciative approach (more positive feedback than constructive criticism) is adopted if the confidence of people is to be strengthened.

Coaching skills are important too – asking questions so that the people being supervised or delegated to can try to find answers and solutions for themselves rather than being told. This builds self-confidence as well as important skills for problem-solving.

When to delegate

Before delegating, you need to analyse and categorize the types of work to be delegated. Some tasks may be repetitive, routine and procedural where there are prescribed methods, documented processes and online templates or standards. Some may be unusual or unique problem-solving activities where a degree of critical thinking is required. Other tasks may require a broader and deeper range of commercial knowledge and skills and an ability to deal with tricky situations or challenging people.

Where work for others is involved, you need to check that they will be happy with the work being delegated to someone else and are properly informed of the individual's background and contact details.

While people often consider delegating when they are busy and overstretched, it takes time to properly delegate tasks – to provide clear instructions, to support the person or team in learning how to tackle a new or complex task and to check-in regularly on progress. Ensure that you delegate work when you have sufficient time to provide the necessary support – or identify someone else who can do so.

Why don't people delegate more?

The business case for delegation is very strong. But there are many people who fail or refuse to delegate. There may be many reasons for this. It's worrying when people don't delegate because they lack confidence or trust in the skills and abilities of those available for delegation. Some people 'work hug' – perhaps due to a fear that if work is delegated that they will have insufficient work to do themselves or other people will receive more visibility.

Whereas some leaders will delegate happily to their team until someone indicates that they have too much work, other leaders may be overprotective and take on more work themselves to avoid making their team members work too hard. A good leader will achieve a balance once they fully understand the capabilities and limits of their team members.

Delegation steps

Consider the suitability of the individual for the task – their skill level, workload and personal style. And also consider the suitability of the task for the individual – there are occasions when things shouldn't be delegated.

There are numerous models to help you delegate. In *The Art of Delegation* by Ros Jay and Richard Templar, the following guidelines are suggested:

1 Review the task and set the objective

2 Decide to whom to delegate

3 Set parameters

   a) Objective

   b) Deadline

   c) Quality standards

   d) Budget

   e) Limits of authority

   f) Details of any resources available

4 Check they understand

5 Give them back-up

I propose a slightly different approach:

1 Clarify your expectations

   a) Explain what needs to be accomplished and why it's important

   b) Help them see the 'big picture' or context – if possible, connect the task to organizational, team, client or personal development goals

2 Establish checkpoints

   a) Plan how you're going to ensure that the work is being completed by establishing checkpoints – these might be more regular for a junior tackling a task for the first time

b) Manage the risk of mistakes occurring by being proactive and staying in the loop at critical points within the task

3 Delegate the results, not the process

a) Focus on the end result and, unless the person is inexperienced or there are prescribed regulations, allow him/her to determine how best to achieve it

b) If you dictate exactly what to do, when to do it and how to do it, you limit the learning potential

4 Define roles

a) Explain how much support you'll provide and when and how

b) Let the person know when to wait for your instructions or make independent recommendations and decisions – the more authority you give, the better the end result will be – however, use your discretion, depending on the task and individual

c) Make sure the person understands the extent to which independent initiative is allowed

d) Encourage questions and be available to offer help and guidance

e) Signpost other sources of help and support

f) Describe the situations when they should definitely check or report back to you

5 Talk about consequences

a) Reassure them about time – it may take them longer to complete an unfamiliar task.

b) If you allow people to have authority over their work, inform them of the consequences of both successful and unsuccessful results

c) What rewards can they expect if they do a great job?

d) What will happen if they don't achieve the expected results?

6 Confirm their understanding

a) Ask them to repeat back their understanding of the task – possibly even to email you with the key points and schedule the checkpoints in your diary

b) Ask them what they are likely to tackle first (and why) and ask them what they perceive to be the most challenging aspects of the task

Mutual responsibility in delegation

Those delegating tasks have a responsibility to provide clear instructions, context, support and help. However, those who are being delegated to also have responsibilities. They should be honest about their skill level and their workload if they think that this may have an impact on their ability to complete the task.

Delegatees are responsible for asking questions for clarification or seeking support if and when they need it. They are also responsible for speaking to the person who delegated the task if they foresee any difficulties – particularly where they suspect that critical dates or quality levels might not be achieved. They are also responsible for ensuring that they report back on the agreed checkpoints and do not exceed their limits of authority.

Best practice in delegation

There are some other useful things to remember when delegating, which are covered in more detail elsewhere in the book:

Empathy – Try to remember when you first tackled a new task and were at the receiving end of delegation. Put yourself in the shoes of the person you are delegating to and try to address their likely questions and concerns.

Non-Verbal Communication (NVC) – Watch the NVC of the person to whom you are delegating. Watch whether their body language changes and at which point. Consider when they are signalling either resistance or a desire to ask a question.

Personality differences – People are different. Some are more focused on the task and others on relationships, some are introverts and others are extroverts. Take care when delegating to those who have a different style to yourself, as the way they prefer to communicate or work may be different to yours.

Reassurance – Explain that elements of the task are tricky and that you yourself experienced some difficulty when tackling the task for the first time. Give the delegatee permission to express their concerns.

Reflection – Once you have explained the task, allow the delegatee some time to reflect on what needs to be done and come back for further clarification or help a short while later.

Feedback – Once the task is completed, ask the delegatee for feedback on how you might improve the way you delegate tasks in future.

31

Motivation and leadership

Motivation has been described as 'the passion to work for internal reasons that go beyond money and status; an inner vision of what is important in life, the joy of doing something, the curiosity in learning, being immersed in an activity and the pursuit of goals with energy and persistence'. In positive psychology, Mihály Csíkszentmihályi coined the term '**flow**', also known as 'the zone'. This is like an extension of motivation – it is the mental state of a person when he or she is fully immersed in a feeling of energized focus, full involvement and enjoyment in the process of the activity.

A motive is a person's reason for doing something and comprises three elements:

- Direction (What a person is trying to do)
- Effort (How hard a person is trying)
- Persistence (How long a person continues trying)

Direction means that there needs to be a clear objective. Ideally, there should be alignment between the goals of the organization and/or team and what individuals are doing for people to feel involved and contributing. We saw in the section on stress earlier (see p. 61) that if people feel that they are doing meaningless work and that they are working under pressure, then they may experience stress.

Effort and persistence will be affected by the recognition and reward systems. Of course people's salaries and benefits are important, but the motivating factors are often to do with other issues such as recognition, responsibility and progression. This is particularly important for Millennials who will want to see short-term progress steps and immediate impact rather than simply long-term promotion prospects.

One of the most famous theories about motivation comes from Abraham Maslow. He suggested that there was a **hierarchy of needs** and that people respond to the most basic needs before addressing those higher up the hierarchy.

- Self-fulfilment and self-actualizing – being the best you can be
- Ego needs – receiving respect and strengthening self-esteem
- Need for recognition – love and belonging
- Safety needs – protection from danger
- Basic physiological needs – food, water, sleep, temperature

Some will be familiar with Frederick Herzberg's model of **hygiene and health** approaches to motivation. You should ensure that the 'hygiene' basics are OK (e.g. job security, pay and benefits, working conditions, supervision and autonomy) before trying to increase motivation through 'health' issues such as achievement, recognition, job interest, responsibility and advancement. This relates to intrinsic and extrinsic motivation. **Extrinsic motivation** relates to external rewards based on the task, whereas **intrinsic motivation** is often a greater motivation – pride in a job done well, pleasure at seeing a customer situation resolved speedily, satisfaction at achieving a good result in difficult circumstances and respect from co-workers.

This is supported by Dan Ariely, a behavioural economist, who argued that people are not rats in a maze, as behaviourists would have us believe. At work, they do more than exchange time for money. He said that there is evidence that we are driven by meaningful work, the acknowledgement of others and the amount of effort we put into something (i.e. the harder we work, the prouder we are).

Recent research by Dr Nelisha Wickremasinghe has identified three main motivational centres of the brain – the threat, drive and safe brain motivators. Her research indicates that most of our problems in the workplace arise because our body and minds are overexposed to real or imagined threats. People often respond to threat by moving to a drive-based response – working harder, trying to win and striving to achieve. While this may work in the short term, in the longer term it isn't sustainable and leads to stress and burn-out. To get into safe brain mode you need to feel calm, connected, safe and secure. This is particularly important where you want people to be creative (see the material on thinking environments by Nancy Kline).

The culture of an organization is important for motivation too. Consider Douglas McGregor's '**Theory X and Theory Y**'. Theory X suggests that people cannot be trusted. They must therefore be controlled and need financial incentives and threats of punishment. If you apply this approach to intelligent and hard-working professionals then they will often rebel against it. Theory Y suggests that people seek independence, self-development and creativity in their work. If treated right, they will strive for the good of their organization. Henry Mintzberg suggested that professionals and knowledge workers respond better to inspiration than supervision – so vision will be more important to them than control.

The later development of this theory – **social motivation** by Edgar Schein – indicates that behaviour is influenced most fundamentally by social interactions. People are responsive to the expectations of those around them, often more so than financial incentives – and this suggests the need for cultural change and the development of team goals, plans and actions. Peer pressure is important.

Expectancy theory (Victor Vroom) attempts to explain how people choose which of several possible courses of action they will pursue. The choice process is seen as a cognitive, calculating appraisal of:

- Expectancy (If I tried, would I be able to perform the task I am considering?)

- Instrumentality (Would performing the action lead to identifiable outcomes?)

- Valence (How much do I value these outcomes?)

Justice theories of motivation are concerned with equity theory, which suggests that a person is motivated to maintain the same balance between his or her contributions and rewards as that experienced by salient comparable people. They will consider two types of justice:

- Distributive justice – Whether people believe they have received or will receive fair rewards

- Procedural justice – Whether people believe that the procedures used in an organization to allocate rewards are fair

There is the need for clarity around how people are rewarded for their efforts and to ensure that there are systems to ensure that people are treated equally.

Goal-setting theories of motivation (Ed Locke) are also useful. Locke defined a goal is 'what an individual is trying to accomplish; it is the object or aim of an action', and offered some interesting insights:

- Difficult goals lead to higher performance than easy goals

- Specific goals lead to higher performance than general 'do your best' goals

- Knowledge of results (feedback) is essential if the full performance benefits of setting difficult and specific goals are to be achieved

- The beneficial effects of goal-setting depend partly on a person's goal commitment (determination to try to achieve it)

P. C. Earley suggested that goal-setting may be harmful when a task is novel and where a considerable number of possible strategies are available to achieve it. J. Kuhl distinguishes between action orientation (where people use self-regulatory strategies to achieve desired goals) and state orientation (where they do not). In addition to supporting the need for clear objectives, the need for regular feedback is highlighted.

In the book *The Small Big – Small Changes that Spark Big Influence*, by Martin, Goldstein and Cialdini, there are lots more insights into motivating people. For example:

- Use people's first name in communications to increase their motivation to do something

- Include examples of task significance such as case studies and personal stories

- Set a goal with a low to high range that averages the same as an original goal. This engages both challenge and attainability influence factors

- Use the small area hypothesis – highlight the smaller area of attainment achieved or remaining

- Optimize incentives by offering rewards that fall into two distinct categories – and then allow the team to access the second category only after they have earned one reward from the first category

Motivation will also depend on the **psychological contract** (the unwritten set of expectations of the employment relationship as distinct from the formal, codified employment contract) that people have with their organization and the role models that they follow.

The manager's role in dealing with conflict

There is a dedicated section on conflict management in this book (see p. 156). However, there are seven key principles to guide supervisors and managers in dealing with conflict in their teams:

1 **Prevent unnecessary conflict** – Conflict can be caused by creating competitive environments or failing to clearly define roles and responsibilities and areas and lines of authority. It can also occur when you do not consult stakeholders.

2 **Be courageous in the face of conflict** – Deal with conflicts openly, constructively and quickly.

3 **Practise 'management by walking about'** – This allows you to see where conflicts may emerge before they do. It also provides insight into how conflicts are managed at present. It makes you more available to answer questions that may avert conflict.

4 **Promote informal resolution** – Create policies that encourage resolution by discussion amongst those concerned although with authority and processes specified for making final decisions.

5 **Put formal processes in place** – There should be documented procedures for addressing grievances and disciplinary issues. But note that these are usually adversarial processes and you should avoid over-reliance on them.

6 **Assess and improve organizational culture** – See above on this point. Related to culture is organizational climate, which is how it feels for employees to work in an environment. The communication climate is how the organization works to invite or prohibit constructive communication ('the conflict climate').

7 **Model the behaviours you desire** – Do what you want others to do – be a good role model.

A common complaint is that supervisors don't deal with conflicts when they arise. To promote effective conflict management, supervisors must give regular informal feedback to employees. Supervisors and managers must take care to notice any bullying or where there is repeated mistreatment of an individual.

Leadership and leading people

There is some confusion between management and leadership. Warren Bennis offered the following comparison:

Management	Leadership
Administers	Innovates
Is a copy	Is an original
Maintains	Develops
Focuses on systems/structures	Focuses on people
Relies on control	Inspires trust
Has a short-term range	Has a long-term perspective
Asks when and how	Asks why
Has eye on the bottom line	Has eye on the horizon
Imitates	Originates
Accepts the status quo	Challenges the status quo
Classic good soldier	Own person
Does things right	Does the right thing

Peter Drucker, in his book *The Effective Executive*, makes a distinction between efficiency and effectiveness: 'Efficiency is doing things right; effectiveness is doing the right things.' This resonates with the difference between management and leadership.

Early models of leadership saw that leaders were either motivated to achieve the task or motivated to support people. One of the simplest and most popular models of leadership is enshrined in the approach advocated by John Adair. For both operational and strategic management, he argued that the leader's role is to constantly balance three things – the task, the team and the individual. Focusing on any one of these will be to the detriment of the other two.

There are many definitions of leadership and a wealth of management material on the subject. There are generally recognized leadership skills – many of which are covered with emotional intelligence (see p. 7), which has been found to be a predictor of leadership effectiveness. A leader must:

1 Build vision

2 Communicate vision

3 Set goals

4 Coach and support

5   Build coalitions

6   Network

7   Facilitate

8   Deal with conflict

9   Negotiate

10 Monitor and control

No one style of leadership is perfect for all occasions. There is considerable evidence of the need for **situational leadership** – adapting your leadership style to different scenarios. For example:

- Dictatorial – Where you tell people what to do when facing a crisis and urgent action is required and there is no time for consultation

- Analytical – When there is time pressure or threat and the right decision must be made quickly by analysing the available information which is likely to be imperfect

- Opinion seeking – Asking stakeholders and team members to show that you value people's views. This builds confidence in the team

- Democratic/Consultative – Where you regularly seek the views and solutions of others, thus empowering them and building their commitment

The latest leadership studies reveal further types of leadership:

- Visionary – Providing a guiding vision, persuasive stories, passion and integrity

- Transformational – Raising people's sense of purpose and motivation through charisma, inspiration, intellectual stimulation and individual consideration

- Adaptive – Challenges and takes people out of their comfort zone and exposes them to conflict

- Connective – Searches for meanings and makes connections

There is an interesting piece of research from the Centre of Creative Management which shows that success in an early management position is associated with rather different factors to those associated with success in more senior leadership positions.

Success in early management	Success in senior leadership positions
Independence	Being a team player
Ability to control short-term results	Having longer-term strategic vision
Creativity	Managing the creativity of others
Ambition and high standards	Self-esteem
Speciality strength	General management skills
Being contentious and taking a stand	Creating unity and cohesion

SECTION SUMMARY

THIS SECTION EXPLORED SOME OF the most common internal relationships with your boss or line manager, with your team members and with others in the organization. It then moved on to a number of issues related to managing and leading people.

Exploring the business relationship with your team leader, we considered the impact of his or her leadership style, the workplace or corporate culture and internal politics. Particular types of 'difficult' behaviour including stubbornness, bullying and micromanaging were explored as well as techniques to help you improve your assertiveness. Ideas for building buy-in and consensus were examined.

Then we considered groups and teams – how you integrate within them and ideas around social identity theory and ingroups and outgroups. Team roles and relationship styles – with tools such as Belbin – were considered as well as ideas around how teams form, linking back to Part 3. Ideas on how to find coaches and mentors were shared.

The focus then shifted to managing teams and virtual teams and the creation of safe, appreciative and thinking environments to encourage high performance, creativity and development. Guidance on giving feedback, coaching, delegation and motivation was provided as well as the manager's role in dealing with conflict. Finally there were some thoughts about leadership and leading.

PART SIX

EXTERNAL RELATIONSHIPS AND SELLING

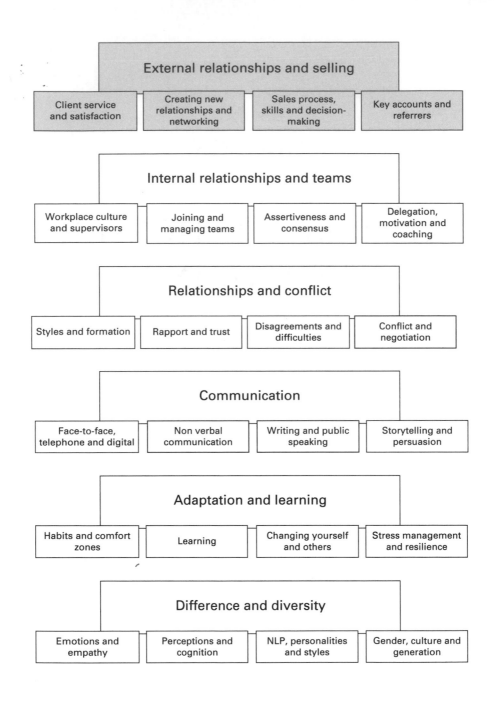

32

Working with customers and clients: expectations and satisfaction management

In previous sections we have considered human diversity, how we adapt to others, the fundamentals of communication, how relationships are formed and the dynamics of internal relationships, and it is now time to turn our attention to external relationships.

There are many types of external relationships – for example, with future recruits, suppliers, competitors, affiliates, partners, shareholders, professional and trade bodies and the government. My focus will be on customers (usually consumers buying things for themselves) and clients (typically individuals buying on behalf of an organization) and those who recommend or refer business.

Some people are in roles where a major part of their work is talking to customers or clients. If so, they will probably receive specialist training in customer service, selling, relationship management or account management. However, there are many jobs where communicating and working with customers and clients is not the primary focus yet there is still a need to establish effective business relationships.

Whilst it is always necessary to understand customer and client requirements with good communication, the focus on customer service is often passive – responding to ad-hoc requests. However, with clients there is often a longer-term relationship where communication, mutual understanding, persuasion and selling skills are required.

Customers make decisions based on what they want – and may be motivated by things like price, brand or experience. Clients are in a different organization and can choose to use another supplier – and often there are several people involved in the decision and the buying process may take longer.

The relationship dynamics – particularly the power or 'upper hand' that the customers and clients have – are different. So the onus is on us to take the lead in establishing and nurturing the relationship and in meeting the needs of the customers and clients.

Customer experience management (CEM)

Customer care is the identification, management and control of **critical incidents** when customers come into contact with the organisation and form their perceptions of the organisation's service quality, expecting their needs to be satisfied. It involves a complex series of relationships and interpersonal interactions between customers, individual employees and the organisation and must cover every aspect and activity of the organisation's operations to make it work.

Preece and Shafieie

Many organizations focus on ensuring that customers have a good experience whenever they come into contact with the organization. There might be many **'touch points'** along the **customer journey** – whether online through social media, on the website, when they telephone or visit, at meetings and when they receive invoices, make payments or seek help.

The customer experience has a number of elements (Ian Golding):

- Functional – Does it do what people want it to do?

- Accessible – How easy is it for people to do what they want to do?

- Emotional – How does it make people feel?

Other research (Paraduraman, Zeithaml and Berry) suggests that people use five determinants of quality:

- Reliability

- Assurance

- Tangibles

- Empathy

- Responsiveness

The client journey (sometimes called the client life cycle) has a number of stages:

- Choosing – people deciding to buy from you

- Using – people experiencing your products or services

- Paying – people paying for the products or services

- Staying – people remaining with you and perhaps buying further products or services from you

Each customer experience can be great, good, average or bad. Organizations want every '**moment of truth**' to be positive to create a good impression. This is difficult when an organization has thousands of customers talking to hundreds of its staff. Each member of staff needs to know how to behave appropriately whenever they interact with a customer.

In a 2017 report by KPMG Nunwood it was suggested that the pillars of customer experience were:

1 Personalization (individualized attention drives emotional connection)

2 Integrity (being trustworthy)

3 Expectations (managing, meeting and exceeding)

4 Resolution (turning a poor experience into a good one)

5 Time and effort (minimizing customer effort)

6 Empathy

When an organization has thousands of consumers, communications may be numerous, brief and through digital channels or telephone calls. This is a **business-to-consumer** (**B2C**) operation. There may be short interactions – enquiries, requests for help or complaints – and then the relationship is over. Here is some guidance for these quick interactions:

- Be polite – Provide a short and friendly greeting and your name at the outset as well as a question along the lines of 'How may I help you?' Address people by their titles (e.g. Mr Smith) to demonstrate respect. Say 'Please' before you put them on hold and 'Thank you for waiting' afterwards.

- Be a good Ambassador – You are the voice of your organization – the way you behave will have an impact on the organization's reputation as well as your own. Some organizations enshrine their values on how to interact with clients in brand or communication guidelines to ensure consistency.

- Listen – Give your full attention and listen carefully to what the person says. Do not interrupt. If the person is angry, let them speak. Validate their emotions by acknowledgement. Thank them for bringing the issue to your attention. Apologize that they are upset, without necessarily accepting blame.

- Help – Either provide the help that they are seeking or explain how they may get help. If you need time to investigate, note their details and say when you will contact them again. Set realistic expectations.

- Escalate if necessary – If you need input or authority from someone more senior, then advise the caller and take responsibility for getting back to them.

- Check everything is covered – Confirm that they have everything they require and that they are happy for the interaction to end. Thank them for their enquiry. Update systems about the interaction.

In some organizations, there may be fewer clients where there are important, complex and ongoing relationships. This is particularly true in organizations which sell their products or services to people in other organizations (**B2B – business-to-business**).

Client satisfaction

Organizations want clients to be satisfied – to retain them, for repeat purchase and recommendation and for cross-selling and up-selling.

Anderson et al. suggested that there were two aspects to **client satisfaction**: transaction specific and cumulative. Unhappiness at a particular transaction or interaction is more likely to be forgiven if there is a long-term cumulative amount of goodwill and satisfaction from a relationship.

Some organizations measure client satisfaction – either for a particular interaction with questions delivered by email, telephone call or text, or for the overall relationship. A frequently used method of measuring satisfaction is the **Net Promoter Score (NPS)**, where clients are asked to rate their likelihood of recommending the organization on a scale of 0–10. Those who score 0–6 are considered detractors, those scoring 7–8 are seen to be satisfied but not delighted, and those scoring 9 and 10 are seen as promoters.

Expectations will have an impact on satisfaction. If a client anticipates that your organization's response will be slow and unhelpful then they will be delighted if they find you fast and helpful. Similarly, if in the past they have found your organization to be fast and helpful, then they will be disappointed with the service if the experience doesn't match up. This shows that the same interaction can be perceived negatively or positively depending on the client's past experience and expectations.

Client expectations are influenced by many factors. Parasuraman, Zeithaml and Berry suggested they were grouped into:

- Word of mouth communications
- Personal needs and preferences

- Past experiences

- External communications

Organizations with a strong error management culture – who empower staff to take corrective action when clients experience problems – are four times more likely to be among the most profitable in their industry. The highest satisfaction ratings are not from those who report a seamless service but those who experienced a service stumble that was immediately put right by staff.

33

Establishing new relationships: self-esteem and self-confidence, first impressions and personal power

We will focus here on B2B organizations who rely on clients, but many of the ideas will be applicable to consumer relationships.

You are likely to establish new relationships with potential and existing clients in a variety of ways – through social media, emails, telephone calls, at events and at meetings. Some interactions will be by chance – you meet people at events – and others will be deliberate, where you have targeted people to meet. The focus here will be on face-to-face interactions.

When we were children, we were often told 'Don't talk to strangers', so it is not surprising that some people are nervous about meeting new people. And it can be particularly nerve-racking if forging successful relationships with people is important to your reputation and success. Often, people are unsure of the etiquette – or rules – of meeting new people in a business context. Sometimes, people are afraid of saying the wrong thing or experiencing an awkward situation and embarrassment.

We need to feel confident and to convey confidence when meeting new people. We want to make a good impression by giving an accurate portrait of ourselves and our organization. We have to communicate effectively and create rapport and trust (see p. 148).

Developing your self-confidence

Self-confidence is internal – it is what we feel. Confidence is external and what we convey to others. It is possible to feel one thing and convey another.

To build you **self-confidence** you can:

- Get training – From degrees and professional qualifications which can take a long time to achieve, to training courses and e-learning tools that can be completed quickly.

- Prepare properly – Research and read all the information you need in advance. Prepare your questions. Anticipate what will be discussed and the concerns that are likely to arise so that you are ready for whatever happens. Know what you might say and what you want to achieve.

- Engage in positive self-talk – Rather than thinking about your inexperience and failings, direct your inner conversation to be more positive – your strengths, past achievements, your successes and your track record.

- Look after yourself – Get enough sleep, exercise and avoid too much caffeine, which can make you feel edgy. Forgive yourself if you make a mistake – correct it and move on, don't dwell on it.

- Avoid perfectionism – 80 per cent of the result usually comes from 20 per cent of the effort (this is called the **Pareto effect**). Too many people invest too much time striving for perfection. Accept that 'good enough is good enough'.

- Focus on what you can do – Don't let big issues that are beyond your grasp upset you; focus on the things that you can influence, change or control. Remember the **Serenity prayer** (Reinhold Niebuhr): 'God, grant me the serenity to accept the things I cannot change, courage to change the things I can, and wisdom to know the difference.'

- Surround yourself with positive people – Negative people can be wearing and depressing. Spend time with upbeat and enthusiastic people who choose to see your strengths and opportunities rather than problems.

- Enjoy yourself – Find time for the things that you enjoy and find pleasure in small steps and successes.

To present high self-confidence (although remember the need to be authentic – see p. 4):

- Use Non-Verbal Communication (NVC) – Be aware of the messages you are conveying unconsciously. Confident people in Western cultures adopt an open and upright posture, avoid folding their arms and crossing their legs, use a large amount of body space, maintain eye contact, smile and speak at the right pace and at a good volume. There is more on NVC on p. 82.

- Acknowledge your successes – Acknowledge your past successes, what you have achieved and learned, what obstacles you have overcome and your strengths.

- Accept the facts – You were chosen for your job and you are capable of performing well.

- Know you will survive – Whatever life throws at you, know that you will survive.

It's helpful to know how to present a confident image, even if you don't feel it. Lots of people suffer from imposter syndrome (see p. 6). There is an excellent TED video by psychologist Amy Cuddy who talks about an experiment in which people adopted one of five '**power poses**' for just two minutes and effectively changed their physiology by releasing the chemical testosterone into their systems, which actually made them feel more confident.

Self-esteem

Self-confidence is connected to **self-esteem**. Self-esteem is something we develop when we are young – it's the difference between how we see ourselves (our self-image) and our 'perfect self' or how we think we should be. If parents criticize the child ('You are lazy') rather than the child's behaviour ('You are acting lazy') then their self-esteem will be low.

For a strong self-image and high self-esteem, parents need to help children learn that everybody makes mistakes and gets things wrong sometimes, everyone feels negative emotions and feels angry, sad or lonely at times, nobody is perfect and adults aren't always right, looks aren't everything and internal qualities are important and that the child is loved regardless of their errors or faults.

Children need to reflect and learn, as self-esteem comes from within. Children need clear boundaries, lots of praise when they do things well and the promise of rewards for when they achieve things. They need to know when they do things wrong, to be asked about what more appropriate behaviour might be and given responsibility for doing so in future.

There are two models of self-esteem – the enclosed circle model shows that the individual is the most important person in their own life, but accepts that others are their own most important people. Enclosed circle people are reassured about all the things that they are and do and it doesn't matter what other people do or think. The linear model only allows an individual to feel good about themselves by comparing themselves favourably with others. It divides everything up – everyone can't be equally good, there has to be a hierarchy with someone being the best.

A **perfectionist** is someone who has to get everything right – they have excessively high standards (read more about control freaks on p. 208). Perfectionists have difficulty letting things go and varying standards to the time available and the effort needed. Perfectionists often have unrecognized fears and needs – they are motivated by a fear of failure and are never satisfied by achievements. They also keep emotions under tight control and fear showing vulnerability or losing control. Healthy people are motivated by enthusiasm and generally feel OK about themselves, show vulnerability and aren't afraid of making mistakes.

Brené Brown remarked that 'connection gives purpose and meaning to our lives' and pointed out that we are neurobiologically wired to connect with people. We feel a sense of shame and fear at the prospect of disconnection as it makes us feel unworthy. She added that 'what makes you vulnerable makes you beautiful' and suggested that – to support connection – we let ourselves be seen more clearly, which includes revealing some of our vulnerabilities. This relates again to authenticity.

Understanding and managing perceptions

Sensation occurs when our eyes, ears, noses and mouths absorb energy from something physical in the environment. This energy is converted into neural impulses in the brain and perception is the process which organizes that information and interprets it as something meaningful. The same sensory material – for example spoken words – can be perceived differently by people. We talked about self-perception, perceptions and authenticity in Part 1 (see p. 4)

When it comes to business relationships, there's a pertinent quote from my favourite psychologist William James: 'Whenever two people meet, there are really six people present. There is each man as he sees himself, each man as the other person sees him, and each man as he really is.'

In business relationships we need to be aware of who we really are and accept that people may perceive us in an entirely different way. Ideally, we should aim to be authentic and convey ourselves honestly. But in some business relationship situations – for example, when we are trying to establish a dialogue – there may be conventions and etiquette to follow. We may need to establish a level of rapport and trust before we take the risk of relaxing and exposing our real selves.

We can use empathy (see p. 7) to try to see ourselves as others might see us. And we can work hard at paying real attention to other people and reading both their non-verbal communication as well as their spoken words to understand the real person they are. The old saying 'Don't judge a book by its cover' might help us guard against making instant and possibly erroneous judgements.

Creating a good first impression and impact: the power of non-verbal communication (NVC)

Consider how we perceive people when we first meet them – how we allow **first impressions** to shape our perceptions.

It only takes a fraction of a second for people to form a first impression – and this is typically formed by non-verbal signals. Evidence suggests that it is rare that an initial impression is changed.

Critically review how you look and the impression you create. This includes what you are wearing – clothes, shoes and hair style. There are often expected norms for business dress – for example, a suit or smart clothes and discreet accessories. Of course, in newer and younger businesses – and those in the digital space – there may be a less formal style of attire. The 'chinos and casual shirt' uniform is common in the tech sector in the United States.

Whilst it may feel unfair that people judge you on what you wear, we must accept that it happens. To maximize our chances of creating the right impression, be aware of in-group and out-group bias – so to try 'fit in'. Persuasion scientists suggest that we should aim to dress a little higher than those we are meeting.

Beyond what we are wearing, how we are standing or sitting – our stance or posture – is important. We need to be straight rather than slumped and with no crossed arms or legs that create a barrier. Eye contact is important in Western cultures.

Whilst a smile is a friendly and welcoming facial expression in many cultures, we should be aware of personality differences addressed in Part 1. Some personalities are more 'dog' – lots of smiles and chatter and warmth, while others are more 'cat', with a distant and cooler disposition. Facial feedback theory says that the expression on your face helps to control the way you feel inside. Your NVC will show people how you feel about yourself (see Part 3). Some people use NLP (Neuro-Linguistic Programming) techniques to help them generate more positive feelings, which translate into more positive NVC.

Greetings are a potential issue. In formal business situations in the West, people shake hands – the only occasion when physically touching someone is permitted. Handshakes and touching are very powerful – some people talk about how you can anchor names or feelings by combining them with the handshake. The strength, style and length of a handshake may be interpreted by others to have certain meanings too. But in other cultures, the greeting may be a bow or a kiss – or even two or three kisses!

When speaking to a group of people, you can increase everyone's involvement by '**light housing**' – moving your eye contact around all the individuals in turn. Eye contact is an important way of connecting with people and – along with eyebrow raises – to indicate that you expect another person to speak. Eye contact is often used as a cue for turn-taking in conversations.

There are three ways to achieve personal power:

- Presence – By being physically attractive or having strong personal presence, although this can be intimidating

- Authority – By having knowledge and expertise, although the danger is that you then want to always be right

- Impact – The ability to create change by asking incisive questions

Recent research by Heidi Grant Halvorson suggests that when someone meets you for the first time they are likely to assess you in two phases. The initial assessment is quick and without conscious thought using non-verbal cues to fill in the blanks. The second phase involves closer attention and information gathering to draw informed conclusions applying three lenses:

- Trust lens (to decide if you are friend or foe)

- Power lens (to assess your influence)

- Ego lens (to confirm a sense of superiority)

Amy Cuddy, in her new book *Presence*, explains that when someone meets you for the first time they ask two critical questions:

- Can I trust this person?

- Can I respect this person?

34

Building your contact base: networking, targeting, messaging and social media selling

In many careers and businesses, there is a high value placed on who you know and who knows you. Having a strong network of contacts within and beyond your organization can help in a number of ways.

For help with careers, you may find mentors and others who can provide advice and job opportunities. Despite the advent of social media, many jobs are never advertised but filled by people using their contacts to identify suitable candidates.

There's value in knowing people who work in similar jobs, businesses and industries. They can be a source of knowledge, market intelligence and even comfort. It's helpful to talk to people who have faced or are facing similar challenges to your own.

In the digital age, there is a saying that says, 'It's not who you know or who knows you, but it's who knows what you know.' This highlights the value of self-promotion – if people in your network know your skills and knowledge then they will be able to contact you or connect you with the relevant people when suitable opportunities arise. Personal recommendation is still a great way to win new clients and business (see **referrer management** below). You can build your reputation by having the right connections who know your expertise, what you do and for whom.

Anyone involved in selling will know the value of a strong contact base. You need to know who buys and recommends products and services, who are the influencers and decision-makers and who might have insight into the relevant people or organizations. There's information on the **Decision-Making Unit (DMU)** below. It also helps to know your competitors – so you can differentiate and position yourself and your organization.

Word of mouth (WOM) is a powerful way to win new clients and work – see below. And the digital age has given word of mouth a shot of steroids, as it is so much easier using tools like LinkedIn and Twitter to connect with the relevant people or to move through your first-degree contacts to reach their contacts.

Having a strong contact base is often seen as an important part of your personal armoury – along with your qualifications, skills and experience. And rather than leave it until later in your career – when it can be hard to build contacts at a senior level – it is good to start building your network as soon as possible. When you are at the start of your career, it is easy to connect with your peers who will also be seeking contacts, and there is less pressure. Then you grow your own network – you all mature and gain responsibility at the same time.

Business relationships become a form of currency. Especially if your role involves some element of promotion or selling – as many jobs do in our increasingly connected world.

Knowing who you need to know (targeting)

Everyone will have some contacts – people who attended the same school or college, friends and acquaintances, those you worked with in other organizations, family members and their friends and those you encounter as you pursue hobbies and sports. The range of situations where you will have connections is immense.

There are two approaches to building your contact base further – you should attempt to blend the two approaches.

The first approach is to simply be interested in other people and to form connections with anyone that you come into contact with. Regard everyone as having some value in terms of their connections, knowledge, skills or interests. You approach each person with an open mind and a desire to initiate a conversation. You will seek areas of common interest. Anyone might be your next best friend! In some industries, for example in the real estate world, everyone seems to know everyone else, so all contacts will be valuable.

The other approach is more focused. It is adopted by those who have selling as a major part of their role. It involves thinking carefully about who you need to know and finding ways to meet these people. This targeted approach means that you go to events – industry conferences, training courses and membership associations – with the specific intention of meeting the people you want to connect with. Typically, you will have a marketing or sales plan to combine this activity, using the likes of **content management** (preparing written materials or videos) and online communications.

Whichever approach is adopted, you need to maintain information about your contacts. Some people rely on their smart phone. Others use contact lists within Microsoft Office on their PC. Some may prefer to manage private and public lists on social media platforms. Some people may work at organizations where their contacts are held in a centralized system such as a **Client Relationship Management (CRM)** system.

Most systems allow you to store more information than just the names and contact details. You may have notes about where you met them and their interests. You may keep a log of when you last saw them and may keep details of their interests and family. You might categorize them depending on when or where you met them or their roles or industries, and might even grade them in terms of importance. Your system may automatically capture email correspondence with them. All this information helps you to maintain and grow business relationships.

However, you need to be aware of the rules about keeping personal and sensitive information. Check your organization's policies and training and be familiar with the privacy and data protection rules that exist. Across Europe these are enshrined in the General Data Protection Regulations (GDPR) which came into effect in May 2018.

Clarity, differentiation, messaging, value propositions and BrandMe

When people meet you, they will form an initial impression of you. As you build a relationship, their understanding of you will develop and deepen. Of course, you can let this process happen naturally, but if you are building business relationships for a specific purpose – to be known as an expert, to be contacted when the right opportunity arises, to be recommended or to be in the frame when your products are being purchased – they need to know what sorts of connections or opportunities you are seeking.

You need clarity in the message you share about who you are and what you do. You could ask yourself 'What do I want to be famous for?' or 'What are the three things I want people to think about me?'

You will need others to know how you are similar to others who perform the same role, but also how you are different too. That will be the memorable part for most people – how you are different. In marketing language we call this **differentiation** – and it is as important for the brands of major organizations as it is for individuals. Some people call this '**BrandMe**', and it is increasingly important in the digital world.

When selling, you must define your **value proposition**. There are numerous definitions of value propositions (sometimes known as a unique selling proposition or USP) and this is because you can consider value propositions from the perspective of a corporate brand, through particular markets and segments, for particular products, services or thought leadership campaigns and then also for a specific opportunity with a particular client.

Some definitions concentrate on the perception of value from the buyer's perspective when considered against the alternatives (including doing nothing). This reminds us of the need to see things from the client's point of view (and thus the need for empathy skills) and the translation of features and advantages into benefits.

Translating features into benefits sounds easy but requires an in-depth understanding of the real needs of the other person. To get to this understanding requires informed and probing questioning in the context of a strong relationship of trust. This was elaborated on by some marketing experts to explore the various quality-price combinations that might be relevant in a particular segment. For example, Professor Nirmalya Kumar suggests the use of value curves to compare competitor offers for each segment of the market.

Barnes, Blake and Pinder have a definition of value propositions that focuses on the experience that a client receives and the need to calculate a measurable value (benefits – costs × 2). Their Value Proposition Builder takes you through an analysis of bad, neutral, good and Wow! value experiences. The use of service mapping and blueprinting might provide a mechanism to get to the heart of service value propositions.

Adrian Payne's definition sees value residing in the reassurance that the supplier will continue to provide a stream of tailored products/services – thus continually providing superior client value in an extended relationship.

Daniel Priestley, in his book *Key Person of Influence – The Five Step Model of the Most Highly Valued and Highly Paid People in Your Industry*, explains the entrepreneurs' journey and provides a model for how to establish your own personal brand (BrandMe) effectively. He argues that you need to shift from functionality (what you do) to vitality (how you do it) by using the **SALT process**:

- Social footprint (your social connections and how far they reach)
- Awards and associations (awards you have won and associations you belong to)
- Live appearances (appearing at networking events and speaking live in person or online)
- Third-party media mentions (getting others to write or talk about you)

Once you get past introductions, you need to develop the dialogue and convey your messages in an engaging way. Storytelling is covered in Part 4.

Networking skills

Effective **networking** to build new contacts draws on a range of skills that are described in this book, such as non-verbal communication, rapport building, asking questions and active listening. There are some excellent books on the subject. I particularly like one by Will Kintish. However, here are some of the key elements.

Understand the principles

Networking is just a tool. And you can do it in person (face-to-face) or online. It is just one tool within business development, so you should consider what you need to do both before and after networking to ensure it is effective.

Have realistic expectations. Networking is rarely a source of instant results – you have to make a concerted and continued effort to realize any payback. Networking can also be made more comfortable if you remove the pressure of expecting immediate results. Most networking takes place by putting other people together ('joining the dots') or providing information that may have no short-term benefit for you or your organization.

Networking should be seen as a way to widen the pool of contacts (the beginning of a pipeline) and as a starting-point for the development of a potentially long 'courtship'. A sustained effort to maintain contact (perhaps through a marketing programme) will build familiarity, trust and knowledge with a new contact.

If you really don't like meeting new people then choose another method to generate new contacts – otherwise you will communicate your discomfort unconsciously though your non-verbal communication.

Networking is about communication – face-to-face and two-way communication. It has uncontrollable elements – you don't know who you might meet or how they might react. You must be prepared to deal with unexpected situations.

Each person has his or her own network – some small and some extensive. By enlarging your pool of contacts you increase your networking ability hugely – because you connect with the networks of others. Networking is aimed at the 'capturing' end of the business development process. You need to understand the pipeline or business development model (see below) in its entirety for networking to be effective.

Think about your aims

Networking can be used for personal reasons – to learn about people, about their businesses and their industries and to learn about life. It can help you build your contact 'bank', which could be used for future career opportunities. It can help you make connections with the 'right sort of people' (which you define!). And it is a way to have fun.

On the business side of the equation, it can help you meet new clients, suppliers and referrers. It enables you to renew old acquaintances in a time-efficient way. It can raise your own or your firm's profile and help you collect valuable market and competitor intelligence.

But it can also be important to network within your own organization. This is particularly important for those starting out in their careers. It is also a key tool to improve **internal communication** and collaboration in larger organizations (see Part 4).

Think about what you expect to achieve with your networking and remember that your specific aims should be dictated, in part, by a proper marketing analysis and plan. Otherwise you could invest a lot of time networking at the wrong events and end up looking for needles in haystacks.

Preparation

Most people feel a little nervous about going out to meet new people. And many networking situations feel a little awkward and socially uncomfortable

– especially if you have a personality that is more inwardly than outwardly focused.

Try to obtain a list of attendees before you attend an event so that you can be familiar with the types of individuals (and their organizations) you are likely to meet, and this will help you prepare a few topics of discussion or questions that will help smooth introductions. Ask your existing contacts or the organizers to help you identify and meet targeted people.

First impressions and introductions

This was discussed above (see p. 268).

Try not to make quick initial impressions about whether someone at an event is worthy of your attention. Sometimes people who look uncomfortable and remain on the periphery are there because they want to meet people but dislike the networking scene as much as you do. Introducing yourself, showing an interest and helping them to network will put them at ease.

The way you introduce yourself will have an impact on the impression you create. Pronouncing your name, role and organization clearly (and with a smile) and providing conversation hooks are things that can be practised and rehearsed. Learning to introduce your colleagues (rather than yourself) provides the opportunity to offer much more information.

Remember your key messages – some people call this an **elevator speech** (if you had 90 seconds with someone in a lift, what would you tell them?). There is a **SHREK model** for developing interesting personal introductions:

- Say who you are
- Hook – include any connection to make it warm
- Reason statement – what you do, with an example for similar organizations
- Effect – specific fact or example with value of benefit
- Key question – to get the conversation started

Practical tips when networking

'Hunt in a pack.' Networking in pairs or small groups is easier, and 'lone' guests can feel and look a bit distant. Working together means you are unlikely to be left alone and that you can more easily join other groups of people. You can also use the introduction of your colleague as a way to start new conversations and perhaps move around the room.

Show interest. Many people feel inadequate at making 'small talk', although it is better to ask interested questions about other people's views, roles, organizations and industries. Non-verbal cues can be used to show interest.

Develop your memory. You may worry that you will not remember names or points discussed at a networking event. Excuse yourself occasionally to write notes on business cards or on your phone – and immediately after the event. There are techniques that can be learned to improve memory.

Adopt a positive mental attitude. Neuro-Linguistic Programming (NLP) involves understanding whether people's preferred mode of communication is visual, audio or kinaesthetic and then matching their style (see p. 15). It uses visualization techniques to help people regain the positive feelings from good experiences to apply in new situations. Think positively before attending an event and the positive mental state will be reflected within more positive body language. People tend to avoid individuals who are emitting negative or uncomfortable vibes.

Enhance your conversational skills. Some people may feel inadequate because they feel they cannot make 'small talk'. Not everyone is a born raconteur who can keep an audience enraptured for hours, but everyone can develop the confidence to make interesting conversations in any situation. Focus on the positive, feel good about yourself, be sincere, don't interrupt and use positive non-verbal communication. Avoid talking excessively about yourself, tell stories (see p. 94), see opportunities to learn, provide conversational hooks, ask questions, make people feel important and listen carefully.

'**Givers Gain**' is an important idea in networking and business relationships. It means that you make an effort to always be focused on giving something

– time, advice, help, connections, information, praise – that is helpful to others. Help other people rather than looking for how others can help you. If you develop a reputation as someone who is generous with their time then people will come back to you again and again.

Learn techniques for ending conversations and moving on to other people. Moving between groups can be challenging. Look for 'loose threes' – people who are standing with some space between them. Or take a colleague to join other groups. Watch for non-verbal cues such as eye contact to see who would welcome you joining the conversation. Or simply ask 'May I join you?' – with a smile.

If you think there is value in continuing the conversation or remaining in contact after the event, then you can exchange business cards or contact details. Offer low-commitment follow-ups – for example, suggesting you connect on social media or that you arrange to meet at a future event. This is more likely to appeal than a high-commitment offer of a meeting or lunch – which is probably premature at such an early stage of the relationship. It is also a good idea to have a range of things that can be sent to people met in this way shortly after meeting.

Following-up

After a networking event, you need to complete any follow-up actions as soon as possible. This may be as simple as adding the person as a connection on social media or dropping them a quick email saying how much you enjoyed meeting them. You may add them to a list or database so that they receive information from your organization in the future.

It may take time and several conversations before you get to meet the person again. Building business relationships is a long-term process and you need to be patient and consistent in your contact. Therefore, use a system (such as a CRM) to enable you to organize the information you gather about networking contacts, what their interests are, when you last contacted them and what you need to do next and when.

Online networking and social media selling

Increasingly, people are networking online and using **social media selling**.

Obtain training on the social media platforms you intend to use. In the UK, LinkedIn is the preferred platform for professional and business networking, although Twitter and Facebook are used by some sectors. Spend time watching and listening to how others communicate on social media to pick up on what engages and what deters.

Establish a good profile – with an appropriate photograph and emphasizing your key messages. Then connect with people you already know (on LinkedIn you can import your email contacts) and identify or target the sorts of people you want to contact. You should also get into the habit of connecting with all the people on social media whom you have met in real life.

Then comes the tricky bit – the interaction. You need to share relevant content – both business-related and perhaps some personal material – but without being too pushy or appearing to be doing 'a hard sell'. Think about what other people might want to read rather than simply what you want to say or share.

Get the right balance between posting your own material and sharing material (or curating it) from others. Some suggest a balance of 30 per cent of your material to 70 per cent of other people's material. Your content might include articles, blogs, videos, infographics, diagrams and photos. Typically, you will be encouraging people to visit your website for further information, to download information or to sign up to a newsletter so that you can progress the relationship beyond social media. In marketing terms, this is referred to as a **Call to Action (CTA)** – and it means that you will also be able to measure the effectiveness of your social media activities.

Be aware of the 'social' element of social media. In addition to liking, commenting on and sharing other people's content, you also need to engage in online conversations. So whilst some people think it is good to have thousands of connections, in reality there will be a limit to how many people you can communicate with online in a meaningful way.

Most social media platforms are public (at least to all of your connections if you use your settings correctly) but have a mail or messaging facility which you can use for private conversations. Although it's good practice to remember that even private messages can be shared publicly – so, as with emails, if you wouldn't want other people to see it then don't put it in writing.

With social media you can build your reputation as an expert (and receive third-party endorsements and recommendations), stay in contact in an unobtrusive way and draw people into conversations through the content you share.

As well as communicating with your direct connections, you can reach a wider network of people by using online communities of people with shared interests, for example in LinkedIn Groups. These offer great opportunities for becoming known by and connecting with people you don't know personally. It is generally considered bad form – certainly on LinkedIn – to try to connect with people that you don't know or with whom you have no common group memberships. Cold calling is just as uncomfortable online as it is on the telephone.

You can measure your online reputation with tools such as PeerIndex and Klout – they provide a measure of your profile and the subjects on which you communicate.

35

Selling yourself and your ideas: sales processes, decision-making and cognitive bias

Selling is a concept that makes many people feel uncomfortable. That's often because they have the wrong idea about selling. Usually, we are only aware of people selling to us when they do it badly – when it is pushy and focused on the product or service and with a lot of words spoken at us regardless of our interest.

But whether you are selling yourself (for example, at an interview or a promotion panel), your ideas (for example, at an internal meeting) or the products or services of your organization in a sales situation, you will need to appreciate the fundamentals of selling, some key concepts about good selling practice, an understanding of sales processes and also a wide variety of skills. Many of these selling skills are those which underpin better business relationship described throughout this book.

I like to reframe selling as being about 'helping people to buy'. One of the earliest models of selling I liked was empathy selling. It explained that bad selling is where there is high projection (i.e. a lot of talking by the salesperson) and low empathy. Good selling is where there is high empathy first and then appropriate projection that is tailored to the needs of the other person.

Empathy is a constant theme throughout this book – it is a fundamental concept for better business relationships. It is also fundamental for good selling. If we develop good empathy with the person we hope to sell to, we will get to know about them and what interests them and what their needs are so we will only present information to them that is relevant and useful.

The initial stages of selling focus on establishing a good business relationship by achieving rapport and trust so that productive two-way dialogue can take place.

Needs and motivation are important. A lot of sales models and processes focus on helping you to identify (or create) needs before attempting to offer a solution. You could view the sales process as a sort of detective job where you need to uncover the needs or diagnose the problems before offering possible solutions. Many sales process models are called diagnostic, consultative or solutions selling.

Selling is a vast subject – and my first book was devoted entirely to the subject – so I am only able to share a few key ideas here to get you started. But first let me share some advice from one of my personal heroes. Dale Carnegie, who wrote *How to Win Friends and Influence People,* made this famous observation: 'You can win more business in two months by being interested in other people than you can in two years trying to get people interested in you.' You should be curious about other people – questioning and active listening skills are important in selling. And remember that you have two ears and one mouth – aim to listen at least twice as much as you speak.

Selling skills

How do you know who is likely to be good at selling? There are lots of psychometric and aptitude tests that can assess personalities, traits and skills that are relevant for selling. A useful 'rainmaker' assessment employed in professional service firms was devised by Cliff Ferguson and has four elements:

1   Focus – Clarity on who you are trying to reach and where they are (see targeting on p. 272)

2   Awareness – How well you understand your own personality and style
    and how good you are at adapting (Part 1 covers this)

3   Implementation – The processes and systems you use to establish
    contact, build relationship, explore needs and win business. The
    training and other systems to support you

4   Application – Being motivated and disciplined to sell consistently

Classical vs consultative sales processes

Some people think that if they do enough of the right sorts of activity –
networking, meeting people, etc. – then they will win the sale. But you need a
process to guide you through sales situations.

In the past, the classical approach to selling suggested the following
stages:

1   Identify the buyer(s) and learn about them

2   Establish contact and build rapport and a relationship

3   Confirm they have the authority to make decisions and have a budget

4   Identify or create a need and explore it

5   Adapt a product/service or solution

6   Demonstrate you can solve the problem

7   Convince them that you are the best provider with the best solution

8   Persuade the buyer to purchase now

9   Overcome any objections

10 Close the sale

11 Deliver the promised solution

Some of these ideas are explored in more detail below.

However, although there are plenty of models that illustrate the buying
process from the client's perspective, in reality it doesn't necessarily follow a

linear process and often sales processes don't map onto whatever process the buyer has anyway.

To illustrate a possible client buying or purchasing process, consider the following:

- Identify the problem

- Define (scope) the problem

- Specify the possible solutions

- Search for information about solutions and providers

- Evaluate the alternatives

- Select the best option

- Negotiate the terms of the agreement

- Monitor progress and evaluate success

Clients may have a number of different buying situations. For example, they may be seeking a product or service for the first time or they may have bought similar products and services in the past. They will approach the buying–selling process differently. So we need to approach the selling situation differently – adapting our approach.

While we like to think that we are rational creatures, making important business decisions on a logical basis, emotions play an enormous part as we assess whether we like the people who are selling to us and whether they share a similar culture and values.

There are many sales process models to guide us through the maze of business relationships for selling – some are suitable for simple sales scenarios (for example, a relatively low-value purchase by an individual) and more complex ones (for example, an international corporation sourcing major capital expenditure items across several countries).

In recent times there has been a shift to more diagnostic and consultative approaches where a tailor-made solution and package of benefits needs to be crafted to meet the different needs of various individuals and teams involved in a complex buying scenario. An elegant model is as follows:

- Prepare – Develop a game plan
- Prospect – Identify targets with new business opportunities
- Partner – Build rapport, credibility and trust
- Probe – Uncover discontent and pain
- Present – Deliver client-focused solutions
- Problem-solve – Overcome objections
- Pilot – Navigate terms and close the sale

But these are transactional models – they appear to end when the sale is agreed. In many sales situations there are important ongoing relationships where further up-selling and cross-selling is required and even a partnership arrangement sought. It is here that relationship management, account management and key account management (KAM) techniques are deployed (see below).

The differences between transactional selling and relationship selling are compared here:

Transactional selling	Relationship selling
Focus on the selling organization	Focus on the buying organization (client)
Emphasis on features	Emphasis on benefits
Price and availability are key	Price is less important than value
Salesperson adds little value	Salesperson defines benefits and value
Relationship is one-sided	Relationship is mutual
Commissions are low	Commissions are high
Quotations are used	Tailored proposals are developed
Sell more by working harder	Sell more by working smarter
Tactical and fast	Strategic and significant

Exploring and understanding needs (features and benefits)

If the sales process can be redefined as detective work where you must uncover what the buyer really needs, it becomes obvious that a key role of the salesperson is research. You need to understand as much as possible about the individuals and their personal and business needs, their roles and departments and how they support their organizations to achieve their objectives within their particular markets, sectors and countries.

Some people use the metaphor of an iceberg to show how complex the sales process can be. Like an iceberg, a client may only reveal very limited information about his or her requirements. The job of the salesperson is to win trust and probe carefully so that all of the personal and business needs that are hidden below the surface – and perhaps not even known to the client – can be uncovered.

The process is further complicated by the fact that different people within a client organization may play different roles in the decision process – so then the detective work becomes more complex. Selling can then be seen as identifying information – and filling gaps in the information – so that a clear picture of the client organization's decision-making people and processes is obtained.

Many organizations invest in databases and other systems that enable them to undertake this research more easily and to record and share what is learned from both formal and informal sources so that the relationship can be developed, opportunities can be identified and a sale can be achieved.

People rarely buy for the features of a product – but for the benefits. This can be illustrated by a famous example from an electric drill manufacturer whose leader explained that customers do not buy drills but a method to make holes. So, for example, if you are selling a car then the features (e.g. braking systems, fuel economy, reliable engineering, multiple seats, large storage, etc.) will stay the same but different buyers will focus on different benefits such as safety, environmental friendliness, status or thrilling adventures.

The sales discovery process is about learning client needs – what problems they want to solve and what opportunities they want to grasp – and presenting whatever product or service you are selling as a series of benefits – the value that will be delivered by the product or service.

Sometimes the client has no immediate requirements or needs. Some salespeople either give up or try to forge on regardless. Inexperienced salespeople will continue to talk to and meet with the client (this is called a **continuance**) without having a long-term strategy or techniques for moving the client closer to needing its services (this is called a **progression**).

In cases where an opportunity is anticipated in the longer term, the role of the salesperson is to keep strengthening the relationship, building mutual understanding and trust, positioning their organization appropriately and continuing to explore future issues or opportunities that the client will want to address.

Exploring the buying process/buying decisions (DMU)

The Decision-Making Unit (DMU) will have an impact on the decision-making people and processes and therefore the likely length and success of the sales process.

The DMU concept suggests that people in the buying organization adopt different roles for each buying decision. The roles in the DMU – and therefore the need for different types of business relationships and sales approaches – are as follows:

Gatekeepers – People who support or assist but do not have the authority to make decisions. Their role is to protect senior people from interruptions and approaches from salespeople. Whilst these people have little ability to help you sell (they can be valuable as sponsors), if they are upset they can thwart your efforts to reach others in the DMU.

Users – People who will use the product or service but have little say in the decision process. Again, if you build strong relationships with these people they can become sponsors who help you gain knowledge of and access to decision-makers. If enough of the users are dissatisfied, this will be fed back to those in decision-making roles who may then wish to change supplier.

Buyers – People trained or qualified in buying processes. Many organizations have procurement or buying departments who specialize in sourcing and comparing suppliers and agreeing favourable prices and terms for their organization. Sometimes buyers are not procurement specialists but people who are qualified in the product or service being purchased. For example, general counsel are trained lawyers who may assess credentials and offers from external lawyers. Buyers may want different information – so adapt your approach and the value proposition. Buyers may run formal tendering or bidding processes and keep control of the sales process.

Influencers – People within the organization (perhaps at a senior level or a non-executive director) who do not make buying decisions but are able to influence the decision-makers. This can be a positive influence – if they know or like you and your organization – or a negative influence. Sometimes an organization's bankers or professional advisers may be influencers.

Decision-maker – The person(s) who makes the decision to purchase. However, they are likely to draw on the views of their gatekeepers, buyers, users and influencers.

Sponsors and anti-sponsors – Anyone in the DMU can also adopt the role of a sponsor (someone who wants to help you win business and will provide information and assistance) or an anti-sponsor (someone who will work against you and try to prevent you winning work from the organization).

The process that organizations use to buy may be quite different. Some are organized on a centralized basis and others are more distributed. Some organizations will have detailed policies and procedures for purchasing, while others may have less formal approaches where each decision-maker has autonomy. Some organizations will have structured budgeting and resource allocation processes. Some may have detailed criteria against which all suppliers must be measured. Some will operate panels of approved or preferred suppliers. The job of the salesperson is to gather information about both the decision-making unit and the decision-making processes. And this is why in business-to-business sales situations the average time to close a deal is nine months.

If you are selling products and services that are different, you may have to identify and connect with a range of different people in the organization. And you might use those in the original DMU as your sponsors to help you make connections in other DMUs.

Decision-making theory

Behavioural science offers a large body of knowledge about how we make decisions. I only have space to mention a few ideas.

In the first section of the book we saw two cognitive systems – one for fast, instinctive thinking from the emotional brain and the other for slower, deliberate thinking from the logical brain. In selling situations we are appealing to the quick, emotional brain with habit and brand loyalty for consumers and more rational thinking for business purchase decisions. But in reality both systems are deployed in buying decisions.

Choice is relative. People may make different decisions when there are two or three options available. For example, if offered just two prices we might opt for the lower, but when given three prices we tend to omit outliers and go for a middle price. This is the reason why sometimes there are decoy prices – a very expensive option that no one really chooses but is there to focus on the mid-priced item.

Cognitive bias

Cognitive bias can be thought of as 'rules of thumb' – general principles we adopt in the absence of adequate information. Daniel Kahneman is credited with the discovery of many cognitive biases. A famous one is the **framing effect** – people will give different responses depending on how a question is framed.

There are all manner of cognitive biases – tricks that your brain plays on you even when you think you are making a rational decision. We explored some in the section on persuasion but there are others, for example:

- Affect heuristic – decisions based on emotions not facts

- Anchoring bias – over-reliance on the first piece of information received. If we are told to expect to pay £100 for something, we will compare all other prices to this £100 'standard'

- Availability heuristic – overestimate the importance of available information

- Bandwagon effect – tendency to do what everyone else is doing (a form of Groupthink)

- Bias blind spot – seeing biases in others but not yourself

- Catastrophizing bias – the consequences of a worried-about scenario are imagined to be negative in the extreme

- Choice-supportive bias – feel positive about choices even if they are flawed

- Clustering illusion – see patterns in random events

- Confirmation bias – tendency to seek information that supports our existing beliefs. We form mental models of the world and search for information to support our existing view. Leon Festinger explained **cognitive dissonance** as the human need for consistency: 'Mental stress or discomfort is experienced by an individual who holds two or more contradictory beliefs, ideas or values at the same time or is confronted by new information that conflicts with existing beliefs, ideas or values.' In these situations we either deny the new information or change our opinion

- Conservatism – slow to accept new ideas

- Decoy effect – different decisions depending on whether there are two or three options

- Estimating and forecasting – overly influenced by vivid memories when we are estimating or forecasting
- Fundamental attribution error – attributing situational behaviour to fixed personality
- Halo effect – a first positive impression sticks. There is a tendency for a positive impression created in one area to influence opinion in another. If you see an organization favourably for one of its products, you are likely to consider its other products in a similarly positive way.
- Horn effect – opposite to the halo effect
- Ideometre effect – our thoughts can make us feel real emotions
- Information bias – seek information when it does not affect action
- Loss and reward – we tend to prefer a small reward now compared to a bigger reward in the future
- Ostrich effect – hiding from impending problems
- Outcome bias – judging a decision based on the outcome
- Overconfidence – too confident in own abilities
- Overestimation bias – the odds of a worried-about scenario are imagined to be high
- Placebo effect – believing something will have an effect on you causes the effect
- Planning fallacy – tendency to think that we can do things more quickly than we actually can
- Primacy effect – first information is most valued
- Pro-innovation bias – supporters of an innovation overvalue its usefulness
- Reactance – react to rules and regulations by exercising our freedom
- Recency – most recent information is valued most
- Repetition – we are likely to be persuaded when a piece of information is repeated on numerous occasions

- Salience – the tendency to use available traits to make a judgement about a person or a situation

- Status Quo – we favour options that perpetuate the existing approach

- Sunk cost – we avoid losses and prefer decisions that justify past actions – even when they are flawed

In the section on change management (see p. 46), we saw that there can be **decision fatigue** – a point in the day when the quality of our decisions declines. Psychologist Roy Baumeister demonstrated that there is a finite store of mental energy for exerting self-control and making quality decisions.

David J. Cresswell has shown that we make better decisions, especially when dealing with complex information, when a period of distraction is introduced. In creativity exercises, we often ask people to take a small 'excursion' – to do something completely different – so that when they return to the problem-solving exercise their brains have done some background processing to come up with better solutions.

Scott de Marchi and James T. Hamilton, in their book *You Are What You Choose*, suggested that people approach decision-making across different aspects of their life in the same way. They devised a method called **TRAITS** to measure how we make decisions: Time (how future focused), Risk, Altruism, Information, meToo and Stickiness. They found that most people scored highly on two or three approaches. So even in decision-making, there are personal differences.

36

Selling skills: questions, active listening, persuasion, closing, objections and trusted adviser

Questions are a major tool in selling. Most people are aware of the difference between closed questions (where the answer is usually only 'Yes' or 'No') and open questions (using Who, What, Where, Why and How), which elicit a longer response.

Some people think of the questions in a funnelling way – broad questions at the outset (which encourage divergent thinking) and increasingly narrow questions to focus in on the critical issues (convergent thinking).

There are different types of questions to use in selling situations. For example, questions can demonstrate your understanding or expertise in a particular subject. Questions can combine two familiar questions in an unfamiliar way to prompt a person to think more carefully before automatically responding with their usual answer.

Some sales methodologies focus entirely on a structure to ask questions in a particular way. For example, **SPIN™ selling** was developed by psychologists at Huthwaite International after researching how successful salespeople ask questions. The question structure they use is Situation (understanding the broad context), Problem, Implication and Need/payoff.

There's a simpler model by Dugdale and Lambert which applies **SHAPE** (Surface, Hunt, Adjust, Paint and Engage). Both models help you to discover the client's problem, and guide the client to think about the value of resolving the issue and the cost and benefits of doing so.

You might recall that structured questions underpin the coaching process (see Part 5) – where they encourage someone to find a solution to an issue themselves. Selling in a consultative way is similar – although obviously you hope that the person comes to the conclusion that they need you and your products or services!

Attention and active listening

Asking questions is only one part of the equation. A good salesperson will pay close attention to the responses and will develop their active listening skills. Some people underestimate how much skill and effort is required to be a really active listener. The National Center for Biotechnology Information in the US found that our average attention space is eight seconds – less than a goldfish at nine seconds. When people train as therapists, a significant part of their programme focuses on how to listen really carefully. And it can be exhausting.

Often when we are listening to people our brains are working hard on thinking about what we might say next. Our mental model of the world means that we might perceive things differently to how the person who spoke the words intended. Our brains can trick us by picking up on one or two familiar words and not hearing what else might be said. There are all sorts of cognitive biases that can get in the way of properly hearing what others say.

Or we may be nervous and jump onto the first thing that the client says that allows us to talk about something that we know about. This can make the person shut down and cease to share further information and may lead a sales conversation down a dead-end path.

Our brains work at about 500 words a minute and we listen at 150 words a minute. There is a lot of spare capacity, so we can be tempted to think about other things while listening to someone. And that limited attention means that we might miss vital information – also, the speaker may detect that we are not giving 100 per cent of our attention to them.

Some 50 per cent of our brain's capacity is dedicated to vision, so non-verbal communication is important for both the speaker and the listener. You might watch for a discrepancy between what someone says and their body language. Some salespeople are skilled at observing non-verbal language and identify buying signals, resistance or discomfort and focus their questioning accordingly.

As well as demonstrating that you are respectful, open-minded and paying attention, active listening skills can help probe issues at a much deeper level – revealing beliefs, internal frames of reference, values, limiting assumptions, unconscious needs and other perceptions.

Here are just a few techniques to enhance your active listening skills:

Non-Verbal Communication – Maintain steady eye contact without appearing to stare and mirror or match posture. Nods and smiles or paralingustics ('ahh' and 'mmm') encourage people to continue speaking. Watching for inconsistencies between what someone is saying and their non-verbal communication may provide insight to their true feelings and opportunities to explore contradictions.

Silence – People need time to think and reflect on a question before offering a response. Showing your tolerance for a comfortable silence gives others time to explore and articulate their feelings and thoughts more fully. Some salespeople jump into silences too quickly.

Restating or Reflecting – Repeating back words and phrases that the person has spoken confirms that you are listening and encourages them to speak further. It helps to build trust, as the person can continue to speak without fear of you making (premature) judgements.

Paraphrasing – Saying what the other person has said in your own words demonstrates that you are absorbing the information and understanding. It offers an opportunity for the other person to reflect on how their words are being perceived and to correct the emphasis or meaning.

Summarizing – Summarizing helps to show that you have grasped all the main points and are effectively tracking what they are saying. The other person also has the opportunity to indicate if anything has been overlooked.

Focusing – This is similar to summarizing, but offers a way to prioritize further discussion. Alternatively, you might encourage the person to focus further on something that they said in passing which may have greater importance.

Professor Schultz Von Thun offered a **four ears model** of communication:

1 Factual – the information and facts being shared

2 Self-revelation – information about the person making the communication

3 Relationship – information about the relationship between the sender and receiver of the information

4 Appeal to action – the action being suggested

Persuasion in sales

Part 3 (p. 116) covers influence and persuasion. Martin, Goldstein and Cialdini, in their book *The Small Big – Small Changes that Spark Big Influence*, also found psychological evidence that suggested the following:

- When meeting someone for the first time, dress in a style that is similar to the group you wish to influence but at one level higher of authority

- Position messages in a way that first focuses the client's attention on the potential future benefits your proposal offers, followed by examples of what your organization has previously delivered

- Advice and recommendations from an expert who are themselves uncertain is most compelling, as the source's expertise, coupled with a level of uncertainty, arouses intrigue

- Build in a peak-end effect – something pleasant at the end of an experience

Their evidence suggests that the longer we know someone, the less likely it is that we will be able to accurately predict their preferences. So occasionally invite a colleague who knows a client less well to uncover new information and opportunities. If you expect something in return for something (reciprocity), they suggest that what you give first is unexpected compared to the norm.

Closing the sale and handling objections

In classical selling, there was the idea that you had to 'close' the sale – persuade the client to sign up. This can feel a bit 'pushy'. So it's preferable to adopt a more consultative approach where there should be no need to 'close' since it should happen naturally. However, people often ask about closing techniques so here are some examples:

- Trial close – 'So if we can agree a flexible pricing system, you will sign up?'

- Assumptive close – 'As you seem happy, we will start working on it . . .'

- Directive close – 'We will start on this tomorrow'

- Alternative close – 'Shall we start on Monday or Wednesday?'

- Questioning close – 'How would you like to proceed now?'

- Probing close – 'You appear to be happy with most of the arrangements?'

- Summary close – 'Now we have covered all the relevant points, the price is acceptable and the contract process is clear it looks as if we are ready to start'

In classical selling, it was expected that you would encounter objections. I think that objections occur when the sales process has failed in some way – where you did not identify sufficient need or motivation and tried to close prematurely.

While some people fear objections, others consider them natural and inevitable. They may simply be an indicator of a misunderstanding or lack of information. They are an opportunity to continue the sales conversation if managed correctly. I learned a technique early in my sales career that helps me classify and respond appropriately to objections.

- Pause and think
- Clarify
  - Confirm your understanding of the issue
  - Convert it into a question to obtain more information
- Classify
  - A false objection might be when someone says 'Your company is too small', when really they mean that they do not have the authority to make the decision
  - A hidden objection might be when someone says 'Your company is too small', when really they mean that they prefer another supplier with whom they are friends
  - A misunderstanding means that they need more information
  - A real objection is just that – a real reason why they can't proceed. For example, 'Our head office makes those decisions' (in which case you need to find out how you engage with people at head office)
- Counter, answer or agree
- Confirm that you have responded adequately. Always end on a positive note

Adding value and providing insight

One of the things I advise people to do when they are selling is to try to add value to the client at every interaction. This means that every email, call or meeting should include something for the other person to show them that you are thinking of their interests rather than your own. We touched on this idea in the networking section with 'Giver's Gain'.

I was excited to learn a few years ago about research by psychologists John E. Doerr and Mike Schultz in their book *Insight Selling* that showed the difference between those salespeople who were successful and those who came second or third. The difference was in the amount of insight that they brought to the sales process.

Doerr and Schultz found that the factors separating those who came first in sales situations and those who came second were:

1   Educating with a new perspective

2   Collaboration

3   Persuasion that results would be achieved

4   Listened

5   Understood needs

6   Helped avoid potential pitfalls

7   Crafted a compelling solution

8   Depicted purchasing process accurately

9   Connected personally

10 Overall value superior to other options

Many of these themes are covered in this book. What is perhaps a little surprising is that while consultative, hard-working, lone wolf and relationship-building sales approaches were still deemed successful, it was those who emphasized challenging, educating and insightful approaches that were more so.

The authors argued that the value added by the salesperson during the sales process is the differentiator. They describe the **value proposition** as 'the collection of reasons why a buyer buys. In essence, the factors that affect their desire to purchase and from whom.' They contend that the salesperson and the insightful sales process are part of the value proposition. They also recognize the importance of emotion in the sales process when they describe the three legs of the value proposition as:

- Resonate (both rationally and emotionally)

- Differentiate (from other providers)

- Substantiate (how results will be achieved and risks minimized)

This shows just how important better business relationships are in the world of selling. The model they propose is elegant and simple, suggesting that in each sales situation you follow the **RAIN** framework:

- Rapport

- Aspirations and Afflictions (explore goals and challenges)

- Impact (Inquiry and Influence – what would happen as a result of achieving goals or resolving challenges)

- New reality (understanding of what the future might look like when the goals are achieved or the challenges addressed)

Doerr and Schultz also offer a simple sales process:

1   Connect – Join the dots and connect people

2   Convince – Demonstrate yours is the best choice with maximum return and minimum risk

3   Collaborate – Find what to collaborate on and how for the future relationship

Commercial and trusted adviser

Similar to the ideas in consultative, solutions-based and insight selling is the concept of being a commercial adviser. This is a special form of business relationship that encompasses selling and consulting. The seven habits of a commercial adviser are:

1 Understand the client's desired outcomes (know what they want to achieve in the short and long term)

2 Understand the client's business (understand their business plan, strategy, industry or sector trends)

3 Understand the economics (be fluent in the client's financial information)

4 Understand the people (both internal and external stakeholders as well as management and operational staff)

5 Agree the scope (define what you will actually do for them, manage their expectations and prepare and communicate work plans)

6 Build practical solutions (remove complexity and advise them on what they need to do and when)

7 Communicate for impact (gain buy-in from sponsors, management and stakeholders and engage people through workshops, presentations and meetings)

An even deeper and closer type of business relationship is that of the trusted adviser who exhibits the following:

1 Authenticity

2 Puts clients' interests first, rather than their own

3 Is genuinely interested in their clients and their businesses

4 Believes it is important to understand the client's underlying needs (not just wants)

5 Reliable (keeps promises)

6 Credible

7 Connects emotionally

8 Passionate and enthusiastic

9 Focuses on the long-term relationship (not short-term gains)

37

First meetings

Throughout this book we've covered a lot of ideas and advice about business relationships and selling. So now we will see how they all fit together in one particular situation – the initial sales meeting.

Before the meeting

1   Conduct research – There is a wide range of information required and external and internal sources to be interrogated. There's value in preparing a synopsis of the information both to brief the rest of the team if others are involved and to identify what questions to ask the client and what insights to share.

2   Agree aims and agenda – While first meetings are usually about developing rapport and exploring the client and their needs, it is helpful to think about your aims for the meeting. This might be to gain particular information about the client's decision-making process. Think about what you want to happen after the first meeting – so you can gain agreement while you are there. If you send an outline agenda to the client in advance, it shows that you are enthusiastic about the opportunity and that you respect their time. It might also flush out information about the client's expectations for the meeting.

3   Anticipate questions – Anticipate what the client is likely to ask you so you can be ready with the necessary stories (case studies, etc.) and evidence. Naturally, you need to be ready for the question 'Why should we consider/appoint you?' – dealing with your value proposition. You may not have sufficient information before the meeting to have this

nailed down. Consider the questions you want to ask the client. These should be ranked in order so that the most important questions are asked early in the meeting. Your questions should convey your expertise and understanding.

4   Identify how to provide insight – We saw that insight selling is the most effective, so you need to identify how you will add value, provide ideas or insight at the first meeting so that the client values the experience and invites you back again. Applying the idea of Giver's Gain and reciprocity, it would be good if you could offer the client a personal or business opportunity that they would value. This may take some creative thinking, strategic consideration and additional research.

5   Consider what to take along – Do not take a large pile of material to the first meeting. At this stage you don't really know enough about what the client is interested in. It would be better to send some materials over as a follow-up after the meeting that reflect the topics you discussed. However, it helps to take along explanatory charts and diagrams that describe your approach or methodology – these you can discuss with the client to help pinpoint their particular areas of interest.

During the meeting

6   Arrive early – This is helpful for two reasons. First, you will have time to recover from the journey and adopt a calm and confident attitude. Second, you can look around and chat with any staff (e.g. receptionists). These gatekeepers can relay to others how they found you and may be able to help you in the future when you need access to decision-makers.

7   Manage time – Time is precious and there is much to do at a first sales meeting. Identify what needs to happen and how much time should be allocated to each activity: greetings and small talk; introductions; aims and agendas; questions and answers (the main bulk of the meeting should be dialogue about the client's 'aspirations and afflictions');

summarizing; demonstrating expertise; discussing possible solutions; conveying key points; providing insight; dealing with misunderstandings and objections; agreeing next steps; stressing the benefits; and thanks/goodbyes. You might request a tour of the premises or ask to be introduced to other people who were not at the meeting. If you have an agenda and a plan, you need to be flexible to adapt to the client's needs and any unexpected developments.

8   Build rapport – Selling is as much about emotion as it is rational choice. People buy people. Business relationships are paramount. You need to quickly understand the nature of the people you are meeting and adapt your approach as necessary. But don't sacrifice authenticity.

9   Use emotional intelligence (EQ) – Body language (NVC) is important. Balance eye contact with note-taking and take care with your tone of voice. Remember that what you say is often less important than how you say it. Emotional intelligence supports sales effectiveness, as you need to demonstrate empathy with the client's point of view. Emotional intelligence also helps establish trust.

10 Ask questions and listen attentively – Know what type of questions to ask at each stage of the sales process. Questions promote interaction – remember that 'telling isn't selling' and that you need to focus on being 'interested rather than interesting'. There are various frameworks to structure questions but a key point is to start with broad, open questions and resist the urge to focus in on specifics too early. Show interest in people – rather than boring them with lots of detail about your organization, its products and services. Formulate questions that challenge the client and make an impact. Skills and techniques involved in active listening must be deployed. A key part of professional selling is to find or create a need before attempting to offer solutions. You need strategies (and patience) for dealing with clients who seem entirely satisfied with their existing advisers and therefore have no motivation to consider switching.

11 Explore the Decision-Making Unit (DMU) – In complex selling situations, there are often many people involved in making decisions and at first meetings you need to obtain as much information as possible about who makes such decisions and how. It may be that your first meeting is with gatekeepers and buyers (e.g. procurement) – and that you need to win these people over before they introduce you to users and decision-makers. Think too about different buyer motivation types and how to adapt your approach to each of the styles.

12 Tell stories and offer solutions – It can be dull for clients to listen to lots of technical information – especially if they are not an expert in the product or service they are buying. Tell stories to convey information. This increases retention of information as well as a positive attitude towards the storyteller. There's a wealth of information about persuasion science. Whilst it is unlikely that you will complete the entire sales process in the first meeting of a complex business service, you will have to communicate about price, handle objections, negotiate and close the deal at some point.

After the meeting

13 Confirm key points quickly – There are several reasons why you should send a short summary email quickly. You want to do so while the meeting is fresh in your mind. A fast follow-up shows that you are keen and responsive. You can also add extra ideas and insight that occurred to you after the meeting. The client may use your email to communicate with others in the organization – effectively selling you to other members of the decision-making unit, so be aware of the 'invisible audience'.

14 Complete any agreed actions – This could be simple things like providing links to information you mentioned or introducing them to people they would like to meet. It might also be the preparation of a proposal or pitch.

15 Update your systems – Whether you use a simple spreadsheet to manage your contacts or a sophisticated CRM to co-ordinate your sales pipeline, you should update your systems. This way you will track your sales activity, plan follow-up activity and manage your opportunity pipeline. In larger organizations there may also be internal communications systems for reporting and co-ordinating sales activity across teams.

16 Telephone to gauge reactions – Whilst emails are time efficient, in sales situations you really want the interaction of a live conversation. You can pick up on nuances and hesitations, people are likely to be more candid and share more information when speaking and a telephone call enables the next step to be agreed.

38

Pitching and tenders

In many business sales situations, you will be required to provide a pitch to win business. Pitches and tenders come in many shapes and sizes – some are informal and short, others are formal and drawn out. In some pitch and tendering situations, the buying organization will do everything it can to remove the opportunity for personal interaction and business relationships to have an impact on the final decision. What's interesting though is that even in formal tendering scenarios, existing business relationships still have a significant impact on the outcome. Smart people will aim to develop a relationship well ahead of any pitching or tendering situation.

A pitch or tender condenses the entire sales process into a short period of time. There may be initial forms to complete, group briefings, telephone calls and meetings, the preparation of documents as well as formal presentations perhaps to a panel of decision-makers. In some situations, there may be an online auction where the price is the final determinant between the shortlisted suppliers.

There is a lot to be aware of when attending preliminary meetings (see Chapter 37, above) and when preparing written material for pitch and tender documents (see the material on written communications on p. 107). So here I concentrate on how to present at a pitch meeting, although there is general material on presentations on p. 98.

Research, plan and prepare the content

If you want me to speak for two minutes, it will take me three weeks of preparation. If you want me to speak for thirty minutes, it will take me a week to prepare. If you want me to speak for an hour, I am ready now.

Winston Churchill

The research and preparation stage of a winning pitch presentation is important for many reasons – to ensure that your messages are properly joined up into a compelling value proposition, to increase the confidence of everyone participating and to enable those pitching to gel as a team so that the client sees cohesion.

Empathy – focus on the needs of the audience

Can you imagine what it is like to have to sit through half a dozen presentations that all follow the same structure and content? Having been on the selection side of the panel on many occasions, I can tell you that it's boring. So the first job in preparing for a pitch presentation is to use some empathy and put yourself in the shoes of the audience.

Research – go beyond the brief

The client will need to hear rational information. And you will have done extensive research as you talked to the client at scoping meetings and obtained the wider commercial context about the project or work to respond to their brief and submit a tender document.

Extend the research into the deeper values of the client organization, its history, its aims and strategies, its other work, its business reputation, other business relationships and the people who will be present at the pitch presentation.

The more information you gather the more likely you will be able to identify additional value points and innovative ideas and to tailor the material more closely to the needs, style and language of the client.

Concentrate on the differentiating value proposition

In a pitch, you will draw on the material in the original brief and in whatever documentation you have been asked to submit. Ideally, your tender or pitch document will have made your compelling value proposition crystal clear so that the client is in no doubt what unique blend of attributes and benefits you contribute. Select and reinforce the key message.

Focus on three key points

The presentation is likely to be short – perhaps only ten to fifteen minutes of your allotted time (you'll need as much time as possible to pose and answer questions and interact with the client – to simulate the future working relationship). So less is more. Most presentation experts advise you to identify no more than three key points.

Structure and signpost your content

I encourage people to prepare a mind map of all that they might want to cover in a presentation. Then they can easily see the main points and perhaps a logical structure. There are many different ways of structuring content – to differentiate your presentation, to make it easy for the audience to follow, to emphasize those critical three key points, to present solutions to problems, etc.

You will need to signpost the content so that the client knows exactly where you are in the presentation and what comes next. Repetition and reinforcement are important – and support retention through the primacy and recency effects.

KISS – Keep It Simple Stupid

Products, services and projects are likely to be complex. There will be lots of detail on what is to be done, how it will be done, who will do it, the likely challenges and, of course, the cost proposals and contractual issues.

But your task is to make things simple. Later discussions and questions will allow the client to get through to the nitty-gritty. So be assured and convey your key points as simply as possible.

If you can't explain it simply, you don't understand it well enough.

Any fool can make things more complex. It takes a touch of genius to move in the opposite direction.

Everything should be made as simple as possible but not simpler.

Albert Einstein

Choose the best presentation method and audio-visuals

As your value proposition differentiates your firm's offer from those of the competitors, so must your presentation stand out from them too. For many firms, PowerPoint (or Keynote) is the tool of choice. More adventurous presenters will use tools like Presentia.

Some will be brave and work with models or simulations. Others will use music, flowcharts, handouts, flipcharts, actors, videos and all manner of other props and aids. Your choice will depend on the facilities available, the client expectations and the experience of your presenting team.

The critical thing here is to rehearse. And rehearse again. Then everyone knows the content really well and everything moves smoothly.

Prepare for questions

Anticipate all possible questions that the client may ask – even the difficult ones. And consider who is best in the pitching team to answer them so that the chair knows how to direct questions. Rehearse tricky responses so that everyone is on the same page.

You are usually invited to ask the client panel questions, so prepare some. Questions should demonstrate your expertise and insight. Questions allow you to show you've done your homework and have thought above and beyond the brief. Questions should add insight and make the client reflect on their ideas. Questions can make your team stand out.

Anticipate disasters

Be prepared in case there is a power or equipment failure – or a critical no-show in your team or in the client's team. And be ready to go completely off-script if the client decides to take the pitch meeting in a different direction.

Ensure that you deliver well and connect emotionally

> I've learned that people will forget what you said, people will forget what
> you did, but people will never forget how you made them feel.
>
> Maya Angelou

You've addressed the rational element of the decision. But the client's choice
will depend on a raft of emotional factors too – how well you understand
them, whether you speak their language, the extent to which you make them
feel confident and valued and so on. The latest research (insight selling) shows
that the way in which clients experience the sales process is a major determinant
of who wins.

Some research shows that an existing relationship can have an impact
on the purchase decision by up to 30 per cent. So business relationships are
critical in helping you win pitches and tenders.

Adapt to the clients' personality types

Research and understand the role that each member of the client team plays in
the decision-making unit (DMU) and the decision-making process.

Think about the different personalities and preferences of those people.
Personalities and information-processing preferences (visual, auditory and
kinaesthetic – from neuro-linguistic programming) differ.

Throughout your presentation and discussions, recognize different
personality styles and adapt your style to ensure that they feel comfortable –
whilst remaining authentic and congruent with whom you are.

Feel and look confident (NVC)

Manage the first impression you make. This is largely based on non-verbal
communication (NVC) such as your voice and your gestures. These are highly
dependent on culture so take care in a global or multinational environment.

If you don't feel confident (you will if you prepare and rehearse) then find ways to reduce nerves (for example, breathing and visualization exercises) or increase confidence (e.g. watch the fabulous TED video by Amy Cuddy on power poses).

Craft a great introduction

Every member of the pitching team will need to introduce themselves and explain their role on the pitch team and during the work. Think about three key messages for each person – otherwise the client will become overloaded with information. In some cultures, an 'expertise and credentials' introduction is expected. In other cultures, a less formal and more personal introduction is the norm.

You should also consider how to tackle the initial handshaking and greeting routines – it can get complicated if there are lots of you. And think about the psychology of the seating arrangements – you want to avoid a 'them vs us' scenario if possible.

Tell stories

Neuroscience tells us that when people listen to a story that they connect to, a whole host of cognitive functions take place. During the presentation and interview use stories, anecdotes and case studies to bring material to life. Stories also offer a great way to simplify complex ideas – perhaps through the use of metaphors or analogies (see storytelling on p. 94).

Create rapport and trust

The way that humans connect and develop relationships is addressed elsewhere in this book (see Part 3). Understanding non-verbal communication, empathy, active listening and showing an interest in others are the main routes to creating rapport and trust (see p. 148).

Influence and persuade

Understanding the science of influence and persuasion will assist you in making a strong case in a way that has impact. Understand the difference between features and benefits and remember that 'telling isn't selling'. Influence and persuasion are covered in Part 3 (see p. 116).

Control – time keeping and strong endings

You must finish on time – especially in Western cultures. And before you finish there should be a strong summary reinforcing the key points of your proposition and making it clear why the client should choose you.

Debrief the team after the presentation and contact the client to find out how you did, whether they need any further information and what the next steps will be.

39

Key account management

Key Account Management (KAM), which is sometimes called Key Client Management (KCM), is where there is a structured business relationship with your most important (or potentially most important) clients. It is concerned with more than simply retaining critical relationships. It is a specialized form of selling.

Some see KAM as looking after the 'crown jewel' clients, developing a deeper understanding of clients' objectives and needs, a process to capture and leverage client knowledge, a way to move to a partnership where the client is more securely 'locked in' and a plan for developing the long-term growth of key existing and target clients.

Reasons to invest in a Key Account Management programme

There are many reasons to focus on your most important client relationships:

- According to the Pareto principle, 80 per cent of a business's revenue and profits will come from 20 per cent of its clients. It is therefore sensible to focus attention on these major clients as part of a risk management strategy. Tailoring your service to specific clients is often part of a differentiation strategy and can 'lock in' critical clients. It's also worth considering that your competitors may target your largest clients, so it would be foolhardy to lose them through complacency.

- Research indicates that clients that use a variety of services are more profitable and that it costs six to seven times more to generate work from a new client than an existing client. For example, in a recent book (*Professional Services Marketing Handbook* by Nigel Clark and Charles Nixon) it was revealed that for an international law firm client work involving five or more countries was 30 per cent more profitable than single-country domestic work. KAM is an effective way to improve cross-selling and up-selling.

- Major clients are often a valuable source of referrals. It may be because they have a strong reputation or because the nature of the work you do for them is critical or innovative. If you expect a major client to devote time to providing testimonials and acting as a reference site, then it is only fair that they should receive some benefit from doing so. A KAM programme will ensure that the balance is maintained.

- A firm's systems are often inadequate at recording and managing the vast amount of information about a particular major client, so someone needs to be tasked with collating and maintaining the information and sharing it with the relevant people so that appropriate and timely action is taken. Furthermore, some clients may have specific contracts or service level agreements and these will need to be monitored.

- A major client is likely to require a variety of products and services from numerous teams and offices in a firm. Someone needs to have responsibility for co-ordinating these services, assessing the satisfaction of the client and planning its future development. The role of Relationship or Account Manager will require time that is essential for the delivery of service even if it doesn't generate income in its own right. KAM programmes measure the investment and return of this time.

- Key clients move through stages – for example, from seeing you as commodity provider, to service provider, to strategic partner to trusted adviser. As clients form partnerships with suppliers, there needs to be a greater focus on the relationship – to ensure that there is ongoing deep mutual understanding, to take proactive development steps and to promote collaboration and the co-creation of new products and services.

- Whilst synergistic KAM is rare, the most advanced programmes have large dedicated teams of staff focused entirely on a key client. These teams often have a deeper knowledge of the client's business and market than many of the client's own staff and it is from this position that they are able to provide insights to senior management and craft initiatives that add value to a true strategic partnership. These KAM teams bid for and win major investment from their businesses and often lead the innovation and new product development initiatives.

Growing your business is like filling a bucket – if it is leaky and you continue to lose clients it will take even more effort to generate new clients to fill it. Some research indicates that a reduction in client churn (i.e. many clients stop using the organization and have to be constantly replaced with new clients) by just 5 per cent can lead to a profit improvement of 50 per cent. Research also shows that a 10 per cent increase in loyal clients can generate a 20 per cent increase in profits. So a bird in the hand really is worth two in the bush. Client retention is affected by many factors including service delivery excellence, proactive added-value services and pricing, but KAM can be a critical way to retain and develop major clients.

Elements of a Key Account Management programme

Introducing a KAM programme requires significant investment and even long-term structural and cultural change in an organization. And it can take a significant amount of time. However, the rewards are potentially huge.

The elements of a strategic KAM programme might include:

- Clear objectives and an organization-wide strategic plan
- Stakeholder buy-in and cultural adaptation (including reward systems – often reward systems focus on winning new business rather than retaining and developing existing business)

- Information and research systems

- Internal communication

- Skills training programmes

- Agreement of criteria and identification of key accounts

- Client research and listening programmes

- Creation of teams and allocation of roles and responsibilities

- Development of client plans

- Implementation of client plans

- Investment in collaborative research and development (R&D) projects with clients

- Monitoring, measurement of results and reporting

There are many challenges in introducing a KAM system, including lack of vision; unrealistic expectations; poor internal communications; loss of momentum; inward focus; short-term sales focus; client protectionism; and lack of time. There are many other cultural, strategic and marketing issues that need to be addressed in a systematic way as well as buy-in and stakeholder management.

KAM meetings

How do you sustain and develop the business relationship in a KAM programme? There are potentially hundreds of interactions that can have an impact on multiple relationships over the lifetime of the KAM. My observation is that at the start of a KAM programme there is a lot of enthusiasm and people are keen to have meetings with the clients to tackle tangible and concrete issues. They are also keen to have conversations where they can explore cross-selling or up-selling opportunities or identify short-term new business opportunities. But once these initial meetings have taken place, they are unsure how to proceed, the programme falters and enthusiasm wanes.

This problem is caused by a number of factors – most of which stem from an inadequate understanding of the KAM process:

- Short-term view – People are busy and are likely to focus on winning business in the short term. If there are no immediate opportunities they often don't know how to engage with clients.

- Inward sales approach – The business has decided to 'squeeze the lemon' and get more work out of major client relationships. It's an internal agenda and insufficient research and effort is made to understand what the client really wants and needs – both now and in the future – and how to really add value to the relationship.

- Lack of goals – Goals are likely to relate to additional revenue within the current financial year. In a strategic and structured KAM there will be long-term goals relating to the strength and breadth of the relationship and how to achieve partnership status by making a real difference to the client's business. Strategic goals might relate to how much money might be saved for the client, how much revenue is generated for the client or how you and the client might collaborate to develop innovative new ways of working together.

Most businesses consider KAM in a simplistic way. However, KAM is described as a process to achieve long-term profitable relationships with key clients by making consistent, measureable contributions to their profitability and their customer relationships.

The need for a key client plan

A thoroughly researched and comprehensive key client plan will help people know what they are trying to achieve in the short, medium and long term and therefore inform them of the nature of the discussions they should be holding with their clients at any point.

If the client knows that the firm is truly interested in helping their business succeed then they will make time for meetings – knowing that the provider will make every effort to ensure that any meetings add value to their knowledge, perspective or ideas in exchange for their time. Where clients suspect that suppliers are purely out for their own short-term gain then they are likely to resist meetings.

Client life cycle determines meeting aims and content

The nature of the conversations at key client meetings will be determined by the stage in the **client life cycle**.

In the early stages the meetings will be about getting to know the client – its aims, strategies, operations, preferred working and cultural styles. There may be many different initiatives discussed to achieve this, including seminars, shadowing and secondments. Early conversations might be guided by the information required by the provider in order to 'fill the blanks' in their knowledge that cannot be obtained from public records.

Later on, meetings will focus on ensuring that the client is happy with the products or service provided and how the supplier can improve service delivery. Service reviews and client listening programmes come to the fore. There may be ongoing meetings to address critical service elements, reporting requirements and the integration of systems.

As the relationship matures and trust grows, the shift might be to exploring the Decision-Making Unit (DMU) for the purchase of other products and services – the cross-selling and up-selling scenarios. Conversations at this stage will be about enlisting the client's people as sponsors and champions and finding ways to gain access to decision-makers in other parts of the organization. However, the providers will need to make a strong case that they can add value when offering these other services – particularly if the client has a 'horses for courses' approach to buying products and services. Providers will also need to be aware of the fact that their client contacts may have no relationship or knowledge of other parts of the organization and are therefore limited in their ability to help.

Throughout these conversations, in addition to understanding the rational needs of the people, departments and organization, the provider needs to be alert to the personal motivations of the individuals – their own profile and aspirations – and to gain an appreciation of the sometimes delicate internal politics. Sometimes it may be appropriate to ask the client about providing case studies, testimonies, joint conference papers and other PR-related activities that put the client and the provider in a positive light in wider industry initiatives.

Many suppliers will look to sector research, thought leadership and benchmarking studies to see how they can help their clients compare themselves against their competitors or industry norms and identify opportunities for them to achieve savings or competitive advantage. Education initiatives and workshops might be the main topic of conversation here.

Another stage of the relationship building might be the organization of social events where other members of the supplier's team and the client's team are brought together. This is driven by the use of the classic **bow tie to diamond** approach to increase peer-to-peer relationship networks.

Later still, where the relationship is strong, providers may organize meetings where they present ideas for how they can provide new insight, co-create innovative solutions or establish partnerships for mutual benefit. Here the topics of conversation might move to the joint development of extranets, tailored software, online solutions or platforms that could be licensed to third parties.

Use research and empathy to imagine the aspirations and pains the client organization is facing and to consider new ways to help them succeed. This requires a commitment to really get to know the client's organization and to invest time and money in research to explore problems and opportunities that may be beyond the area of technical work being undertaken.

One simple technique is to gather the client team together, provide them with wide-ranging commercial information about the client and its markets and ask them to come up with '60 ideas in 60 minutes' for how the client organization can improve. Some of the ideas generated can be worked up and presented to the client. The essence here is a proactive attempt to help the client – even if there is no immediate prospect of work for the service provider.

Too many key clients?

Many businesses try to tackle too many key client relationships. It should be apparent that those managing relationships need a really in-depth knowledge of the key client and must commit time on an almost daily basis to keeping abreast of developments in the client's market and organization.

Some firms have sophisticated analysis and research systems – which provide relationship managers with briefing materials on a daily basis about key clients and their markets and developments that are likely to have an impact on them. Yet the relationship managers still need time to read the information, consider its impact on the client and to consult with other members of the client team – or other experts – about that potential impact. Then they have to communicate with the key client – through emails, telephone calls, teleconferences, visits, meetings and social events. This is not something that can be done for more than one or two key clients at any time.

Another observation about why having these conversations is so tricky is that not many of the people who are charged with developing key client relationships have had structured training in professional selling – whether using consultative solutions or insight selling approaches. Similarly, few have had training in structured Key Client or Key Account Management.

40

Generating recommendations and referrals

Many organizations generate work from **word of mouth** (**WOM**) recommendations and referrals. These recommendations may be from consumers – as we see with reviews placed in systems such as TripAdvisor for hotels and holidays; Amazon for consumer products; and CheckaTrade.com for domestic trade services.

But many businesses rely on recommendations and **referrals** – some of which are formal through business directories, websites and social media platforms and others which are less formal where it is simply someone recommending your organization where they either have first-hand experience of what you do or have heard that you have a good reputation.

The power of word of mouth

Word of mouth recommendations – particularly in the fast-moving world of social media – are a valuable source of work for businesses which sell to other businesses. Statistics show that at least 13 per cent of a B2B (business-to-business) organization's work is generated this way. In some business services – for example in professional services for lawyers, accountants and surveyors – it can be as high as 90 per cent.

Paula Bone has argued that word of mouth recommendations can be considered from a number of perspectives:

- Direction – People seeking opinions about you or people sharing their views about you

- Valence – Whether the experience was positive or negative

- Volume – The number of people receiving the message

Bad news travels further and faster than good news. There are estimates that people will talk about a good experience to two other people but up to fourteen people about a bad experience.

As well as obtaining positive word of mouth recommendations from existing customers and clients, many organizations rely on third parties or other professional and business organizations for their recommendations. In these situations, the marketing and business development is not so much focused on the end users, customers and clients – often because their needs are unpredictable and/or infrequent – but on those organizations who come into contact with these people or businesses first when they experience a problem. An example might be a business that is experiencing financial difficulties and approaches a bank. The bank then might suggest they contact a specialist accountant such as an insolvency practitioner or a legal adviser. The bank's recommendation as to which to approach will carry a lot of weight.

In these situations, it is worth developing good business relationships with those people who might recommend and refer clients to you. In simple terms, this could merely involve thanking them when they refer someone to you. Alternatively, you might adopt a targeted approach – much as described in the selling sections above – to identify the most desirable potential recommenders and referrers and develop a plan to contact them, find out what they are interested in and how you can help them and to form a strong relationship perhaps involving collaborative or joint marketing initiatives.

Referrer management is almost as big a topic as selling. But here are some key tips about setting up a referrer management programme.

Plan – back to basics on referrer management

Referrer management programmes and activities are often managed by individuals as part of their networking and contact-building and there are no strategic aims, organization-wide systems or co-ordination. Analyse what is currently happening across your organization or department, establish goals for what results or performance improvements are required and develop a focused plan to achieve the desired results. The plan should have specific actions to be undertaken at specific times. With a plan you can measure how much you invest in referrer management, and how much you receive in return.

Target – focus efforts on the right referrers

While networking activities (see p. 271) may generate a wide contact base of referrers, it is impossible to devote the same level of attention to all of them. Furthermore, you are likely to need a more proactive approach to identifying and making contact with the referrers most likely to be of value – rather than simply hoping you will connect with them at events or online.

Analyse where the best referrals are likely to come from, compare this with what is happening at present and carry out research to identify the most suitable referrers for the future. Explore the criteria that you might use to select and assess the most suitable referrer organizations and individuals for targeting. You will need good information systems to manage referrer relationships – for example a Client Relationship Management (CRM) database.

Research – understand referrer aims

Use different ways to research referrers' needs and interests. Identify gaps in your knowledge about referrer organizations – how they are structured, the appropriate people to target, their core and target markets, their particular strengths, potential conflicts and their aims and strategies. Such research also provides input into referrer segmentation, grading and prioritization strategies.

Explore – reveal referrer perceptions and preferences

Ask current referrers why they refer clients and to whom. Understanding how referrers think and feel about your firm can uncover incorrect perceptions about your strengths and weaknesses and target clients and gaps in their knowledge. Some referrers may incorrectly 'pigeon hole' organizations for particular types of clients, product and services.

Develop the relationship – add value

Without sales training, people may be tempted to approach referrers with a 'We're good at this so please refer work to us' approach – on their own agenda. You need empathy and to focus on understanding the needs of the referrer. Prepare to add value to the referrer at every interaction – whether on the phone or at meetings. Ideas include providing information; offering insights into their clients or competitors; facilitating introductions; suggesting leads and opportunities; and promoting them in valued communities, etc.

Let it go – sunk costs

Whilst it is impossible to identify which referrers may refer the best clients and work in the future, there is a tendency for people to continue to invest in potential referrer relationships over a long period of time without receiving any referrals.

'**Sunk costs**' is where people have invested so much time and effort in a business relationship in the past that they are reluctant to cease activity as this means that effort is written off. Instead, they continue to maintain the relationship hoping that some work will emerge in the future. Hope is not a strategy!

Gently investigate whether the relationship is likely to generate results in the future and different ways to drive the conversation forward and progress the relationship – for example, by requesting introductions to other people in the referrer organization. It's worth thinking about the Decision-Making

Unit (DMU) model mentioned above and also about polite ways to take a back seat where the prospects are poor.

Reciprocity with referrers

In the section on persuasion, we saw that reciprocity – the need to repay a kindness – is a strong human drive. It's obvious that people are more likely to refer clients or work to you if they perceive that you will refer clients back to them.

But how to reciprocate when you are unable to refer work back? There are many things you can do to repay a kindness – for example, say thank you; ask how you can help; raise their profile by sharing their content in your social media channels; invite them to provide content for your communications; introduce them to people they may find interesting or useful; provide them with information that they value; invite them to events and make them look good to guests; provide complimentary services to their clients; include them in your training and marketing programmes; and invite them to participate in collaborative projects.

SECTION SUMMARY

THE SECTION STARTED BY CONSIDERING relatively short interactions with customers and clients as part of the service experience and we explored ideas around satisfaction. As we started to think about developing new relationships, we considered self-confidence (and its relationship with self-esteem) and perceptions. This led to ideas about how we can use non-verbal communication to create a favourable first impression and impact. In order to build a contact base we considered the need for targeting and clarity of your message, value proposition and differentiation – including your personal brand ('BrandMe'). Networking skills were broken down into those needed in advance, during and after an event as well as in online and social selling situations.

Then we moved on to material about how to sell yourself and your ideas. Classical solutions and consultative selling models were explored. The need to use research and empathy to understand needs and convert features into benefits followed. Then concepts on the decision-making unit, decision-making processes and cognitive biases were examined. Questioning and active listening skills were explored, with information on persuasion, objection handling and closing. The need to add value and more recent selling models such as insight selling were considered, as well as ideas around commercial and trusted advisers.

Then all of the ideas in the book were applied to two particular selling situations – a first meeting with a client and a competitive pitch. We looked at key client programmes – why they are important and the elements of a programme. We considered how conversations with clients might alter as the relationship becomes stronger and closer. Finally, we looked at the power of word of mouth recommendations and ideas to support referrer management programmes.

FURTHER READING

Better Business Relationships covers a wide range of topics and this list signposts just a few of the many books that provide more detailed information.

Topic	Title	Author	Publisher/Date
Anxiety	*Feel the Fear and Do It Anyway*	Susan Jeffries	Vermilion (2007)
Assertiveness	*Assertiveness*	Terry Gillen	Chartered Institute of Personnel & Development (1997)
	Assertiveness at Work	Ken Back and Katie Back	McGraw-Hill Education / Europe, Middle East & Africa (2005)
Change management	*Making Sense of Change Management: A Complete Guide to the Models, Tools and Techniques of Organisational Change*	Esther Cameron and Mike Green	Kogan Page (2016)
	Psychological Change – A Practical Introduction	John Mayhew	Palgrave (1997)
	Switch: How to Change Things When Change is Hard	Chip and Dan Heath	Random House Business (2011)
	Transitions – Making Sense of Life's Changes	William Bridges	Nicholas Brealey Publishing (2017)
Coaching	*Coaching and Mentoring – Practical Methods to Improve Learning*	Eric Parsloe and Monika Wray	Kogan Page (2000)
	Coaching for Performance	John Whitmore	Nicholas Brealey Publishing (2009)
	Key Coaching Models	Stephen Gibson	FT Publishing International (2016)

(*Continued*)

Topic	Title	Author	Publisher/Date
	The Manager as Coach and Mentor (Management Shapers)	Eric Parsloe	Chartered Institute of Personnel and Management (1999)
Cognition	*Blink: The Power of Thinking Without Thinking*	Malcolm Gladwell	Penguin (2006)
	Time to Think: Listening to Ignite the Human Mind	Nancy Kline	Cassell (2002)
Communication	*Confident Conversations – How to Talk in Any Business or Social Situation*	Lillian Glass	Piatkus (1991)
	Interpersonal Communication	Peter Hartley	Routledge (1999)
	Listening Skills	Ian Mackay	Chartered Institute of Personnel and Development (1998)
Conflict	*Conflict Management*	Baden Eunson	Wiley-Blackwell (2013)
	Conversational Riffs – Creating Meaning out of Conflict	Neil Denny	Eldamar Ltd (2010)
Cultural differences	*Kiss Bow or Shake Hands, 2nd Edition: The Bestselling Guide to Doing Business in More Than 60 Countries*	Terri Morrison	Adams (2006)
Difficult behaviour	*Coping with Difficult Bosses – Dealing Effectively with Bullies, Schemers, Stallers and Know-alls*	Robert Bramson	Nicholas Brealey Publishing (1993)
	Dealing with Difficult People	Roy Lilley	Kogan Page (2016)
	Dealing with Difficult People – Proven Strategies for Handing Stressful Situations and Defusing Tensions	Roberta Cava	Piatkus (1999)

Digital marketing	*Understanding Digital Marketing – Marketing Strategies for Engaging the Digital Generation*	Damian Ryan and Calvin Jones	Kogan Page (2016)
Emotional intelligence	*Chimp Paradox: How Our Impulses and Emotions Can Determine Success and Happiness and How We Can Control Them*	Steve Peters	Vermilion (2012)
	Emotional Intelligence 2.0	Travis Bradberry and Jean Greaves	TalentSmart (2009)
	Emotional Intelligence – Why it Can Matter More Than IQ	Daniel Goleman	Bloomsbury Publishing PLC (1996)
Influence	*How to Win Friends and Influence People*	Dale Carnegie	Vermilion (2006)
Key account management	*The New Successful Large Account Management*	Robert B. Miller and Stephen E. Heiman with Tad Tuleja	Kogan Page (2011)
	The Seven Keys to Managing Strategic Accounts	Sallie Sherman, Joseph Sperry and Samuel Reese	McGraw-Hill Professional (2003)
Leadership	*Effective Leadership – How to be a Successful Leader*	John Adair	Pan (2009)
Management	*Fast Thinking Manager's Manual*	Ros Jay and Richard Templar	Financial Times Management (2004)
	The One Minute Manager	Ken Blanchard and Spencer Johnson	Harper (2011)
Negotiation	*Getting to Yes – Negotiation and Agreement Without Giving in*	Roger Fisher and William Ury	Random House Business (2012)
	The Leader's Guide to Negotiation: How to Use Soft Skills to Get Hard Results	Simon Horton	FT Publishing International (2016)
Networking	*Business Networking: The Survival Guide*	Will Kintish	Pearson Business (2014)

(Continued)

Topic	Title	Author	Publisher/Date
Neuro-Linguistic Programming	*Frogs into Princes: Introduction to Neurolinguistic Programming*	Richard Bandler and John Grinder	Eden Grove Editions (1990)
	Introducing NLP	Sue Knight	Chartered Institute of Personnel & Development (1999)
	NLP: The New Art and Science of Getting What You Want	Harry Adler	Piatkus (1995)
	NLP – The New Technology of Achievement	Steve Andreas and Charles Faulkner	Nicholas Brealey Publishing (1996)
Non-verbal communication	*Body Language: How to Read Others' Thoughts by Their Gestures (Overcoming Common Problems)*	Allan Pearse and John Chandler	Sheldon Press (1997)
	Body Language at Work	Adrian Furnham	Chartered Institute of Personnel and Development (1999)
	Peoplewatching: The Desmond Morris Guide to Body Language	Desmond Morris	Vintage (2002)
	People Watching	Vernon Coleman	Blue Books (1995)
Online communication	*Managing Online Reputation – How to Protect Your Company on Social Media*	Charlie Pownall	Palgrave Macmillan (2015)
	Mastering Story, Community and Influence: How to Use Social Media to Become a Social Leader	Jay Oatway	John Wiley & Sons (2012)
Persuasion	*Influence: The Psychology of Persuasion*	Robert B. Cialdini	Harper Business (2007)
	The Small Big – Small Changes that Spark Big Influence	Steve J. Martin, Noah J. Goldstein and Robert B. Cialdini	Profile Books (2014)

Presentations	HBR Guide to Persuasive Presentations	Nancy Duarte	Harvard Business Review Press (2012)
	The Presentation Book – How to Create It, Shape It and Deliver It	Emma Ledden	Pearson Business (2013)
	Presenting with Power – Captivate, Motivate, Inspire and Persuade	Shay McConnon	How To Books (2006)
	TED Talks – The Official TED Guide to Public Speaking	Chris Anderson	Hodder and Stoughton (2018)
Promotion	Key Person of Influence – The Five-Step Method to Become One of the Most Highly Valued and Highly Paid People in Your Industry	Daniel Priestley	Rethink Press Limited (2014)
Relationships	Working Relationships Pocket Book	Fiona Elsa Dent	Management Pocketbooks (2009)
Selling	Conceptual Selling	Robert B. Miller and Stephen E. Heiman with Tad Tuleja	Grand Central Publishing (1972)
	Dynamic Practice Development – Selling Skills and Techniques for the Professions	Kim Tasso	Thorogood (2003)
	Empathy Selling	Christopher C. Golis	Kogan Page (1992)
	Insight Selling: Surprising Research on What Sales Winners Do Differently	Mike Schultz and John E. Doerr	John Wiley & Sons (2014)
	The New Strategic Selling	Stephen E. Heiman and Diane Sanchez	Warner (2005)
	Selling With Integrity – Reinventing Sales Through Collaboration, Respect and Serving	Sharon Drew Morgan	Penguin Group (SA) (Pty) Ltd (1999)
	Smarter Selling: Next Generation Sales Strategies to Meet Your Buyer's Needs – Every Time	Keith Dugdale and David Lambert	Financial Times/ Prentice Hall (2007)
	SPIN Selling	Neil Rackman	Routledge (1995)

(Continued)

Topic	Title	Author	Publisher/Date
Stress	*Crazy Busy – Overstretched, Overbooked and About to Snap*	Edward Hallowell	Nightingale-Conant (2004)
Transactional Analysis (TA)	*Games People Play: The Psychology of Human Relationships*	Eric Berne	Penguin Life (2016)
Writing	*Business Writing – How to Write to Engage, Persuade and Sell*	Ian Atkinson	Financial Times/ Prentice Hall (2011)
	Hypnotic Writing – How to Seduce and Persuade Customers With Only Your Words	Joe Vitale	Wiley (2002)
	Persuasive Writing (How to Harness the Power of Words)	Peter Frederick	Pearson Business (2011)

SUBJECT INDEX

NAME INDEX